THE TEACHER INSURGENCY

EDUCATION POLITICS AND POLICY SERIES

Series edited by Jeffrey R. Henig

OTHER BOOKS IN THIS SERIES

Challenging the One Best System
Katrina E. Bulkley
Julie A. Marsh
Katharine O. Strunk
Douglas N. Harris
Ayesha K. Hashim

Outside Money in School Board Elections
Jeffrey R. Henig
Rebecca Jacobsen
Sarah Reckhow

Are Charters Different?
Zachary W. Oberfield

The Fight for America's Schools
Edited by Barbara Ferman

Striving in Common
Jennifer Jellison Holme
Kara S. Finnigan

Compete or Close
Julia A. McWilliams

THE TEACHER INSURGENCY

A STRATEGIC AND ORGANIZING PERSPECTIVE

LEO CASEY

Harvard Education Press
Cambridge, Massachusetts

Paperback ISBN 978-1-68253-555-4
Library Edition ISBN 978-1-68253-557-8

Library of Congress Cataloging-in-Publication Data is on file.

Published by Harvard Education Press,
an imprint of the Harvard Education Publishing Group
Harvard Education Press
8 Story Street
Cambridge, MA 02138

Cover Design: Endpaper Studio
Cover Image: John Doukas/Shutterstock.com

The typefaces in this book are ITC Legacy Serif, Gotham Narrow, and Knockout

For Winsome

Freedom is never granted; it is won. Justice is never given; it is exacted.

A. Philip Randolph, "A Vision of Freedom": Remarks at Dinner Celebrating his 80th Birthday

At the banquet table of nature there are no reserved seats; you get what you can take and keep what you can hold. If you can't take anything, you won't get anything. If you can't hold anything, you won't keep anything. You can only take what you need and are entitled to and hold what you need and are entitled to with power, and power derives from organization.

A. Philip Randolph, Keynote Speech to 1961 Convention of the Negro American Labor Council

Contents

CHAPTER 1

From "Teacher Spring" to Teacher Insurgency

AS WINTER SWEPT ACROSS THE UNITED STATES at the outset of 2018, ushering in the bitterest and bleakest days of the year, American teachers and their unions had little to celebrate. The first eight years of the decade had exacted a heavy toll, and still more trouble was lurking on the horizon.

In 2010, a swarm of Republican state governments under the sway of the far-right Tea Party movement had come to power. Across the nation, these "red" state governments had enacted legislation designed to silence the collective voice of teachers and other public-sector workers by eviscerating their unions. Among the most prominent of these states were Scott Walker's Wisconsin, where an epic but ultimately unsuccessful battle was waged by labor against this legislation, Rick Snyder's Michigan, and John Kasich's Ohio.[1]

In the wake of the Great Recession, funding for public education had been slashed across the country, with particularly deep cuts in the red states, many of which were granting massive tax cuts to the wealthy and corporations that reduced state revenues. A growing portion of the funds that remained were diverted from public schools to voucher programs for private schools and to charter schools.

Nationally, teachers had been severely disappointed by a Democratic administration that had turned over its education policy to "reformers" who laid the problems of America's public schools at the feet of teachers and their unions. From the helm of the US Department of Education, this technocratic leadership had promoted a business model of education centered on high-stakes standardized exams, advocating their use to determine whether students would be promoted and graduated, whether teachers were evaluated as unsatisfactory and dismissed, and whether schools would be closed. At the same time, it supported a significant growth in the numbers of charter schools.

Following the calamitous results of the 2016 election, matters in the nation's capital went from bad to worse, and hit rock bottom with the appointment of a billionaire secretary of education who was an open and implacable foe of public schools and unions.

At the beginning of 2017, the Supreme Court had scheduled the oral hearings in *Janus v. AFSCME* for late February. *Janus* had been crafted by anti-union organizations to financially cripple public-sector unions and had been litigated with the financial backing of the Koch brothers, the DeVos family, the Bradley Foundation, and others on the far right.[2] It was widely expected that the five-person conservative majority on the court would rule against the unions, overturning forty years of the court's own precedents. Teacher unions had been preparing for such an eventuality since early 2016 with programs of intensive membership engagement.

For American teachers, the 2010s had been a long, dark night. And at the start of 2018, there had been very few signs that it would end. But, in the words of the old Irish peasant saying, it is always darkest before the dawn.

THE WEST VIRGINIA STRIKE OF 2018

In those early months of 2018, West Virginia teachers, education workers, and their unions found themselves grappling with one of the state governments that had acquired a deep red political hue over the decade. Both houses of the state legislature had solid Republican majorities, with a powerful Tea Party presence. The billionaire governor, whose stake in coal mining had made him the wealthiest person in the state, was a nouveau Republican; he had abandoned the Democratic party soon after he was elected to that office as its candidate. For nearly nine decades, dating back to the beginning of the New Deal, West Virginia had been a Democratic stronghold, a status attributable in no small part to the political clout of its labor movement. But the decline of the state's mining industry and the waning of the once-mighty United Mine Workers had sapped that union strength, and in 2014, the Republicans had swept to power. In 2016, the Republican state government adopted an anti-union "right-to-work" law; only a few years prior, such a measure would have been unthinkable in a state that had been the site of a number of the fiercest battles in American labor history.

As 2018 began, the salaries of West Virginia teachers were near the bottom nationally, and lagged well behind the surrounding states of Kentucky, Maryland, Pennsylvania, Ohio, and Virginia.[3] The salaries, health insurance, and pensions of West Virginia teachers and education workers were decided by the state, and for a number of years the government had been shifting the costs of health insurance onto teachers and other public workers through increased co-pays and premiums. These changes cut into real income as the increased health insurance costs ate away at stagnant salaries. In early 2018, the governor had proposed a token 1 percent raise in teacher salaries in his State of the State address, and another round of cost shifting in health care threatened to further plunder teachers' take-home pay.

The four southernmost counties of West Virginia—Logan, McDowell, Mingo, and Wyoming—had been the center of its coal mining industry and the heartland of the United Mine Workers. It was in these counties, where teachers were often the children and grandchildren of coal miners who had lived and breathed union, that the first rumblings of resistance to the state government's plans were heard.[4] In January, teachers and education workers from these counties organized meetings to discuss what was happening in the state capital—the inadequate salary proposal, the detrimental changes in health insurance, and the underfunding of public education—and what to do in response. In keeping with their rich labor heritage, they made plans for one-day county walkouts in defiance of the law. On February 2, they conducted a one-day strike and held a protest at the state capitol. For the first time in West Virginia history, this action brought together members of the three statewide education unions—AFT West Virginia, affiliated with the American Federation of Teachers (AFT); the West Virginia Education Association, affiliated with the National Education Association (NEA); and the independent West Virginia Service Personnel

Association, a union of school-related support workers such as custodians, bus drivers, and cafeteria workers.

The February 2 walkouts were reported by state and national media outlets. They quickly became the talk of West Virginia teachers in their schools and on social media, and they provided inspiration to teachers from other parts of the state.[5] A Facebook group of West Virginian teachers that was the center of much of the social media discussion grew to over twenty-thousand members in the first months of 2018.[6] In short order, teachers and education workers in additional counties, including Wayne, Cabell and Lincoln, were organizing their own one-day walkouts. A movement was rapidly taking shape and spreading across the state.

Coming as it did in the doldrums of a decade when American teachers and their unions had been under sustained attack and were expecting more of the same, the dramatic appearance of these walkouts on the political stage center was unexpected. No one—not the state government, not the state unions, not even the teachers who organized the first walkouts—had anticipated that this movement would emerge, much less how quickly it would proliferate. But as soon as the walkouts began, the three state unions began to mobilize, with their national affiliates providing key organizational support. Local leaders were asked to assess the potential support for a statewide strike action, and state leaders organized tele-town halls and took to social media to take the pulse of members around the state. Meetings were organized that brought together the members of all three unions in each of the state's fifty-five counties, and a vote was taken on whether to call for a statewide walkout, with an overwhelming "yes" response. On February 22, four days before the Supreme Court would hear *Janus v. AFSCME*, the entire education workforce of West Virginia was on strike and demonstrating at the state capitol. Their slogan was "55 Strong," a statement of the solidarity that had been built among teachers and education workers from every county in the state.

West Virginia teachers were still on strike when the Supreme Court conducted the oral hearings for *Janus v. AFSCME*. They remained on strike for nearly two weeks, faithfully walking the picket lines in the dead of winter. Five days into the strike, the governor announced his support for a 5 percent raise for teachers, education workers, and other public-sector workers, and union leaders recommended its acceptance and a conclusion to the strike. But teachers were profoundly distrustful that the state government would deliver on the governor's promise: the Republican president of the state Senate, an outspoken opponent of the strike, had declared his unwillingness to pass the deal advocated by the governor and was doing his best to sow discord between teachers and other public-sector workers and between public-sector employees and the community. Consequently, teachers refused to end the strike and demanded actual legislation. It was only after the full salary increase was signed into law on March 6 that teachers and education workers ended their strike. They had won their major demand, and they returned to their classrooms the next day.

TEACHER SPRING OF 2018

The sheer audacity of the West Virginia strike captured the imagination of teachers across the United States. Erupting in a deep red state in the midst of the Supreme Court's deliberations over *Janus v. AFSCME*, the strike was a powerful statement that teachers and other public-sectors workers were not prepared to go quietly into the night. The Court's right-wing majority could rule against public-sector workers and their unions, as it would do at the end of June, but it did not have the final word. That belonged to the rank-and-file members of the unions.

The West Virginia strike provided a spark, and in the months that followed, it lit a prairie fire of teacher strikes across the United States. On April 2, Oklahoma teachers and education workers began what would become a ten-day statewide strike for improved salaries and increased funding of public schools. On the same day, teachers in several Kentucky counties held one-day walkouts over the governor's efforts to gut their pensions. On April 26, Arizona teachers and education workers launched a weeklong statewide strike, also for improved salaries and increased school funding. And on May 16, North Carolina teachers and education workers held a one-day statewide strike demanding improved compensation and increased funding for public schools. These strikes, which I collectively call "Teacher Spring," were signs of the dawn of a new day for American teachers, their unions, and America's public schools.

In important ways that I will discuss in this book, the Teacher Spring strikes of 2018 found a template in the West Virginia strike. It had been focused not simply on the needs of teachers and education workers, as important as they were, but also on the chronic underfunding of the public schools and the fiscal policies that provided tax cuts to corporations and the wealthy while starving schools and other public services. Against efforts to divide the strikers from other public workers and the community, it put forward a broad solidaristic vision that fought for all public-sector employees and for the schools that their communities needed and deserved. In one especially telling illustration, West Virginia teachers organized to make sure that students who relied on public schools for the meals were fed during the strike. As a consequence, it enjoyed an unprecedented level of public support, as did the subsequent strikes of Teacher Spring.

The strikes of Teacher Spring were all the more powerful for having taken place mostly in states where they were prohibited by law, making them acts of civil disobedience. Moreover, they had mostly occurred in deep red states with extremely conservative Republican state governments. In four of the five Teacher Spring states—West Virginia, Oklahoma, Kentucky, and Arizona—teacher salaries, health insurance, and pensions were set centrally by the state government, with only a minimal role for local school districts. This system, which is employed by relatively few states, meant that the Teacher Spring strikes were of necessity mostly statewide, a largely unprecedented development in both teacher union history and in American labor history. That statewide strikes were organized is all the more remarkable when one understands that in these deep red states, teacher union membership was less dense and teacher union organizational infrastructure less developed than in most parts of the country. The one exception to this rule was West Virginia, where union density is approximately 75 percent, taking into account all three statewide unions.[7] It is telling that the West Virginia strike had the greatest success in winning its demands.

TEACHER INSURGENCY

In 2019, the wave continued to gather momentum, with four particularly noteworthy strikes. In Los Angeles, the second-largest school district in the US, teachers struck for eight days in January. Teachers in Denver walked out for three days, and teachers in Oakland struck for eight days during February. In Chicago, the third-largest school district in the nation, teachers and education workers walked out for eleven days in the middle of October. These four strikes were by no means the only ones in that year; many smaller districts also experienced walkouts. And on February 19, a few short days before the anniversary of the 2018 strike, West Virginia teachers and education workers struck for one day to stop a bill tying their salary increases to the introduction of school vouchers, the opening of charter schools, and the gutting of teacher seniority. This bill was an unsuccessful maneuver by Republicans in the state legislature, who were smarting from the triumph of the 2018 strike and the November 2018 election defeat of a number of the strike foes who had been opposed by the unions.

The Teacher Insurgency strikes had much in common with the Teacher Spring strikes, but they also broke important new ground. Unlike the 2018 strikes, many of the 2019 strikes occurred in deep "blue" states where the governments were controlled by Democrats. (Even the Denver strike in "purple" Colorado took place after the Democrats had taken control of state government in the 2018 election.) Given the greater likelihood of blue states' public employees having the right to strike, these strikes often took place in the states (only one-quarter of all states) where they were legal.

The spread of the teacher strikes to the blue states indicated that while the issues that generated them may have found their most extreme manifestations in deep red states, they were being experienced across the country. It also demonstrated that the strikes had become a national movement. "What it says is that West Virginia and Oklahoma wasn't sui generis; it wasn't an isolated moment," American Federation of Teachers (AFT) Randi Weingarten told the *New York Times* after Chicago teachers successfully ended their strike. "This is now a strategy."[8]

The Chicago strike was also notable in that it coordinated the teachers' strike against the school district with a strike by education support workers in Service Employees International Union (SEIU) Local 73, and by Passages Academy, a charter school where teachers were also represented by the Chicago Teachers Union (CTU). This coordination followed on a series of successful strikes against Chicago charter schools during late 2018 and the spring of 2019, including the first strikes against entire charter chains in the United States. (The 2019 Los Angeles strike also was coordinated with a strike by the Accelerated Charter School, organized with the United Teachers of Los Angeles.) Together with the issues raised by the CTU, this coordination marked the full emergence of what might be called a solidaristic strike and negotiation strategy, in which the power of the CTU was joined with other workers inside the Chicago school district and other teachers in Chicago to strengthen the bargaining position of all and to take on issues of the students and communities they educated and served.

Finally, the strikes of 2019 were innovative in their demands. Not content to simply raise traditional union demands on compensation and work conditions, and even moving beyond educational issues such as class size that teacher unions had always bargained, the 2019 strikes took up issues such as the impact of excessive testing on education, the need for social and health services for students living in poverty, supports for homeless students to ensure the continuity of their education, the impact of the unregulated expansion of charter schools on public district schools, and protections for undocumented students from Immigration and Customs Enforcement (ICE) raids.

THE SCOPE AND SEQUENCE OF THIS BOOK

In this book, I will employ the term *Teacher Insurgency* to describe the entire movement of strikes in 2018, 2019, and beyond. By reserving the term *Teacher Spring* to describe only the strikes in the spring of 2018, I will be able to distinguish its distinctive features, while also including it in the larger movement of the Teacher Insurgency.

Social movements and protest movements—including the labor movement—are by their nature dynamic and changing, not permanent and fixed. Movements wax and wane: they are born in bursts of activism, and they wither into periods of inertia and even inactivity. On occasion, they completely expire. But these trajectories are life cycles, so a movement can be renewed and reinvigorated, even reborn. And the life of a movement can be long or transitory, productive or barren. A movement can be on the order of the unionism of the 1930s, which remained a dominant political force for decades and dramatically reduced income inequality in the United States, or it can end up like the nuclear freeze movement of the early 1980s, which organized the largest peace rally in American history and then quickly faded, with no meaningful impact on American foreign policy. It can be like the civil rights movement, vanquishing de jure Jim Crow segregation and begetting landmark civil rights and voting rights legislation, or it can be like Occupy Wall Street, which for all the attention it brought to the growth of extreme income inequality, rapidly disappeared without any discernible impact on American economic policy.

In no small measure, these different trajectories are shaped by what the participants and leaders of a movement do. Their actions directly impact how long a movement thrives and what it accomplishes in the way of social, political, and economic changes while it is still vibrant and dynamic. When a movement is young and in the ascendant, as the Teacher Insurgency now is, the interventions of participants and leaders are particularly important in shaping its trajectory and life path. Simply put, there is no law of history, politics, or economics that guarantees that the Teacher Insurgency will continue to advance and impact American education in progressive ways: it will happen because teachers and unionists employ sound strategic and organizing approaches, or it will not be.

As teachers and union activists, our strategic approach must be based on a thorough understanding of the relations of power in education politics and American politics more generally, with the knowledge of how to craft interventions on that political terrain to positive effect; our organizing must be rooted not only in the issues that are important to teachers, but in a deep understanding of *why* they are important to teachers and how they shape a collective "teacher" identity. This book was written to address precisely these questions of strategy and organizing. Its audience is first and foremost teachers and teacher union activists and leaders, but what is has to say about strategy and organizing will have a broader applicability for the larger labor, progressive, and democratic left movements and for those fighting to save American democracy in a moment of great crisis.

This book has three main sections. In the first, "The Origins of the Teacher Insurgency," I start with an analysis, in chapter 2, of the issues that motivated the teacher strikes of 2018 and 2019. These issues fall into two general categories, those that ensue from the underfunding of public education and those that involve the deprofessionalization and deskilling of teaching. Both sets of issues are the product of discrete government policies. In some instances, these policies were long-standing, such as austerity plans that date as far back as the mid-1970s; in other cases they are of a more recent origin, such as the deprofessionalization caused by the expanding role and importance of standardized exams. But all of these policies developed a particularly aggressive intensity in the decade of the 2010s, creating the basis for the Teacher Insurgency.

Issues can provide only a partial explanation for the emergence of a social movement. Equally important are the underlying dynamics that shape the political ground on which they are contested. In chapter 3, I argue that there are three crucial developments that created a ground favorable to the emergence of the Teacher Insurgency: the growing gap between what teachers expect when they enter teaching and what their actual experience is; the emergence of mass protest movements in the US after a period of relative quiescence; and the changing terrain of American educational politics. Through an analysis of both the issues that motivated the strikes and the underlying dynamics that created the favorable conditions for their emergence, I will answer the question of why the Teacher Insurgency has emerged at this point in the history of American education and teacher unionism. The logic of the Teacher Insurgency is fundamentally a political one, with government choices and policies—and resistance to them—being the driving forces.

In the second section, "The Strategic Challenges in Perspective," I take up four key strategic questions that the Teacher Insurgency is confronting. Here I break with the common practice of viewing the Teacher Insurgency and movements of working people only through the particular lens of the labor movement; instead, I locate the labor movement in a wider universe of protest movements and social movements, such as the civil rights movement, that have faced similar strategic issues. This broader lens brings a richer and more diverse set of experiences and resources to bear on the question of how to mount successful collective action by teachers.

In chapter 4, I analyze the first of the strategic challenges—the different roles of mobilization and organization in protest movements—with a particular focus on how the use of social media has transformed contemporary protest movements. While social media can be a powerful tool for mobilization, I argue that it cannot replace but instead must complement face-to-face organizing. Chapter 5 examines the second of the challenges—the relationship between protest and politics; that is, between various forms of direct action, such as strikes and demonstrations on the one hand and electoral politics on the other. Against those views that advocate one pole of this opposition to the exclusion of the other, such as those that promote strikes as an alternative to electoral politics, I contend that there is a productive tension between the two forms of action. Protest and politics each bring distinct capacities and unique strengths to a social change project, and a strategic approach that employs both in their appropriate context is most likely to be successful. Chapter 6 considers the history of teacher union strikes, the third challenge, distinguishing between the conditions and approaches that have resulted in successful strikes and those that have ended in setbacks and defeats. The continued use of the strike as a vital direct-action tactic in the Teacher Insurgency requires a solid understanding of what leads to success, if it is to be replicated. And in addressing the last of the strategic challenges in chapter 7, I assess an important approach to bargaining and contract negotiations that has been highlighted in the Teacher Insurgency—bargaining for the common good—which relies on strong partnerships with community. One of the key threads that will appear in this section is a vision of teacher unionism that is rooted in the republican and communitarian conceptions of unionism that were prevalent in the founding of American unionism.

In the third section, "Organizing Teachers, Teachers Organizing," I move from particular strategic issues posed by the Teacher Insurgency to more general questions of how to organize teachers for collective action. While these questions are certainly central to the 2018 and 2019 strikes, they also have a much broader pertinence for the work of teacher unions. I start in chapter 8 by laying out a vision of organizing as an educational process in which those who are organizing learn about their collective voice and power—how to build and strengthen it and how to use it in ways that fulfill their common purposes. Good organizing, I argue, is akin to progressive education in the Deweyan mold, in which those who are learning are active participants in the learning and organizing process.

I then delve into a little theorized and discussed, but very important, component of organizing—the construction of a collective identity, the *we* of an organizing process. Here I analyze the four main discourses that provide the basis for the collective identity *teacher*—the discourse of teaching as nurturance (chapter 9), the discourse of teaching as professionalism (chapter 10), the discourse of teaching as labor and craft (chapter 11), and the discourse of teaching as democratic intellectual work (chapter 12). I demonstrate that these discourses are not simply ways of thinking and communicating but are materially grounded in social practices and institutions; as a consequence, they have within them implicit programmatic directions and policies that must be teased out and expressly articulated. Moreover, each of these discourses is contested, with different practices and conceptions that are often opposed to each other seeking to define what it means to be a teacher. The point of organizing, I maintain, is to intervene in these ongoing contests and to suture these discourses together, as it is in combination that the best elements of each discourse—the most democratic and solidaristic visions of what it means to be a teacher—are reinforced in a coherent collective teacher identity.

The purpose of this book, therefore, is not to provide one more narrative of the Teacher Insurgency, or even to locate it within larger histories of teacher collective action and the labor movement. While my analysis will certainly be informed by historical antecedents of the Teacher Insurgency, its focus will be on identifying the strategic and organizing approaches that will best situate us to build and sustain collective power—power that is capable not only of defending public education and teaching from those who seek to dismantle and diminish them, but of realizing their rich democratic promise. With the right strategic and organizing approaches, a new day is possible.

PART ONE

The Origins of the Teacher Insurgency

CHAPTER 2

The Issues Behind the Teacher Insurgency

THE MOST COMMON EXPLANATION for the emergence of the Teacher Insurgency is that teachers had reached a point where they had nothing left to lose. They went on strike, often in defiance of the law, because their schools' teaching and learning conditions had deteriorated significantly and salaries, health insurance, and pensions had been underfunded to the point that they could no longer support teachers. While incomplete in a number of significant respects, this explanation does provide important insights into the issues that inspired the strikes. In this chapter, I will identify these issues and trace them back to the government policies that gave rise to them.

The issues that motivated the Teacher Insurgency strikes of 2018 and 2019 can be divided into two categories—those that involved the chronic underfunding of public schools and those that involved the deprofessionalization and deskilling of teaching.

THE UNDERFUNDING OF PUBLIC EDUCATION

Throughout US history, there have been deep disparities in the financial and physical resources provided to America's public schools. These inequities were made possible by how the politics of American federalism played out in education, since it is a governmental function reserved to the states under the Tenth Amendment. Public schools receive separate streams of income from federal, state, and local governments, with the vast majority of their funds coming from state and local sources. Poorer states with smaller tax bases generally contribute less to education, and the states that invested the most per student spend approximately three times as much as the lowest-spending states.[1] (These patterns hold true even after adjusting for state differences in labor market costs, poverty, and other factors.) Within states, most local governments use local property taxes to fund public education, reproducing residential divisions of wealth and poverty in the funding of public schools. While federal government money is as a general rule more equitably distributed, it accounts for the smallest proportion (about 10 percent) of school funding. Taken as a whole, this system has led to the shortchanging of public schools that serve high-poverty communities, especially in rural areas and urban inner cities. Given the contours of the American political economy, these underfunded schools serve disproportionately large numbers of students of color, both native-born and immigrant.[2]

These historic trends were exacerbated by the fiscal crises of state and local government that developed in the mid-1970s. At that time, many state and local governments adopted austerity policies that cut funds for schools and other public services. The draconian cuts experienced by New York City public schools as a result of the 1975 fiscal crisis served as a paradigm of this defunding (and established a template for what many states and locales went on to do after the Great Recession of 2008).[3] On the other side of the country, California passed Proposition 13 in 1978, instituting rigid caps on property taxes that resulted in chronic underfunding of public services, especially the state's public schools.[4]

In the wake of the Great Recession, education funding was slashed across the nation. Many state and local governments enacted extreme austerity policies, starving the budgets of public schools and other public services, even while more than a few states further reduced their revenues by enacting tax cuts for corporations and the wealthy. As budget cuts fell disproportionately on schools serving high-poverty communities and large numbers of students of color, funding inequities grew ever larger.[5] At the moment that the Teacher Spring strikes began to explode, funding of public education still lagged well below its pre–Great Recession: twenty-five states were spending \$19 billion less on public K–12 education than they had in 2008.[6]

These trends were not evenly distributed across the nation; they were most acute in red states with ultraconservative Republican governments, including those that would experience the 2018 Teacher Spring strikes. A number of them—Arizona, Oklahoma, and North Carolina—ranked in the bottom ten states for per-pupil education spending. In addition to the deleterious effects of these austerity policies, funding for public education in many of these states was also redirected into education privatization schemes such as vouchers. However, as the 2019 Teacher Insurgency strikes demonstrated, the problems of inadequate funding were by no means exclusive to red states: the public schools in California, one of the bluest states, were plagued by the cumulative effect of decades of inadequate funding, attributable in large measure to the effects of Proposition 13.

By the spring of 2018, post-recession austerity policies had produced a wide array of problems in America's public schools: oversized classes, outdated textbooks, inadequate learning technology, crumbling school buildings and facilities, old school buses in poor repair, the elimination of enrichment subjects (music, the arts, physical education, etc.) from the curriculum, the cutting of health care and social services for the neediest students, and the elimination of mentoring programs for novice teachers and professional development for the entire educator workforce. In Teacher Spring state Oklahoma, many school districts were so strapped for funds that in 2018 that they reduced the school week to four days; in other states, school districts furloughed teachers and/or shortened the school year.[7]

In the decade between 2008 and 2018, the nationwide K–12 student enrollment had increased by 1.5 million; at the same time, employment in public education was down 170,000 positions from pre-recession levels.[8] In thirty-five states, student-teacher ratios were greater than they were before the Great Recession, which meant that class sizes (which track those ratios but, for reasons of how schools are organized, are higher) were also larger.[9] California, the site of the 2019 Los Angeles and Oakland strikes, had the largest student-teacher ratio in the nation, 24:1, well above the national average of 16:1; in Teacher Spring state Oklahoma, the teacher-student ratio had increased by 20 percent since the Great Recession.[10] The national student-to-counselor ratio in 2018 was 482:1, nearly double what is recommended to provide adequate counseling services. Teacher Spring state Arizona had an extraordinary ratio of one counselor for every 924 students, and California had 760 students for every counselor.[11]

On the 2017 report card of the American Society of Civil Engineers, public school facilities received a grade of D+. Close to one-half of all school buildings were in poor or fair condition, and more than half needed improvements to meet basic standards. Funding to maintain school facilities from all levels of government fell $38 billion short of what was needed.[12] A Council of Great City Schools study reported that these conditions were largely the result of "school districts, financially squeezed over long periods of time, (making) economic decisions" to defer "preventive and predictive maintenance work."[13]

Not surprisingly, empirical studies of the effects of post-recession austerity policies have found significant negative impact on K–12 student academic achievement, including declines in English language arts and mathematics achievement scores on the National Assessment of Educational Progress (NAEP) and reduced high school graduation rates.[14] Following the patterns of funding inequity, the losses were heaviest in schools serving high-poverty communities and students of color. School districts that experienced the greatest teacher attrition also suffered the heaviest academic declines.

Teachers were harmed directly by the austerity policies. As Teacher Spring took shape, teachers' average national salary had declined 4.5 percent since the Great Recession. Indeed, public school teachers' salaries in thirty-eight states were lower than they had been a decade earlier.[15] In 2018, some of the lowest-paid teachers in the nation were found in the Teacher Spring states of West Virginia, Arizona, and Oklahoma.[16]

Equally important, US teachers were experiencing a growing salary "penalty" just for working in their profession. By 2018, the difference between teacher salaries and those of professionals with comparable levels of education had widened dramatically, to a 21.4 percent gap, with a major portion of that gap emerging in the decade after 2008. (This stark difference was a product of an actual decline in the real wages of American teachers—down $21 per week since 1996—combined with an increase in the real wages of comparable professionals—up $323 per week since 1996.) While all states experienced that gap to some degree, it was particularly acute in the Teacher Spring states of Arizona, Oklahoma, and North Carolina, with Arizona topping the nation.[17]

Teachers struggled to provide the essentials for themselves and their families. Over half of American teachers were taking on second and third jobs, and in a number of states, teachers were forced to rely on public assistance programs such as food stamps.[18] At the same time, many state and local governments began to cut back on teacher health insurance and pensions, shifting more of the costs of those benefits onto teachers. According to some reports, teacher pensions were targeted at the urging of conservative think tanks that were financially supported by hedge fund managers and corporations with pecuniary interests in the investment operations of these funds.[19] One of the precipitating issues in the West Virginia strike of Teacher Spring was the state's proposals to increase teacher contributions to health insurance through increased premiums and co-pays, which would lead to significant losses in real income. Similarly, the Teacher Spring strike in Kentucky was in major part a response to the state government's plan to diminish the benefits of public employee pensions.[20]

THE DEPROFESSIONALIZATION AND DESKILLING OF TEACHING

At the same time that austerity policies were decimating education funding, another set of policies was being adopted and implemented that had a negative effect on teachers' professional lives. Starting in 2009, the Obama administration's Race to the Top (RTTT) program gave increased impetus to the top-down, technocratic, and market-driven reforms of American education that had first appeared with No Child Left Behind (NCLB) in 2001. At the very moment that the Great Recession had led to precipitous declines in the tax revenues that funded education, Race to the Top provided financial incentives for states to adopt new, standardized test-driven systems of school accountability, teacher evaluation, and student promotion and to enact legislation and policies designed to expand the number and reach of charter schools. Desperate for financial assistance, most states readily complied.

Race to the Top centered on a "business model" vision of education reform, with test scores functioning as a proxy for the bottom line of the profit ledger in private-sector businesses. Test scores became the basis for personnel and enterprise decisions, displacing professional expertise and judgment to a significant extent.[21] Student promotion and graduation depended on passing standardized tests, and schools could be placed into receivership or closed based on the percentage of students who passed. Teacher evaluation systems were promoted in which the teachers' rating was based preponderantly on their students' performance on exams (even, in many cases, in subjects that they themselves didn't teach), rather than on observations by an educational professional.

As the importance of standardized exams was elevated, demands were placed on teachers to replace rich and varied lessons with test prep and heavily scripted, narrowly focused instruction. Tested subjects, primarily English language arts and mathematics, crowded out other subjects. There was little classroom time left for interdisciplinary and project-based learning. Rigid pacing calendars often micromanaged the details of what was taught, when it was taught, and how it was taught. Since low scores on standardized exams are highly correlated with poverty, schools with high concentrations of poverty bore a heavier burden from these changes.

Taken together, the NCLB and RTTT initiatives worked to undermine the professional authority of American teachers, leaving them increasingly hamstrung in their efforts to provide instruction that was in the best educational interests of students. They engendered in teachers a growing sense of alienation from their work as it became more stressful and less fulfilling.[22] In response, the strikes of the Teacher Insurgency raised demands regarding the role of standardized testing and challenged teacher evaluation and merit pay systems based primarily on student test scores.

TEACHING IN THE GLOBAL ECONOMY

The two sets of issues that motivated the Teacher Insurgency—the underfunding of public education and the deskilling and deprofessionalization of teaching—were the product of discrete policies generated in particular circumstances. But these policies were aligned with structural tendencies in the global political economy. Seen from this vantage point, the Teacher Insurgency has been, in significant measure, a struggle over the extent to which these structural tendencies would determine the work of teachers in the US.

As far back as the first decades of the twentieth century, control over teachers' work has been contested in the American educational system. One of the earliest battles of the newly organized teacher unions was resisting the commercialization of public education and the application of methods for organizing assembly-line production in factories—Frederick Winslow Taylor's "scientific management"—to schools.[23] In a famous speech to the 1904 convention of the National Education Association, "Why Teachers Should Organize," Chicago Teachers Federation and American Federation of Teachers leader Margaret Haley decried "the increased tendency toward 'factoryizing education,' making the teacher an automaton, a mere factory hand, whose duty it is to carry out mechanically and unquestioningly the ideas and orders of those clothed with the authority of position and who may or may not know the needs of the children or how to minister to them."[24] Haley's clarion call marked the advent of what would be a prominent theme of teacher unionism over the course of the following century, inspiring such union-led efforts on behalf of the professionalization of teaching as the National Board for Professional Teaching Standards.

The dawn of the global economy of the twenty-first century brought new pressures to bear on schools and the work of teachers, because the new economy centered on the production of information and knowledge.[25] And the new information era required a substantial retooling of schools that had been built for an era of industrial capitalism, when students could drop out of high school and still expect to find steady employment in factories—jobs that, when unionized, would support a family at a middle-class standard of living. In the new knowledge economy, schools had to educate all students to a substantially higher standard of achievement, providing them with skills indispensable to knowledge work, such as analytical reasoning, critical thinking, and problem solving, or condemn them to a life of economic marginality. What is more, with an authoritarian populism of the far right rising across the globe, schools needed to educate all students into the knowledge and skills of democratic citizenship, so they could understand their democratic heritage and function as a grassroots force for democracy. A critical question is whether the various features of the global economy that has taken shape in recent years—such as the "flexibility" that comes from replacing stable unionized workforces with contingent labor, who struggle to survive economically and turn over at a high rate—is conducive to establishing and maintaining public schools that can meet these challenges.

For teachers, this question takes the form of their place in a global economy, with a workforce that has become increasingly bifurcated along an axis of the production and use of knowledge—on the one side, *educated, self-programmable labor* who produce new knowledge, with significant control over the labor process; on the other side, *generic labor* who use knowledge created by others, executing decisions and engaging in labor processes over which they have little control.[26] Manifestations of this growing divide are found within higher education in the US and other OECD nations, as elite research universities are differentiated from colleges that focus on teaching and the labor of tenure-track faculty with research responsibilities is distinguished from the precarious labor of adjunct lecturers and graduate assistants who do more and more of the teaching. As education professionals, teachers understand their work to fit the description of educated, self-programmable labor provided by Manuel Castells—the "autonomous capacity to focus on the goal assigned to it in the process of production, find the relevant information, recombine it into knowledge, using the available knowledge stock, and apply it in the form of tasks oriented towards the goals of the process."[27] What does a teacher do, after all, but focus on the education of her students, identifying the appropriate subject material and skills to be taught, gathering and assessing the relevant information on the needs and capacities of her students, and connecting it to the pedagogical approaches that will produce the desired learning? This recombination work involves the continual creation of new, practical knowledge. But the effect of both the austerity policies that have underfunded public education and the adoption of market-based education reforms that have undermined teacher professionalism has been to consign teaching to generic labor—with teachers having increasingly less voice in and control over the work that they do.

THE CRISIS OF THE US TEACHING CORPS

While it is important to examine these developments in the work of teachers in the context of the larger dynamics of the global economy, it would be a mistake to understand them as the product of an "invisible hand" of the global economy that enforces its logic on society, irrespective of the actions and intentions of political actors. Rather, these developments are the product of government policies, and as such, they were adopted and enacted through political processes—contests between different political actors, with some more powerful than others. If these contests had ended otherwise, it would have produced a different set of policies, with different consequences for the work of teachers. With changes in the political balance of power, such as those that the Teacher Insurgency has the potential to bring, different policies are again possible.

By the time Teacher Spring erupted, the issues that resulted from the underfunding of public education and the deprofessionalization and deskilling of teaching had come together in a perfect storm, producing a growing crisis in the American teaching corps. The pipeline into teaching had been shrinking at an alarming rate, as college students began to regard a teaching career as less and less desirable. In fact, from pre-recession levels, there had been a 27.4 percent decline in students completing teacher education and preparation programs and an even greater drop—37.8 percent—in students enrolling in these programs.[28]

Simultaneously, teachers were leaving the profession in large numbers. In 2018, the Bureau of Labor Statistics' "Job Opening and Labor Turnover Survey" found the highest-ever recorded rate of educator turnover and job leaving in state and local education.[29] The attrition rate for American teachers has been high for a few decades: 44 percent of all first-year teachers leave the profession in five years, and 300,000 teachers leave every year, two-thirds of them before reaching their retirement age. The annual rate of attrition of American teachers appears to be consistently more than double the average in other OECD nations.[30] So the combination of high attrition rates and a shrinking pipeline was particularly troubling, turning the educational workforce into a "leaky bucket" in which teachers left at a faster rate than qualified replacements could be found. American K–12 schools began the 2018–2019 school year with over 100,000 vacancies, almost doubling the shortage of three years before, and over one-third of the schools with vacancies reported that they found them "very difficult" to fill. As a consequence, open positions were filled with teachers who lacked the proper credentials to teach in their subjects. Teacher Spring states Arizona and Oklahoma had particularly acute teaching shortages.[31]

Reflecting this crisis of the American teaching corps, half of public school teachers told the national 2019 PDK/Gallup poll on education that in recent years they had seriously considered leaving the profession.[32] A majority indicated a willingness to strike for higher pay (a number that went as high as two-thirds among the most poorly paid), for better funding for their schools, and for a greater say in such matters as academic standards and testing. Even a larger portion of public school parents—three in every four—said that they would support such strikes under the circumstances. These sentiments were the kindling that, lit by the spark of the West Virginia strike, created the prairie fire of the Teacher Insurgency.

CHAPTER 3

The Political Context of the Teacher Insurgency

WHEN THE STRIKES OF TEACHER SPRING took place in 2018, there was no shortage of issues for teachers to protest. Yet as historians and sociologists of social movements have often noted, economic hardship and declining social status are not by themselves sufficient conditions for the emergence of popular opposition movements. In the absence of a compelling sense that an alternative is possible, the great mass of the population will simply try to make the best of even the most desperate of circumstances. To understand how and why so many American teachers came to believe that collective action in the form of strikes and other protests could change the conditions described in chapter 2, given all of the sacrifices and risks those actions entailed, we must examine three contextual factors: an expectations gap, the reemergence of mass protests in American politics, and the changing terrain of educational politics in the US. This chapter will analyze all three of these trends, with the objective of answering the question: *Why is the Teacher Insurgency taking place now, at this particular moment in the history of American education and American teacher unionism?*

THE EXPECTATIONS GAP

Since the rise of teacher unions in the 1960s and 1970s, if not before, Americans who became teachers had two modest sets of expectations:

(1) that while it would not make them wealthy, teaching would provide a middle-class standard of living for themselves and their families, including comprehensive health insurance and a pension that would make it possible to retire in security and dignity; and (2) that in their classrooms and schools, they would be able to engage in meaningful and rewarding labor that allowed them to make a positive difference in the lives of their students. Over the course of the last two decades, a growing gap has opened between those expectations and the lived reality of American teachers.

Part of this expectations gap is unique to teachers, the product of deteriorating teaching and learning conditions that came with the underfunding of schools and the growing teacher alienation from their labor that resulted from education reforms premised on a business model of schooling. But another part of the gap reflects a wider development among all college-educated workers, especially millennials. Coming of age in an era of exploding economic inequality marked by stagnant wages and declining economic mobility, and living through a "recovery" from the Great Recession in which the benefits were directed to the wealthiest Americans with little to spare for middle- and low-income wage earners, college-educated millennials found that the middle-class life promised to them as the fruits of education and hard work increasingly appeared to be a mirage.[1]

The growing cost of postsecondary education has been of particular salience for these millennials, as it has saddled many of them with unmanageable student loan debt. Since 2006, that debt has approximately doubled its share of the economy: more than 45 million borrowers in the US now owe student loan debts, totaling $1.5 trillion—more than all sources of debt in the economy save home mortgages. Nearly one in every four student loan borrowers is in default or struggling to repay loans.[2] Given the contours of the American political economy, students from working-class and poor families and students of color are those most often in need of student loans to pay for college, and the burden of loan debt falls disproportionately on them.[3]

What is not generally understood, however, is how especially acute the problem of student loan debt is for millennial teachers. The average student loan debt for an MA in education grew 87 percent between 2002 and 2016, far outpacing the increases for all other MA degrees.

Moreover, over the same period, the portion of students taking out loans for an MA in education increased from 41.4 percent to 56.2 percent of all students.[4] Also, as noted in chapter 2, the teacher salary penalty had burgeoned, so that as the Teacher Insurgency developed, teachers were earning 21.4 percent less than similarly educated professionals.[5] The combination of these two developments—increased student loan debt and diminished real income in comparison with other professionals—left millennial teachers in a particularly difficult economic situation.

Precisely because the depths of the economic straits faced by millennial teachers are a development that was not experienced by prior generations, millennial teachers understand them as product of policy choices made by government; consequently, they also believe that alternative policies can be adopted. The belief that an alternative is possible is decisive for collective action.

The expectations gap has significantly shaped the worldview of college-educated millennials, including teachers. Millennials consistently exhibit the highest generational approval ratings for unions, the strongest support for a union role in the economy, and the greatest interest in organizing themselves into unions where they do not already exist. Their support for strengthening teacher unions and paying teachers higher wages is vigorous, as is their support of public education. (Millennial teachers are generally aware that teacher unions and collective bargaining bring with them a significant wage premium.)[6]

Politically, millennials have increasingly tacked to the left, as seen in their active backing of Democrats in general and for tribunes of the democratic left such as Elizabeth Warren, Bernie Sanders, and Alexandria Ocasio-Cortez. Confronting an economy that does not deliver for them, millennials strongly advocate government action aimed at reducing income inequality, and approximately half of millennials have indicated in polls that they would prefer a socialist economy, presumably along the lines of the social democratic Scandinavian model.[7] (It is worth noting that there has been a general shift to the left by the Democratic electorate of all ages, largely in reaction to growing income inequality and climate change; millennials are the vanguard of that development.[8])

A number of historians and sociologists have focused on the role of unfulfilled expectations in the development of social movements and revolution, pointing to the rising expectations that ultimately found expression in the French Revolution and the civil rights movement of the 1950s and 1960s.[9] In this reading, it is *relative deprivation*—the gap between what one expects and what one experiences—that is important. For millennial teachers, that gap is a chasm.

No wonder, then, that younger teachers were often in the forefront of the organizing for the Teacher Insurgency. For historians of American labor, this is significant: the two great waves of unionization in the twentieth century, the industrial unions of the 1930s and the public-sector unions of the 1960s, were spearheaded by younger generations.

THE REEMERGENCE OF PROTEST MOVEMENTS

Why did the worldview born out of the expectations gap find expression in the strikes of the Teacher Insurgency? Before the Teacher Spring, the one notable instance of a statewide strike in the last half-century was the 1990 strike of West Virginia teachers.[10] In West Virginia—as well as in the other Teacher Spring states of Kentucky, North Carolina, and Oklahoma—teacher salaries, health insurance, and pensions are set by the state government, so statewide action becomes the only route of redress when the government chooses to take advantage of teachers on those matters. Yet strikes against state governments are a rarity in American labor history, so it was far from preordained that they would occur. Almost thirty years after the 1990 West Virginia strike, there was a relatively small number of teachers still in active service who had participated in that action. Its oral history—and that of West Virginia's history of militant mine union strikes—did provide inspiration for the 2018 strikers, but heroic history can take a movement only so far.

The experiences of contemporary mass protests were a more vital and formative force in the development of the Teacher Insurgency than historical memories. While strikes had dwindled to a very few in the American labor movement over the last four decades, with K–12 education as part of this trend, the 2012 strike of the Chicago Teachers Union stood as a powerful example that a strike in the education sector could be organized and won. It transformed the horizons of what teachers across the US saw as possible.

Just as important, since it provided firsthand experience, was the reemergence of the mass protest movement in the US following a decades-long period of relative political quiescence. Many of the teachers who organized Teacher Insurgency had participated in or observed closely one or more such protests, from Occupy Wall Street and Black Lives Matter to the wide swath of resistance to the Trump presidency—the Women's March, the airport shutdowns and demonstrations in response to the Muslim travel ban, the demonstrations and civil disobedience on behalf of the DACA Dreamers and against the separation of immigrant Latino children from their parents, the Me Too movement, and the nationwide school protests and March for Our Lives that followed in the wake of the Parkland school shootings. More than a few of these teachers were involved in the national protests against the confirmation of Trump's secretary of education, Betsy DeVos, which centered on her long-held agenda of privatizing public education. The mobilizing tools and methods employed in Teacher Insurgency, such as the widespread use of social media, were often drawn from the experiences of these protest movements.

To understand the Teacher Insurgency, then, it will be necessary to overcome a major shortcoming in studies of the American labor movement: for reasons that would take us beyond the scope of this study, the prevailing theoretical framework of labor studies has viewed organized labor through the lens of what C. Wright Mills called a "labor metaphysic"—as a sui generis social movement with an organizational logic rooted in economic production that is not only distinct but also fundamentally different from the logic of other popular social movements.[11] Attention has been paid to the intersection of the labor movement and the civil rights and anti-racist, feminist, LGBTQ, immigrant rights, and environmental movements, with a focus on their efforts to win the support of organized labor—endeavors that have been increasingly successful in recent history. Labor studies have, however, adopted a largely unexamined assumption that the organization of a class-based movement is of an entirely different order than the organization of movements against other forms of domination. That has always been an unnecessarily limiting approach, obscuring as much as its reveals, and it is especially unhelpful in understanding the strategic challenges posed by Teacher Insurgency, given the role of mass protest movements in its development.

The Teacher Insurgency brought together protest and politics. The 2018 Teacher Spring strikes were unavoidably political, given their objective of compelling action by state governments; and unlike the 2012 and 2019 Chicago strikes and the 2019 Los Angeles, Oakland, and Denver strikes, they were for the most part illegal. Part of what made them possible and what contributed to their success was the changing political environment.

In an unprecedented sea change, public support for 2018 and 2019 Teacher Insurgency strikes has been very wide and deep; poll after poll has consistently demonstrated an approval rate in the range of 75 percent to 80 percent.[12] (During the 1960s and 1970s, when teacher strikes were fairly common, they engendered considerable public opposition.[13]) Local community support for the Teacher Spring was so strong that in an extraordinary move, many local school districts in Virginia, Oklahoma, and Arizona officially closed their schools during the strikes, protecting teachers from potentially negative legal consequences for striking. When Ronald Reagan's secretary of education, Bill Bennet, and Donald Trump's secretary of education, Betsy DeVos, polemicized against the Teacher Spring strikes, wielding the right-wing trope that teachers did not care about their students, their attacks fell on deaf ears. The criticism of the Los Angeles strike by Barack Obama's Secretary of Education, Arne Duncan, was similarly impotent.[14]

Part of what made the strikes of the Teacher Insurgency possible and gave them the successes they won was the changing political environment in which they took place—and to which they in turn contributed. After nearly two decades of sustained teacher bashing and attacks on unions and public education, the terrain of educational politics in the US was undergoing a major transformation, and the Teacher Insurgency revealed just how different the contours of the new landscape were shaping up to be.

Particularly stark illustrations of this changing topography can be found in the mass media. A decade ago, the cover of *Time* magazine starred then Washington, DC schools superintendent and prominent education reformer Michelle Rhee, broom in hand, to symbolize her "clean sweep" campaigns against the district's teachers and their union. Not long afterward, *The Atlantic* turned over its pages to a manifesto from Joel Klein, who had served as the high-profile education reform chancellor of New York City's public schools. After the strikes of Teacher Spring, the *Time* cover featured a rank-and-file teacher, with the caption, "I have a master's degree, 16 years of experience, work two extra jobs and donate blood plasma to pay the bills. I'm a teacher in America." And in July 2019, *The Atlantic* published an essay by venture capitalist Nick Hanauer recanting his previous support for the education reform precept that schools caused economic inequality.[15]

To understand how the changes captured in those images and articles created a political ground favorable to the Teacher Insurgency, I will first set out the evidence of these changes, and then offer an explanation for why they have occurred.

THE SHIFTING TERRAIN OF EDUCATION POLITICS

A key indicator of a changing political landscape is elections. Even as Donald Trump was winning an Electoral College victory in 2016, signs of changing education politics were appearing electorally, as voters in Massachusetts and Georgia rejected by large margins ballot initiatives that would have dramatically expanded the reach of charter schools in their states. Wealthy education reform outsiders such as former New York City mayor Michael Bloomberg, the Walton family (of Walmart), and Success Academy founder Eva Moskowitz's Families for Excellent Schools poured money into the Massachusetts campaign to lift the cap on the number of charter schools, only to lose by an overwhelming margin.[16] The Massachusetts referendum "marked an important flash point for education reform broadly and charters in particular," a post-mortem memo of the Walton Education Coalition read, "As a test case it was important. And it failed."[17]

In the 2018 primary elections, former Los Angeles mayor Antonio Villaraigosa, heavily backed by charters and voucher advocates, lost the California gubernatorial race to public education supporter Gavin Newsom, and six of the eight members of the Independent Democratic Conference in the New York State Senate, "education reform" partisans who caucused with the Republicans, went down to defeat to progressive, pro–public education opponents. In the general election, Newsom won easily and a progressive Democratic majority took the New York State Senate by storm, winning nearly two-thirds of the chamber. Educators with pro-public education platforms who were friendly to teacher unions won the governorships in Michigan, Minnesota, and Wisconsin, defeating union arch-foe Scott Walker in the process, and Illinois, Kansas, Maine, Nevada, and New Mexico saw Democrats replace Republican governors who had been advocates of school privatization.

The 2016 national teacher of the year, Jahana Hayes, made support for public education a central plank in her platform and won election in a white majority district as Connecticut's first African American member of Congress. The Walton family, Michael Bloomberg, Eli Broad, and Reed Hastings, among others wealthy individuals, funneled over $35 million into the race for the California state superintendent of education, but African American assemblyman Tony Thurmond, a supporter of public education endorsed by the state's teacher unions, still won the election against charter executive Marshall Tuck.[18]

The influence of Teacher Spring was directly felt in the 2018 and 2019 elections. In the red states where the strikes had taken place, the electoral challenges were greatest, but important inroads were nonetheless made. Many analyses focused on how many teachers were elected from these states, but no less important was the defeat of elected officials who had opposed teachers and public education. In West Virginia, teachers were pivotal in defeating GOP State Senate Majority Leader Ryan Ferns, a strident opponent of the spring strike, as well as the Republican house leader. "The teachers certainly hurt Republicans across the state," one GOP state senator conceded. Arizona's David Garcia, an educator who took the Democratic nomination for governor in a surprising primary win, came up short in the general election, but a ballot measure supporting a massive expansion of the state's voucher system was voted down by a 2:1 margin, and classroom teacher Kathy Hoffman was elected as state superintendent of education. In Oklahoma, only four of the nineteen Republican state legislators who had refused to raise taxes to fund public education and teacher salaries during the spring strike made it out of the primary elections; twenty-two educators were elected in November. Inspired in part by Teacher Spring, more teachers stood for public office in 2018 than ever before—across the country, more than three hundred members of the American Federation of Teachers ran, and 60 percent of them won their races.[19] In the 2019 elections, Kentucky governor Matt Bevin, who had been the main antagonist of the state's teachers, driving to cut their pensions and slash public school funding, went down to defeat, with teachers playing a major role.[20]

Changes were also felt in big city mayoral elections, as boosters of market-driven education reform such as New York City's Michael Bloomberg, Chicago's Rahm Emmanuel, Philadelphia's Michael Nutter, and Los Angeles' Antonio Villaraigosa were replaced by mayors who supported public schools.

When elections begin to swing, elected officials and public policy follow in their wake. The Teacher Spring states of Arizona, North Carolina, Oklahoma, and West Virginia saw significant increases in education funding after the 2018 strikes, although the underfunding had been so deep that the gains still lagged below pre–Great Recession levels.[21] Democratic elected officials who had once been among the more outspoken supporters of market-driven education reform, charter schools, and standardized test-driven accountability, such as New York Governor Andrew Cuomo, began to distance themselves from their onetime allies among education privatizers.[22] Reflecting shifts in public opinion, the 2020 Democratic presidential candidates were far more critical of market-driven education reform, standardized test-based accountability, and charter schools than in the past.[23] (The one exception was last-minute entrant Michael Bloomberg.) Nationally, charter advocates have begun to voice concern over what one described as a "flat line" in charter school expansion—a telling apprehension, since it demonstrates that their goal is replacing, not complementing, public district schools.[24]

The Political Vulnerability of the Education Reform Movement

What accounts for these changes in the terrain of educational politics? There is no single cause, rather the convergence of a number of different factors. It is not, however, a case of unconnected causes, spontaneously coming together. At the turn of the twenty-first century, a movement to adopt market-centered and -driven (or, as some would call them, *neoliberal*) education reforms emerged as the dominant presence in American education politics, and it set the parameters of education policy discussions and decision-making. This dominance was the product of a hegemonic political project in which different policies, from vouchers and charter schools to accountability systems based on standardized testing, were woven into one unified political field, intersecting with and reinforcing each other. In the public sphere, this project was given expression through a master narrative of what was "wrong" with American education and how it should be addressed. Teachers, their unions, and public schools were cast in the role of villains, the cause of all that ailed education; the reforms that targeted all three were cast as heroic solutions. Crucially, the education reform narrative represented these market models as a "civil rights" movement that would finally deliver to youth of color living in poverty the quality education that had been the exclusive province of the children of privilege.

It was the unity of this political field and master narrative that facilitated the education reform movement's rise to dominance, as the combination of the different elements in an integrated discourse had a synergistic power. But the very integration of these elements created the basis for their collective decline. As I will outline below, various policies in this field have lost their credibility in recent years, with declining public confidence that they could achieve their stated educational objectives and growing objections to the collateral damage they had wrought. Furthermore, the movement's claim to the mantle of a civil rights movement has proved to be remarkably hollow. Given the way in which these policies and this narrative had been woven together in the education reform movement, the effects of such losses in public confidence were not limited to the discrete policies: the entire political project, with its overarching narrative, began to unravel as its constituent parts crumbled. The result has been what might be properly called a crisis of legitimacy for the education reform movement.[25] While a new hegemonic political presence has yet to be established, the political project of market-centered and -driven education reform is increasingly in disarray. The old world of education politics is dying, but the new world is still struggling to be born.

To understand this process, it is necessary to map the entire field of market-driven education reform and to understand how it came to be unified into a hegemonic political presence. As table 3.1 lays out, the field can be fruitfully conceptualized along three intersecting dimensions—economic, political, and institutional. Each dimension is rooted in a different market modality. The economic dimension is based on the idea that unregulated markets are the most efficacious means for the delivery of economic goods and services, including education, and it generates policies that diminish education as a public good and commodify its delivery. The political dimension rests on the idea that decisions made through markets and by corporations are superior to those produced by democratic modes of governance, which results in policies that undermine democratic voice in education and foster autocratic decision-making. The institutional dimension is based on the idea that the institutional design of business organization and the disciplinary power of the market, especially the effects of competition, provide the best organizational blueprint for spheres of civil society such as education, yielding a business model of schooling. What is essential in understanding the period of political domination by market-centered and -driven education reform is that the unity and coherence of this field was not predetermined or inexorably developed but was constructed piece by piece as a political project.

Among other things, the constructing of this political hegemony involved the capture and transformation of progressive educational innovations that were initially at odds with market-centered and -driven conceptions of schooling. The example of charter schools is illustrative of this process. First developed by the late teacher union leader Al Shanker, the original conception of the charter school laid out a vision of laboratory schools that would be engaged in educational experimentation from which other public schools could learn. In this model, charters would be democratically governed by teachers and parents.[26] Today, only a small minority of charters—largely independent and community-based schools—function in the spirit of the Shanker conception; the great preponderance of charter schools and the national leadership of the charter sector have departed from that vision in dramatic ways.[27] Bereft of educational experimentation, most charter schools—especially the leading charter chains—are fully integrated into all dimensions of

TABLE 3.1
The three dimensions of market-driven education reform

<table>
<tr><th>Economic dimension</th><th>Political dimension</th><th>Institutional dimension</th></tr>
<tr><td>Diminishment of education as a public good; commodification of delivery of education</td><td>Undermining democratic voice in education; autocratic decision-making</td><td>Remaking schools in business model</td></tr>
<tr><td>
<ul>
<li>Austerity:
<ul><li>Underfunding</li><li>Disinvestment in public schools</li></ul></li>
<li>Deregulation:
<ul><li>Charter schools</li><li>"Portfolio" model of schooling in a district</li></ul></li>
<li>Privatization:
<ul><li>Vouchers</li><li>For-profit education management organizations (EMOs)</li><li>Outsourcing of ancillary services, such as transportation and food</li></ul></li>
</ul>
</td><td>
<ul>
<li>Top-down mandates:
<ul><li>No Child Left Behind</li><li>Race to the Top</li></ul></li>
<li>Public school closings without community input</li>
<li>Autocratic view of administrative and management authority—superintendent and principal as CEO</li>
<li>Attacks on teacher unions</li>
<li>Concentration of executive branch power:
<ul><li>Mayoral control/ending school boards</li><li>Removing checks and balances on administrative authority</li><li>State takeovers of school districts</li></ul></li>
</ul>
</td><td>
<ul>
<li>Instrumental view of schooling:
<ul><li>Test-driven curricula</li><li>"No excuses" pedagogy and school culture</li><li>Loss of democratic ends of schooling, such as preparation for citizenship</li></ul></li>
<li>Undermining teacher professionalism:
<ul><li>Teacher as "human capital"</li><li>Loss of professional authority in classroom</li><li>Reduction/elimination of teacher preparation/licensure requirements</li></ul></li>
<li>Punitive accountability systems:
<ul><li>High-stakes, test-driven student promotion</li><li>High-stakes, test-driven teacher evaluation</li><li>High-stakes, test-driven school grading</li></ul></li>
</ul>
</td></tr>
</table>

market-centered and -driven education reform: they utilize "no excuses" curricula and school cultures and employ heavily scripted modes of instruction that allow teachers little professional authority and discretion; they are zealously focused on standardized exams and use them as the basis for high-stakes decisions about students and teachers; they operate with a business model that views teachers as "human capital" and induces their rapid turnover; their boards are dominated by individuals from business and finance, and the decisions of those boards are made without meaningful input from the communities; and they are stridently opposed to the right of their teachers and other employees to organize in unions and bargain collectively, insisting that their administrators be able to function as autocratic decision makers. None of these elements are logically entailed in or necessarily part of the idea of a charter school—a school governed by a board whose members are drawn from civil society, rather than part of elected government, and that operates in a space that is exempt from many existing regulations. Yet through a political process in which proponents of market-driven education reform organized and financed charter schools that utilized them, this model came to dominate and control the charter sector. (A similar process of cooptation and capture took place with the "small school" movement.[28])

The seizure of the legacy of civil rights was central to the education reform movement's ability to present itself as representative of a social justice agenda and broader national interest, even though it was financed and led by the economic elite. Their financial resources, mobilized in a new form of philanthropy that sought to leverage its donations to induce market driven reforms to its liking, did play an important role in the consolidation of this hegemonic project.[29] But it is a mistake to view the dominance of the education reform movement for most of the first two decades of the twenty-first century as simply a "billionaire boys' club" working its collective will or to think that education reformers somehow duped supporters of public education, who were too witless to understand reformer intentions. A hegemonic project requires an element of consensus to dominate; it cannot rule simply through a naked exercise of power.

The cooptation of charter schools, small schools, and the civil rights legacy provides an important window into how the interlocking structure of the education reform movement was put together until it became a hegemonic presence in educational politics. But hegemonic status has its vulnerabilities—when the foundation of a structure is undermined, the entire edifice begins to collapse.

The Crisis of Legitimacy of the Education Reform Movement

Ever since No Child Left Behind, education reform advocates have framed their policies as an alternative to the status quo of public schools. This positioning allowed them to exploit the injustices in American education—the "savage inequalities," to borrow Jonathan Kozol's term, that resulted from government policies of unequal school funding and institutionalized racial and class segregation—even as they found their political support in elected officials who, when not actively promoting these inequalities, were doing nothing to remedy them. The promise of good schools was deeply appealing to families who bore the brunt of those inequalities—especially those in racially segregated communities with high concentrations of poverty.

After nearly two decades in power, however, this brand of education reform is now the status quo, with a record that can be measured against its promises—and found wanting. The gap between the promise and the record is perhaps most evident in the national showcase of this brand of education reform: Washington, DC. When Chancellor Michelle Rhee was instituting evaluation and accountability systems that education reformers held up as a national model, she declared that within five years, DC public schools would be "the highest performing urban school district in the country." But after ten years under Rhee and her close lieutenant and successor Kaya Henderson, Washington was not even remotely close to such status. Using Rhee's own preferred metric of performance on standardized exams, progress has been rather modest, no better than that under Rhee's two predecessors. On the nation's report card, the National Assessment of Educational Progress, DC has moved from dead last—fifty-first among states—to forty-seventh; among urban school districts, DC's 2017 scores remain "significantly lower" than the national average scores in the four benchmarks exams—fourth- and eighth-grade reading and mathematics. A significant portion of the gains that did occur can be attributed to changing student demographics; public schools were impacted by the gentrification of DC during this period, as the numbers of white students and students from professional-class families increased, while DC's race and class achievement gaps persisted unabated. Supporters of

Rhee's policies initially made much of an improved high school graduation rate, but investigations soon revealed that with schools under massive pressure from above to boost their numbers, a third of all DC graduates had not fulfilled the requirements for graduation but had been pushed through nonetheless.[30]

There was, however, one dramatic change in DC public schools as a result of Rhee's policies: a massive decline in the share of African American teachers—over 27 percentage points in a school district where the majority of students are African American and students of color account for more than 80 percent of the total student body.[31] The 2010 electoral defeat of Rhee's patron, Mayor Adrian Fenty—which was attributed by many observers to his unqualified support of Rhee's stewardship of DC public schools—was one of the first signs of a developing public opposition to market-driven education reform. As the disappointing performance of Washington's education reform was repeated elsewhere, this opposition grew.

The record of charter schools across the nation fared little better. Rigorous studies show that despite enrolling many fewer high need students who are the most challenging and costly to educate—primarily English language learners and students with special needs—charter schools have generally performed no better than public district schools on standardized exams.[32] A study of thirty-three charter middle schools across fifteen states conducted by Mathematica and the US Department of Education's Institute of Education Sciences (IES) is illustrative; it found that "on average, charter middle schools that hold lotteries are neither more nor less successful than traditional public schools in improving student achievement, behavior, and school progress."[33] To sustain their advocacy, charter supporters increasingly resorted to claims involving select subgroups of charter schools that had higher scores on standardized exams.[34]

Poor test score performance also bedeviled privatization efforts. In 2016 and 2017, rigorous studies of four flagship state voucher programs—Louisiana, Indiana, Ohio, and Washington, DC—showed that students using vouchers to attend private schools did more poorly on standardized exams than those attending public schools.[35]

Test scores had been the centerpiece of the claim that public schools were "failing" and needed to be replaced. But now, facing evidence that undermined their desired policy objectives, market-driven education reform advocates began to field arguments that standardized exams were inappropriate measures of the value of their preferred schools.[36] To be sure, the problems with using student scores on high-stakes standardized exams to gauge educational performance are quite real and far-reaching—they are just not particular to private schools or charter schools. Compelling research has shown that teachers who have positive impacts on non-tested skills of students, such as emotional and social growth, can have as much as a ten times greater effect on student success than teachers whose students show test-score growth.[37] (The measures of success included graduating high school on time, grade-point average at graduation, taking the SAT, and reported intentions to enroll in a four-year college.) High-stakes, standardized exam–based accountability fails to capture what is truly important in teaching and learning. But if anyone lacked the credibility to make such a case, it was education reform advocates who had been all too ready to wield the crude bludgeon of standardized test scores when it had served their policy goals.

As the testing regime of NCLB and RTTT expanded and additional state, local, and school exams were added to the mix, many parents became increasingly concerned about the effects on their children's education and general well-being.[38] A growing opt-out movement from standardized testing developed, challenging the linchpin of the accountability systems of market-driven education reform. It found allies in educators opposed to the use of test scores in their evaluations. Increasingly, test-based accountability became an agenda whose primary constituency was the business elite that found its bottom-line approach to schooling congenial to its worldview.

Democracy in Education Under Attack

Advocates of market-driven education reform have never been reticent about their intentions to substitute the unfettered rule of the market for democracy in education. In the classic academic brief for school privatization, *Politics, Markets and Schools,* John Chubb and Terry Moe were explicit that the market should supplant the democratic governance of schools, which they described as "inherently destructive of school autonomy and inherently conducive to bureaucracy."[39] For Chubb and

Moe, schools functioned best when managed by principals with the power of a CEO of a non-union, largely unregulated business. In this paradigm shift, the economic and political dimensions of education reform are interwoven as an individual economic right to "exit' is substituted for collective democratic "voice" over schools: the educational citizen is remade into a consumer whose only power is the individual choice to leave.[40]

The drive for autocratic power extended well beyond the school. Over the course of the last decade and a half, market-driven education reformers became the strongest supporters of concentrating educational power in the hands of executives—mayors, governors, state departments of education, the US Department of Education—with few or no checks and balances on their authority. From such positions of unencumbered decision-making, the education reform agenda could be enacted, even in the face of widespread public opposition.

This process disempowered local communities, especially the high-poverty, urban communities of color that were the primary target of education reform efforts. Historically, state and local control of education has been pivotal in the incorporation of schools into the American political economy of class and race: it provided the governmental architecture that facilitated the establishment and maintenance of school segregation by race and class and maintained inequitable funding of schools. Consequently, efforts to address these inequalities have often relied on other sources of governmental power, such as federal courts and the federal executive branch, to counteract state and local authorities. The use of the federal government to end de jure racial segregation of public schools in the South, starting with *Brown v. Board of Education*, was emblematic of such efforts. History had taught communities of color to be suspicious of state and local education authorities and to look to the federal government to protect their interests.

But urban communities of color soon found that the governance changes of market-centered and -driven education reform promoted by the federal executive branch under both the Bush and Obama presidencies—imposition of mayoral control, state takeovers of local districts, and replacement of local district schools and school boards with private voucher schools and charter schools run by corporate-dominated boards—did nothing to address the institutionalized racism and class privilege of segregation and inequitable funding that plagued American education. At the same time, the burden of these changes fell disproportionately on communities of color, with the effect of severely restricting their democratic voice in the important decisions regarding the schools serving their communities.[41]

Indeed, on several crucial fronts, these governance changes led to reversals in efforts to bring greater racial and class equity to American schools. Teacher diversity in centers of education reform such as New Orleans, Washington, DC, and Chicago suffered major setbacks as the numbers of African American teachers plummeted.[42] The education reform center of New York City told a story of deterioration in the educational status of African American and Latino students under the Bloomberg-Klein administration: the numbers of African American and Latino students admitted to the elite exam high schools, already very low, shrank to near-extinction levels; the numbers of African American and Latino students in elementary school gifted and talented programs fell dramatically after these programs were reorganized and based solely on high-stakes testing; and the achievement gap between white students and African American and Latino students on the state's high-stakes standardized exams increased.[43] When questioned about a NAACP lawsuit charging that the admission process for the elite high schools was racially discriminatory, Mayor Bloomberg retorted, "Life isn't fair."[44]

"No excuses" charter schools in communities of color adopted the most extreme versions of "zero tolerance," employing punitive discipline measures on a scale that raised serious concerns that they were contributing to a school-to-prison pipeline.[45] A particularly heavy blow to communities of color was the adoption of so-called portfolio policies that led to the closure of public schools, leaving their communities either without a local school or with charter schools in which they had no real voice.[46] For all of the shortcomings that segregation and inequitable funding had brought, the public schools in communities of color and high poverty had anchored their neighborhoods: they were often one of a very few public institutions directly serving them, and their loss was deeply felt in a way that the technocratic authors of these reforms never cared to understand. When the NAACP and Black Lives Matter took high-profile stands against school closures and school privatization and called for a moratorium on the expansion of charter schools—striking a serious political blow to education reformers who had marketed themselves as an educational civil rights movement—they were reflecting grassroots resistance to the diminishment of democratic voice in schools serving communities of color.[47]

The narrative of education reform never stood alone: it was incorporated into a larger discourse that sought to promote and justify the market-driven policies that had resulted in an explosion of economic inequality in the US and across the globe since the 1980s—austerity, privatization, deregulation, and corporate-directed free trade. The mantra of former New York City Public Schools Chancellor Joel Klein—"Some people say we can't fix schools until we fix poverty, but I say we can't fix poverty until we fix schools"—was music to the ears of the economic elite that had so heartily benefited from that gap.[48] His axiom did more than dismiss the many obstacles faced by youth living in poverty as they pursued their education; by casting blame on schools for the economic condition of their students and the community, it provided an alibi for the decades of market-driven economic policy that had produced that economic inequality, and excused the vast inequities within American education caused by unequal funding and by race and class segregation. It offered as a programmatic solution to poverty more of the very same policies, now applied to public education, with the bonus of attacking one of the few remaining pockets of strength in the American labor movement—teacher unions. Little wonder that Wall Street and Silicon Valley hastened to support this agenda.

But if the narrative of education reform benefited from its symbiotic relationship with this larger discourse of market fundamentalism when it was dominant, it would pay a price as the growing opposition to economic inequality, starting with the Occupy Wall Street movement, sent that discourse into decline.

The Trump/DeVos Effect

The 2016 election of Donald Trump and his choice of Betsy DeVos as secretary of education accelerated the tectonic shifts in US education politics. The divisive political rhetoric regularly employed by Trump, with its continuous appeals to racism and authoritarianism, polarizes public opinion. To the extent that a particular stance on an issue is now identified closely with Trump, opposition to that stance grows among his opponents and the public at large, while support for it becomes more intense in his smaller base.[49] Education issues are not as strongly connected to Trump as his racist views on immigration and Muslims, both of which have generated a counter-reaction—the strongest support for immigration and acceptance of Muslims in the history of polling on those issues. But there has nonetheless been a distinct "Trump effect" in education, to the detriment of the education reform agenda he supports.

While many leading education reformers chose to see in Trump a champion who had promised to invest $20 billion in school privatization efforts, most in education were unwilling to ignore the racism and authoritarianism at the center of his campaign and administration. Trump's opponents included a minority in the ranks of education reformers who were deeply concerned at the damage he could do to their cause. When seeking a secretary of education, Trump met with the two most high-profile and anti-union education reformers, Michelle Rhee and Eva Moskowitz. Instead of lending his support, Democrats for Education Reform President Shavar Jeffries revealed the emerging divisions in the ranks of reformers with an unmistakable shot across their bow: "The policies and rhetoric of President-elect Trump run contrary to the most fundamental values of what it means to be a progressive committed to educating our kids and strengthening our families and communities. No Democrat should accept appointment as Secretary of Education." Those divisions went deep enough that Jeffries would soon leave the board of Moskowitz's Success Academy.[50]

Under intense pressure from education reform circles, both Rhee and Moskowitz publicly withdrew from consideration but still offered their support to Trump and endorsed his nomination of Betsy DeVos, a prominent financial backer of educational privatization from a billionaire family influential in the Republican Party. "Betsy DeVos has the talent, commitment, and leadership capacity to revitalize our public schools and deliver the promise of opportunity," Moskowitz opined, even as DeVos badly fumbled her confirmation hearings and faced massive opposition from American educators. Barely winning confirmation to office through a tie-breaking vote by Vice President Mike Pence, DeVos would go on to consistently garner the lowest approval ratings—in the mid- to low 20 percent range—in a Trump cabinet generally held in poor repute. Her identification with the education reform agenda would compound the negative Trump effect.[51]

After years of prodigious self-promotion, Eva Moskowitz was the face of the charter school sector best known to the general public, and her dalliance with Trump and DeVos became an object lesson in how leading education reform advocates who allied themselves with such politics would damage their movement. Moskowitz's warm embrace of Trump and DeVos, including hosting Ivanka Trump in a post-election visit to her schools, garnered increased scrutiny of her autocratic management of the Success Academy chain. Particular attention was paid to its use of punitive zero tolerance practices and the central role of right-wing Wall Street financiers and Trump supporters in its operations.[52] It was not until Trump's infamous August 2017 declaration that there were "good people on both sides" in the wake of neo-Nazi violence in Charlottesville, Virginia, that Moskowitz finally saw the need to create political distance from him.[53] By then the damage was done: the education reform claim on the legacy of the civil rights movement had become laughable. Education politics were in the midst of a dramatic transformation, one that would play a significant role in changing the balance of power in New York State in the 2020 elections.

THE TEACHER INSURGENCY: WHY NOW?

The issues that inspired the Teacher Insurgency supplied its immediate causes. But movements never arise solely because of issues. In the case of the Teacher Insurgency, most of the motivating issues were longstanding, so they cannot answer the question "Why now?" A full understanding of the emergence of the Teacher Insurgency requires an examination of the underlying trends that I have examined in this chapter—the expectations gap for teachers, especially of the millennial generation; the growth of protest movements; and the shifting terrain of educational politics as education reform lost its hegemonic position over education politics. In combination, these historical and contextual factors produced a political moment where teachers across the US were moved to collective action, having concluded that it—and only it—could address the issues that deeply concerned them.

The careful reader will note that this chapter has not discussed in any detail the role of teacher mobilization and organization and the work of teacher unions in these three trends, although they play a very significant role. That analysis is best conducted in the context of addressing the strategic and organizing questions posed by the Teacher Insurgency. I now turn to these questions in part 2 of this book.

PART TWO

The Strategic Challenges in Perspective

CHAPTER 4

Mobilization and Organization

From Civil Rights to Social Media

THE TEACHER INSURGENCY stands at the nexus of three deep democratic currents in American political life: public education, the labor movement, and protest movements. In this respect, it reflects the history of teacher unions and teacher collective action in which it is embedded. However, while the association of teacher unions with public education and with the labor movement is universally acknowledged, few understand their deep ties to democratic protest movements or the ways in which teacher unions function as a species of protest movement. In particular, far too little attention is paid to the powerful bond of teacher unions and teacher organizing with the one democratic protest movement—the civil rights movement—that has played an important role in the history of these unions and in the history of the American labor movement generally. As a consequence, the strategic cross-fertilization that has taken place between teacher unionism and the labor movement on the one hand and the civil rights movement and other democratic protest movements on the other is rarely examined.

This omission results in a cramped understanding of teacher organizing and collective action, and ill prepares us to understand the strategic issues that confront teacher unionism as a protest movement. Of particular salience in this regard is the strategic question I examine in this chapter: the relationship between *mobilization* (the work of generating mass participation in a particular action, such as a strike or a demonstration) and *organization* (the work of establishing and deploying ongoing relationships and structures that contest for power, such as a union). I will focus on a particular mode of mobilization that is often mistakenly seen as a substitute for the work of organization—mobilization through social media. Using an analysis of how solidarity is created and sustained, I conclude that mobilization, including the use of social media, must be understood as complementary to the organizing work of teacher unions. To be politically efficacious, teacher collective action and teacher unionism require a solid organizational foundation.

TEACHER UNIONISM AND PROTEST MOVEMENTS

Much of the rich history of solidarity and common work between teacher unions and the civil rights movement has yet to be recorded. The history books recount how in 1968, Martin Luther King, Jr., was assassinated in Memphis, where he has gone to support striking African American sanitation workers. Less appreciated is that King's relationships with labor included a strong bond with the American Federation of Teachers (AFT) and its New York City local, the United Federation of Teachers (UFT), which arguably provided more support to the movement in the South than any other union local in the United States.[1] A. Philip Randolph is credited for unique stature in the African American community as the head of the Brotherhood of Sleeping Car Porters and the civil rights leader who in the 1940s organized the first March on Washington movement, but his close relationship with the AFT and its New York City locals is left for the footnotes—despite the fact that one of his most valued partners in organizing both the Brotherhood and the March of Washington project was teacher unionist Layle Lane. Lane was the AFT vice president who led that union's civil rights work as it moved to ban and expel racially segregated locals in the 1950s and became the only national education organization to file an amicus brief in *Brown v. Board of Education*.[2] Perhaps the most light has been shed on the close relationship between teacher unionism and the organizing genius of the civil rights movement, Bayard Rustin, who was responsible for introducing King to the Gandhian discipline of nonviolent direct action during the Montgomery Bus Boycott and who, working with

Randolph, organized the 1963 March on Washington. But even then, accounts usually focus narrowly on Rustin's loyalty to the UFT during the difficult and divisive Ocean Hill-Brownsville strike of 1968 and the political price that Rustin paid for that loyalty.[3]

In the 1960s and 1970s, when teacher unions and other public-sector unions were first established and emerged as formidable political forces, most national and local leaders were active supporters of the civil rights movement, including key leaders who were actually veterans of the civil rights struggle. Sandy Feldman, who went on to serve as UFT and AFT president, is an example; she began as a Congress of Racial Equality (CORE) activist who was arrested for civil disobedience in the Route 50 Freedom Rides and was part of the group of young Socialist Party activists who provided Bayard Rustin with his organizer cadre for the 1963 March on Washington.[4] But Feldman was far from alone. Dick Parrish, who served as an officer of the UFT and AFT, had been Rustin's partner as a youth organizer of Randolph's first March on Washington and was a key organizer of both the Freedom Schools of Prince Edward County, Virginia, in 1963 and the 1964 Mississippi Freedom Summer.[5] Velma Hill, who led the organization of the paraprofessionals into the UFT, was a veteran of CORE and had been injured in her struggle to integrate Rainbow Beach in Chicago.[6] Nat LaCour, who served as president of United Teachers of New Orleans and later AFT secretary-treasurer, had been a leader of the African American students at Southern University during a series of civil rights protests in 1960.[7] Leaders such as Feldman, Parrish, Hill, and LaCour drew on their experiences as civil rights activists in their approach to organizing and leading their local unions and the AFT.

In a similar way, many of the leaders and activists of the Teacher Insurgency have participated in the new protest movements of the last decade, especially the movements that have emerged since Trump's election—the Women's March, the demonstrations against the Muslim travel ban, the protests against the separation of immigrant Latino children from their parents, the Me Too movement, and the campaigns against school shootings. Their experiences helped to shape their approaches to the Teacher Insurgency strikes, including the ways in which they understood the key relationship between mobilization and organization.

CHANGING MODES OF PROTEST MOBILIZATION

To understand the Teacher Insurgency through the lens of a democratic protest movement, it is useful to place it in historical perspective. At the start of the 1960s, there were two pivotal mobilizations: the 1960 strike by New York City's UFT and the 1963 March on Washington for Jobs and Freedom. Both events were portents of significant political change. With the 1960 strike, teachers in the largest school district in the United States won the right to collective bargaining, setting off a wave of collective bargaining victories across the country; the 1963 March set the stage for passage of the historic 1964 Civil Rights Act and the 1965 Voting Rights Act.

Before the 1960s, there had never been a teacher strike for collective bargaining in the United States or a successful national mass demonstration in the nation's capitol.[8] And with good reason: the mobilization challenges faced by the UFT and the March on Washington team were as daunting as they were unprecedented. The UFT needed to convince a significant number of New York City's fifty-thousand public school teachers—spread out across three hundred square miles in nearly one thousand different schools—to engage in an illegal strike for collective bargaining, knowing that this action could cost them their careers. Rustin and the March on Washington team needed to recruit a legion of local organizers in major cities across the country to mobilize hundreds of thousands of Americans; organize a small armada of buses, trains, and cars to bring them to DC; plan for enough water stations and portable toilets; negotiate who would be invited to speak and when; and then conduct a peaceful and orderly rally in which all could participate.

To accomplish these tasks, the organizers of these events depended on established organizational infrastructures. The 1960 strike was made possible by a network of teacher union activists across New York City. Starting from a core of teachers drawn to unionism by their democratic socialist and social democratic politics, this network had been built painstakingly over a number of years of unglamorous union work, from representing individual teachers in disciplinary proceedings to lobbying city and state governments for improved salaries and pensions.[9] The 1963 March was made possible by an alliance of civil rights organizations, African American churches, progressive unions, and liberal and left organizations that had coalesced in support of the civil rights struggles in the South during the 1950s.[10] Of particular importance was the Negro American Labor Council (NALC), a national network of African American trade unionists founded by Randolph that brought together a number of experienced hands expert at union, civil rights, and community mobilizations.[11] Progressive unions, including the United Auto Workers and the UFT, provided essential financial support.

In both events, the technology of mobilization and the means of communication were rudimentary by today's standards. Organizers relied on a limited number of face-to-face meetings; one-on-one telephone calls; and leaflets, letters, and press releases banged out on manual typewriters, run off on mimeograph machines, and distributed by mail or in person. In the 1960 strike, teachers had to commandeer nearby pay phones to let the union offices know what was happening at their schools in real time. As a matter of necessity, most communications had to go through an organizational center.

Information was gathered and deployed in ways that seem quaint five decades later. In the 1960 strike, the UFT adapted the "Delany Card" system (used by high school and middle school teachers to keep track of the attendance and grades of the many classes of students they taught) to organize its pickets at schools across the city.[12] In the 1963 March, the national office put together an index card database of buses that could be rented and train space available so it could provide contacts in the field with the information they needed and keep track of how many participants were coming to Washington from different locations.

The methods used in the mobilizations of the 1960 UFT strike and the 1963 March on Washington were characteristic of the role of organization in the labor and civil rights movement in general. Perhaps no analysis better documents this reality than Charles Payne's masterful history of the civil rights movement in Mississippi, *I've Got the Light of Freedom*, which details how "the organizing tradition" provided the indispensable foundation of the freedom struggle in that state.[13]

Compare these two mobilizations of the early 1960s with two that took place more than a half-century later: the 2017 Women's March and the 2018 Teacher Spring strikes.[14] Revolutionary changes in the means of communication—the development of social media such as Facebook and Twitter, mass emails, and videoconferencing platforms—made it both far easier and less costly to mobilize large numbers of people.[15] These new means of communication expanded the reach of mobilization efforts well beyond existing "real life" organizations and networks that took years to build into the virtual networks that can come together on digital platforms in a viral instant. As a result, the time required to mobilize large masses of people was shortened, and the numbers mobilized grew mightily: the 2017 Women's March, the largest demonstration in the history of the United States, was mobilized to take place in sites across the country in a matter of weeks, and the Teacher Spring strikes spread across West Virginia and into other red states like a wildfire. Organization continued to play an indispensable role in these mobilizations: established unions provided the infrastructure for school and district meetings, called the Teacher Spring strikes, and organized strike activities. And it was established feminist groups, unions, faith communities, and political organizations that rented buses and trains for the central Women's March in Washington and arranged for the infrastructure of the main demonstration and of the sister demonstrations in many additional cities. But mobilization was no longer the sole province of organization, as it had been in the 1960 strike and the 1963 March.

Internet communication transformed how the mobilization's message was transmitted to the larger society. The 1960 strike and the 1963 March took place just as American politics was being transformed by a revolutionary change in mass media—the widespread consumption of television. During the 1950s, the number of Americans who had televisions in their homes grew from 5 percent to 90 percent. By 1960, the new medium had begun to shape public perception of range of subjects in significant ways. Beginning with nightly network news coverage of the 1955 Montgomery bus boycott, the civil rights movement was the first domestic political controversy to be consistently viewed in living rooms across the country. Broadcast scenes of brutal racist violence against nonviolent civil rights demonstrators galvanized public opinion against the Jim Crow regime in the South.[16] The 1963 March received widespread television coverage, with millions of Americans watching Martin Luther King deliver his iconic "I Have a Dream" speech.

The movements of the 1960s quickly became aware of the power of television to frame public perception of their protests—one common demonstration chant of the era was "The whole world is watching."[17] But they also soon discovered that this power could be used to their disadvantage, a reality that would become clear to striking teachers and their unions in the 1960s and 1970s.[18] For all of its extensive reach, television was a unidirectional medium, organized hierarchically, and protesters on the margins of power had limited access to it. By contrast, in the twenty-first century, social media are interactive, and Americans learned about the Women's March and the Teacher Spring strikes as much from posts on social media as from mainstream television and print media. (About two-thirds of all Americans currently report getting the majority of their news from social media.[19])

As the Women's March and the Teacher Spring strikes demonstrate, these new means of communication are extraordinarily powerful. One of the key lessons of the Teacher Insurgency is that any mobilization and public messaging strategy of teacher unions going forward must embrace and incorporate their use. This will not always be easy: unions will need to learn how to work productively in a world where communications between their members occur as much outside of established organizational channels as within them. A positive approach is necessary, one that views online communication not as a threat, but as an indispensable set of tools that can enable greater membership engagement, facilitate mobilization, and extend the reach of the union's message.

SOLIDARITY AND COLLECTIVE ACTION

But we also need to be clear about the limitations of mobilizations that rely too heavily on social media; there is a continuing need for established organizations. In *Twitter and Tear Gas*, a study of social media and protest movements, Zeynep Tufekci writes with insight of the "power and fragility of networked protest."[20] Her analysis focused on the Arab Spring and Occupy Wall Street protests, both of which ended largely in defeat, with marginal moral victories at best. To the extent that the 2017 Women's March and the 2018 Teacher Spring strikes share a mode of mobilization that made heavy use of social media networks with the Arab Spring and Occupy Wall Street, Tufekci's insights are also applicable to them.

What are the reasons for this "fragility" of networked protest movements? They are as fundamental as the solidarity that is the foundation of collective action by working people. *Solidarity* is best understood as the shared commitment that people make to and with each other to stand together in common cause. Unlike the ties of kinship that develop between family members, solidarity is not a natural state of being; it must be self-consciously constructed. (The modern concept of solidarity arose in the French Revolution out of ideas of "civic friendship," of political bonds built between equals across social and cultural differences.[21])

The commitment embodied in the idea of labor solidarity is forged in the crucible of the shared work that people undertake on a daily basis, arising from the relationships of trust and mutual support that they develop as they perform that labor. For teachers, solidarity takes shape in the raw material of their daily interactions with each other—the chats over morning coffee and at the Xerox machine on what they will teach that day; the dialogues on how to teach a particular topic, how to employ a new teaching technique, and how to reach a struggling student; the shared work of designing and writing lesson plans, units of study, curriculum, and assessments; the time spent together at school events looking after their students; the lunchroom conversations dissecting the cluelessness of educational bureaucrats and the informal strategy sessions on how to handle an incompetent or abusive administrator; the Friday afternoon café and bar colloquies on how exhausting and exhilarating teaching can be; and the discussions that occur in many different settings, including union meetings, on how the outside world is affecting their students, their classrooms, and their schools. This is the raw material of a culture of solidarity.

One should not romanticize the workplace culture of schools. There are real forces there that conspire against solidarity, just as there are in every workplace. In their affinity to one of the "caring" professions, teachers are opponents of bigotry and hate in much larger numbers than the general population. But implicit bias—imbued by society's racism, sexism, homophobia, and prejudice against minority religions and immigrants—nonetheless remains a real danger. So do the enmities and rivalries that arise in any human setting, which can be aggravated when employers and administrators see advantage in stoking discord in order to divide and conquer. Decades ago, I received an education in this reality on my first day as a newly elected chapter leader for my high school, a position equivalent to a shop steward in other unions. A physical education teacher approached me with a complaint about the new term's schedule of classes for her department; another teacher had received favored treatment, she told me, since that teacher's classes were on an early schedule, allowing her to begin and end her workday earlier. I asked the complainant if she had requested an early schedule and had not received it; no, she replied, she had the schedule she asked for. She just didn't like the fact that the other teacher, with whom she feuded, had received the early schedule that she had asked for. Personal rivalries such as these make the fostering of solidarity hard work.

Yet even in the face of such challenges, teachers still build powerful relationships with each other in the course of their daily interactions. In difficult struggles, such as strikes, it is the strength of these relationships and the commitment to one another, and not fealty to abstract principles, that make it possible for teachers to withstand intimidation from employers and repression from the state. That is the power of solidarity.

In this respect, there are crucial differences between the relationships that teachers build with each through their work in schools and those they form with other teachers on social media. School-based relationships are what we might call "thick" relationships, characterized by rich emotional texturing. They are direct, face-to-face, and ongoing, and reciprocity and accountability to each other is central. In the school, teachers rely on each other in a myriad of ways, helping each other to educate and care for students. The failure of one teacher to fulfill her responsibilities has real consequences for all of her colleagues. That is why the best schools develop a strong culture of mutuality.

By contrast, social media relationships are what we might call "thin"—characterized by weak emotional connections. They are usually indirect, mediated by the digital platforms on which they take place, and are often very sporadic.[22] Since participants in social media exchanges are unable to see or hear each other, many of the cues that communicate emotion in a face-to-face conversation—facial expressions, body language, the volume and inflection of voice—are absent, making it harder to read intentions, achieve mutual understanding, and build friendship.

The norms that govern face-to-face dialogue—greeting a person at the start of a conversation, modulating one's tone, respecting personal space, looking at and listening to the person who is speaking—are not always readily or easily applicable to online interactions. Moreover, unlike the tacit rules of conversation, the norms of positive interactions on social media have not been part of the socialization processes that make social interactions second nature to us. Since they are not physically present to each other, social media participants may cloak their "real life" identities, making themselves largely unaccountable for their online behavior. There is a quality of anomie and normlessness in many social media settings, and toxic exchanges and "flame wars" are all too common. Thus, when social media is used to mobilize collective action, the capacity to be anonymous allows for provocations and disruptions from those seeking to undermine the effort.[23]

These differences are not absolute. Teachers can experience behavior in their schools that is neither collegial nor supportive, especially when the school is dysfunctional, and they can find social media conversations that provide them with sustenance. When teachers feel isolated in their schools, as teachers of color often do, given their experiences with racism and their underrepresentation in the profession, social media provides a platform for the creation of a supportive virtual community.[24] And just as there are ways to make schools into more collaborative communities, there are methods for nurturing healthy and respectful conversations on social media. The use of emoticons helps communicate feelings and intentions, and formal codes of "netiquette" can exclude the most abusive behavior. But, as a general rule, thick relationships with emotionally rich texturing are much more conducive to creating the commitment to each other and to the common cause that is the essence of solidarity.

It is the thinness of social media relationships that accounts in significant part for both the power and the fragility of networked protests. The power of social media mobilization lies in its capacity to make vast connections with those who already share a common perspective on a question of public import, whether it be opposition to the incoming administration of Donald Trump (the Women's March) or unwillingness to bear the burden of underfunded public schools and the deprofessionalization of teaching (the Teacher Insurgency). In this respect, social media mobilizations have the power to link local solidarity networks across individual states for common action, as well as to establish information sharing between activist networks in different states, as happened during the Teacher Spring strikes.[25] But when a common purpose is tested, as inevitably it will be, the thin relationships on which social media mobilizations are based may lack resiliency.

This weakness is especially evident in the challenge every American protest movement must confront—potential divisions in its ranks due to differing analyses or tactics, as well as to issues of racism, sexism, homophobia, anti-Semitism and Islamophobia, and conflicting cultures of class, among others. It is far easier to work through these issues successfully when a movement can draw on relationships of trust forged in common work and common struggle. Without such trust, acrimony and antagonism are much more likely to fester, even when all participants have the best of intentions. The controversies over anti-Semitism and racism that have embroiled the Women's March are instructive.[26] While there certainly have been some missteps by the March's leadership, it would be a mistake to lose sight of the deeper, structural problems. The March's mobilization developed almost *ex nihilo* thanks to social media, without any previous organizational infrastructure, established processes for democratic decision-making, or history of common work among more than a few individuals. Lacking the crucial resource of trust that had been built up through thick relationships over time, the resulting March organization had limited capacity to navigate these issues in ways that would leave it stronger and more unified.

THE POLITICS OF SOCIAL MEDIA MOBILIZATION

It is necessary, therefore, to temper the most enthusiastic accounts of the emancipatory potential of social media. When Manuel Castells writes of social media that "the more interactive and self-configurable communication is, the less hierarchical is the organization and more participatory is the movement," he overstates the case for egalitarianism.[27] There is no question that interactive social media provides an important vehicle for including many new voices in the public sphere conversations of protest movements and politics, especially the voices of younger generations.[28] But there is a substantial body of research that demonstrates that social media are not innocent of the power dynamics in the larger society. Access to different forms of social media and the ability to mount an influential presence there are mediated by the power of class, race, and sex. The much discussed *digital divide*—the class and race differentials in who owns the latest computers and smartphones and who has access to high-speed internet connections—is only one expression of these dynamics, although it is perhaps the one that is least impactful for "wired" professional labor such as teachers.[29] More important—and far harder to remedy—are the ways in which different social media are "gendered" and "racialized," in that social media exchanges tend to reproduce the "real life" habit of discounting the voices of women and people of color.[30] Our understanding of the digital public sphere (and its potential for expanding democratic discourse on issues of political import) should learn from critiques of Jürgen Habermas's influential study of the origins of the public sphere in eighteenth-century coffeehouses, periodicals, and pamphlets: while there were are vital insights to be found in the emergence of democratic deliberation within civil society, one needs to be cognizant that democratic deliberation of this nature can exclude or marginalize "others" and incorporate relations of domination, as it did in eighteenth-century Europe and North America.[31] Accounts of the utopian possibilities of social media, such as that of Castells, elide their "dark side"—everything from online bullying and rumormongering to the ways in which far-right entities and authoritarian state actors, including Russia and China, have used them to spread false information, engender antagonism against various social "others," and disrupt democratic social movements.[32]

While the use of social media to mobilize protests is a recent development, the underlying issues of the connections between mobilization, organization, and democracy have been long debated. In an oft-quoted adage, the early twentieth century German sociologist Robert Michels wrote, "Who says organization, says oligarchy." With these words, he summed up his argument that unions and working-class political parties inevitably devolved into bureaucracies dominated by elites, a propensity he attributed to the demands of establishing and maintaining an ongoing organizational infrastructure.[33] Early in his career, Michels had been associated with the anarcho-syndicalist wing of the Italian labor movement; and his theory of the innately bureaucratic and undemocratic tendencies of organization owed more than a little inspiration to their worldview that politics and state power were intrinsically corrupting and that spontaneous revolts, mass strikes, and worker self-mobilization were the only truly democratic forms of collective action.[34]

In their influential study *Poor People's Movements*, Frances Fox Piven and Richard Cloward applied the essentials of this theoretical construct to twentieth-century American mass protest movements—the 1930s movements of the unemployed and industrial unionism and the 1960s civil rights and welfare rights movements.[35] They argued that the organizations of these movements "were acutely vulnerable to internal oligarchy and stasis and to external integration with elites," and therefore tended to "blunt militancy."[36] It was disruptive mobilizations—strikes in the 1930s and nonviolent civil disobedience in the 1960s—that brought the historic breakthroughs of these movements. Entirely missing in this account is the role of organization in mounting these disruptive mobilizations and in securing the political victories that anchored them in law and policy.

Versions of this anti-organizational ethos have appeared in American protest movements over the course of twentieth century, and were quite evident in Occupy Wall Street, the first of a new generation of protest movements in this century. In its origins on social media, Occupy was an unalloyed form of "crowd-enabled connective action"—a protest movement that emerged directly from networks of individuals on social media platforms, without the mediating presence of an organizational base.[37] Throughout its short existence, Occupy resisted all attempts to develop an organizational infrastructure. Insisting on a leaderless "horizontal" movement, free of all hierarchy and repelling every effort to develop a political program and make specific demands, the movement restricted itself to general condemnations of economic inequality and countless individual testimonies.[38] The experience of Occupy provides an instructive lesson in the limited efficacy of a protest movement that is rooted so deeply in social media mobilization. Despite its extraordinary success in raising the issue of economic inequality, it stumbled and fell on organizational questions. It was unsuccessful as an exercise in democratic self-governance and as an effective model for generating political change. Those lessons are directly applicable to the Teacher Insurgency.

MOBILIZATION, ORGANIZATION, AND POLITICAL ACTION: THE LESSONS

Three critical lessons can be learned from this examination of mobilization and organization in protest movements.

Lesson 1: The democratic character of a movement requires an elected leadership that is accountable to its base. The absence of a democratically elected and accountable leadership does not produce a leaderless movement, but—as Jo Freeman explained in her critique of "structurelessness" in the 1960s women's movement—an unauthorized and unaccountable leadership.[39] Within the movement, leadership emerges informally through friendship groups and who-knows-whom networks; externally, commercial mass media identify individuals within the movement who can be used as spokespersons, making them into movement celebrities. Precisely because such leaders were not elected, there are no clear mechanisms of accountability to the movement, no political way to replace them in these roles, and no way to change the political approach they have decided to pursue. When leadership functions through informal social networks, many conclude that the only path toward change is to undermine the personal relationships on which leadership is based; as a consequence, opposition often ends up taking the form of personal attacks rather than political criticism, ultimately damaging and dividing the movement. (This dynamic is all too present on political social media, given the role of informal relationships in exercising influence.) The anti-organizational and utopian notion that it is possible to eliminate "representative democracy" and function as a pure "direct democracy," without leaders and a division of labor, invariably ends up in division and anti-democratic (and eventually authoritarian) practices.[40]

For a protest movement to be democratic, then, it must develop an organizational infrastructure that functions under the norms of representative democracy, with an elected leadership that is accountable to its base. While the Teacher Insurgency has certainly benefited from the expansion of participation through social media, the democratic character of the movement requires that this participation be partnered with the organized representative democracies—teacher unions.

Lesson 2: Social media politics confuses personal expression and political agency. Occupy's refusal to make specific demands or develop a political program, justified by its vision of thousands of different voices each expressing their personal and particular concerns, accentuated an unfortunate feature of social media politics.[41] In this confusion, one finds a problematic understanding of politics. Political action is a communal, not an individual, endeavor: the blood and sinew of the body politic is found not in a collection of unorganized *I*'s, but in choruses of *We*'s, organized into collective political subjects. These collective political subjects can be as broad as "the people," "the citizenry" or "the nation," but they can also take shape in more defined class- and community-based groups, such as "working people" or the neighborhood "Lower East Side." And they may appear in different identities based on interests, occupation, race, ethnicity, religion, sex, and sexual and gender identity, among others. (In part 3 of this book, I will examine the construction of the collective political subject and identity of teachers and what that means for organizing teachers.) Politics is enacted through contention and conflict between these different collective political subjects, with a focus on questions of power. Since the lasting impact of Occupy was its popularization of the idea of the "99 percent"—the overwhelming majority of Americans who had been disadvantaged by the extreme economic inequality that worked to the benefit of the "1 percent"—it is ironic that it refused to give that category any political content in the form of a statement of demands or a program of reforms, and so failed to become a vehicle for actual political change. When politics is misconstrued as a form of personal expression, it becomes an exercise in individual catharsis, in which political emotion is drained and dispersed rather than combined and concentrated into effective action.

In chapter 5, I will examine the question of the relationship between protest and politics in some detail, making an argument on why the Teacher Insurgency needs to be directly involved in politics if it is to address successfully the issues that brought it into being.

Lesson 3: An anti-organizational model of protest lacks political efficacy. Tufekci's analysis of this model points to the danger of what she calls a "tactical freeze" of social networked protests, meaning the difficulty such movements have in adjusting their tactics, establishing and negotiating their demands, and pushing for policy changes. For an Occupy movement that allowed itself to be defined not by a political program or actual demands but by the tactic of "occupying" public spaces such as Zuccotti Park near Wall Street, this tactical freeze meant that that its expulsion from those spaces effectively ended the movement. As I will discuss in chapter 5, tactical freeze can be particularly problematic when strikes are seen as the sole strategy to be employed by a protest movement or a union, an important issue for the Teacher Insurgency.

In a passage that provides the epigraph for this book, A. Philip Randolph declares that power—the capacity of working people to "take and hold" what they "need and are entitled to"—comes from the power of organization. The experience of protest movements with social media–based mobilization proves that Randolph's maxim continues to be true in the digital world of the twenty-first century: to be successful, social media mobilizations need to be partnered with organizations. Of all the Arab Spring protest movements that arose eight years ago from social media mobilizations, only one—Tunisia's—persists today, and it does so because of the power of the Tunisian trade unions.[42] Of all of the 2018 Teacher Spring strikes, the one that was most successful in winning its objectives was West Virginia's, where the teacher and public employee unions were the strongest—collectively holding 75 percent density in the state, even after having a "right to work" law imposed on them—and where the unions were able to leverage their power in the state capitol to achieve the movement's immediate goals. The lesson is that of the importance of ongoing organization, and the need to build organizations where they do not exist and to strengthen them where they do.

Mobilization through social media is most politically effective when combined with organization. Jen Schradie's analysis of digital activism in North Carolina sets forth some useful guidance on how to successfully deploy social media in progressive campaigns and social movements and provides a healthy antidote to the utopian accounts of the emancipatory power of political social media. In her account, the use of social media by the North Carolina teacher union, an affiliate of the NEA, is a positive exception in a generally bleak landscape. Part of the reason is that teachers, unlike the base of most of the other unions and progressive organizations she examines, are more "wired" into social media. But an equally important piece is that the union had developed expertise in digital activism, and so was able to mobilize its membership to maximum effect.[43]

By the same token, organization is most politically effective when it embraces the tools of social media, with its capacity to extend organizational reach. The most forward-looking unions, including those among teacher unions, are experimenting with techniques of "organizing the unorganized" that combine online and off-line approaches—using social media to make initial contacts, then following up with intensive, face-to-face connections. That is an approach that the Teacher Insurgency should take.

CHAPTER 5

Protest and Politics

Syndicalism and Labor History

EVERY DEMOCRATIC PROTEST MOVEMENT working to achieve change, including the Teacher Insurgency, invariably faces a key strategic question: What should be the relationship between protest and politics—that is, the relationship between various forms of direct action such as demonstrations and strikes on the one hand, and the contest for the political power to govern through electoral campaigns on the other? Some insist that protests are the primary, perhaps even exclusive, vehicle for achieving change and that political transformation follows in the wake of protest. (This is a perspective held by some on the left who have written about the Teacher Insurgency strikes.[1]) Others assert that without electoral victories and the power of government, no real change can be accomplished, so electoral contests are the only real game in town. And still others contend—as I argue in this chapter—that there is a dynamic relationship between protest and politics that, properly understood and leveraged, provides a path to accomplishing deep and sustained change.

To frame this discussion, I will begin as I did in chapter 4, by examining how the civil rights movement of the 1960s grappled with the strategic question of protest and politics. But to properly understand the question as it was debated in the 1960s, some intellectual archeology is required; we must dig back into the debates over strategy in the early twentieth-century American labor movement. As we will see, the strategic approach of the civil rights movement as it emerged mid-century harkened back in important ways to the strategies of those earlier labor movement debates. Of particular importance here is a strategic approach, known in the history of the labor movement as *syndicalism*, that promotes protest and direct action to the exclusion of electoral politics. While there are facets of this approach that are worth recovering in the form of nonviolent direct action, its fundamental opposition to contesting the political power to govern is ruinous. Syndicalism is generally a strategic dead-end for the labor movement and democratic protest movements, but nowhere is it more problematic, I will argue, than in the case of public-sector workers who have the government as their employer, including the teachers and education workers of the Teacher Insurgency.

PROTEST AND POLITICS IN THE CIVIL RIGHTS MOVEMENT OF THE 1960S

In February 1965, in the period between the passage of the 1964 Civil Rights Act and the 1965 Voting Rights Act, Bayard Rustin took to the pages of *Commentary* magazine to discuss the strategic question of protest and politics. Rustin's essay, "From Protest to Politics," was widely read and influential, offering what is now a classic understanding of this question.[2] It provides a useful point of departure for discussing the issue as it involves the Teacher Insurgency.

As Rustin was writing, it was evident that the protests of the civil rights movement, from the bus boycott and freedom rides to the sit-ins and marches, had already accomplished a great deal—nothing less than the end of the de jure segregation of the Jim Crow South. Arguably, the nonviolent direct-action tactics of the civil rights movement had been more successful in achieving their objectives than those employed by any previous protest movement in American history—and any movement since. Yet the civil rights movement was now entering a new phase, and Rustin believed that to complete the work of emancipation, it would have to take on the economic, class dimension of African American oppression. An economic agenda to achieve full equality demanded a strategic turn to politics—to winning the power to govern.

There had been a growing recognition among the more progressive parts of the civil rights movement of the need for a broader agenda to address the entrenched economic inequality of African Americans. The 1963 March on Washington had been officially titled "The March on Washington for Jobs and Freedom," and it had included calls for a massive federal jobs program, a major increase in the minimum wage, and prohibitions of discrimination in employment and housing. After the March, Rustin had joined A. Philip Randolph and Martin Luther King in developing a "Freedom Budget for All Americans" aimed squarely at establishing a full-employment economy and ending the poverty that afflicted so many African Americans.[3] Embodying a broad social democratic agenda, the Freedom Budget contained provisions for: a guaranteed income for all; increases in the minimum wage; universal health care; full educational opportunities in integrated schools; the replacement of millions of units of deficient housing; and the creation of a million new jobs to abate problems of air and water pollution. With the backing of the New Deal economist Leon Keyserling (one of the drafters of the Social Security Act and the National Labor Relations Act) and democratic socialist Michael Harrington (author of *The Other America*, which would inspire the Great Society's War on Poverty), Rustin, Randolph, and King organized a "coalition of conscience" in support of the Freedom Budget. It included the AFL-CIO and a wide swathe of organized labor, civil rights organizations, and religious leaders, along with some three hundred prominent intellectuals. Lyndon Johnson's 1964 landslide victory had brought large Democratic majorities, including many progressives, into both the Senate and House of Representatives, and Rustin believed that the political moment held promise for the enactment of the Freedom Budget. But he also knew that if this moment was not seized, the window of opportunity would soon be slammed shut.

The nonviolent direct-action tactics that had ended de jure racial segregation had been successful, Rustin believed, because their targets were "anachronistic" and "relatively peripheral" to the "American socio-economic order." As a consequence, the movement could achieve its goals within the balance of existing political forces. By contrast, the Freedom Budget agenda was striking at the institutional core of the market economy and corporate power: in Rustin's words, "the struggle for Negro equality" had become "essentially revolutionary." It would therefore require a much more substantial political force to be enacted. The civil rights movement would have to be part of a majority political coalition with organized labor, religious groups, and liberal organizations to achieve enactment. While the struggle to achieve legal equality remained urgent, achieving full equality required the movement to shift "from protest to politics."[4]

The logic and thrust of Rustin's argument is compelling. In fact, because of its power, many who read the essay do not fully appreciate how radically his strategic thinking was changing. In the decades Rustin had spent in the civil rights, pacifist, and socialist movements before 1965, he had engaged in nonviolent direct action to the exclusion of politics and had been arrested on many occasions for acts of nonviolent civil disobedience. As a Quaker and a pacifist, he had spent two years in federal prison during World War II as a draft resister. While on staff for the Fellowship of Reconciliation (FOR), he had been one of the primary organizers of the Congress of Racial Equality (CORE) and was arrested as part of the first freedom rides CORE sponsored in 1947. He had studied the techniques of Gandhian nonviolent resistance in India and introduced the discipline to Martin Luther King during the Montgomery bus boycott, helping to build direct action into a movement for mass action. And now, at the moment of the greatest success of these tactics and techniques of nonviolent direct action, Rustin was advocating a turn away from them. To understand the reasons why, and to put the strategic question of protest and politics in context for the Teacher Insurgency today, it is necessary to understand how Rustin's evolution in thinking emerged from the historic debates of American labor and the American left.

SYNDICALISM IN AMERICAN LABOR

Until 1965, Bayard Rustin was deeply enmeshed in a strong—at times dominant—tradition in the American labor and protest movements, one which can best be described by the term *syndicalism*. This perspective sees protests and direct action, such as strikes, job actions, sit-ins, picket lines, boycotts, demonstrations, and various forms of civil disobedience as the path to winning change. What is always present in this approach—sometimes unspoken and sometimes explicit—is a related refusal to contest for the power to govern and in particular, the refusal to take on electoral work in a serious and sustained way by supporting candidates for elected office. One can make demands on the government, but not contest for governmental power itself, the logic goes, as it is an innately corrupting and repressive force.[5]

In the American labor movement of the early twentieth century, opposition to involvement in elections and politics was widespread, appearing in two distinct but related forms, a conservative doctrine known variously as *voluntarism* or "pure and simple" unionism and a revolutionary philosophy of syndicalism. Voluntarism was the official policy of the American Federation of Labor (AFL) in the early 1900s.[6] At the turn of the century, AFL President Samuel Gompers generally opposed electoral endorsements and campaigns by unions, arguing that "economic action, through the trade union, is the only effective means for the wage earners of our time to achieve anything like progress and success."[7] In line with this view, the AFL wrote into its Constitution a prohibition of any convention discussion of political party campaigns and endorsements.[8] In its overriding focus on independent workplace organization and collective bargaining as the means for labor to address the extreme inequalities of the Gilded Age, the AFL's pure and simple trade unionism often resisted government intervention in and regulation of the workplace: the AFL would goes so far as opposing laws to establish an eight-hour work day, a minimum wage, and health insurance on the grounds that unions should negotiate such issues directly with the employer.[9] Writing such provisions into law, the AFL argued, would harm efforts of unions to negotiate for shorter hours.

A revolutionary syndicalist version of this opposition to involvement in politics and achievement of goals through legislation took shape in the Industrial Workers of the World (IWW), known colloquially as the Wobblies.[10] In the Wobbly pamphlet "Political Parties and the IWW," General Secretary Vincent St. John elaborated its view that workers could free themselves from "wage slavery" only through industrial action—principally, the strike. Politicians of all stripes, even socialists, used electoral campaigns to lead workers into a "cul de sac," Vincent wrote, in which they lost "all idea of ever being anything but a slave for generations to come."[11]

Both of these anti-political postures developed in reaction to the laissez-faire capitalism that dominated the American polity and economy at the time. Neither the AFL nor the Wobblies were immune to the prevailing anti-statist ideologies: elements of Social Darwinism found their way into the worldviews of both unions, with the battles between employers and workers portrayed as a struggle for the "survival of the fittest." But more important in the development of union hostility toward the state and political action was the fact that during this era, government regularly sided with employers in labor disputes. Courts would issue injunctions against picketing, strikes, and boycotts and police, state militias, and federal troops often acted as strikebreakers. In what came to be known as its Lochner era, the Supreme Court used antitrust legislation against unions; it consistently struck down laws that regulated the workplace to the benefit of workers, such as those limiting child labor and the length of the working day and those that established a minimum wage and outlawed "yellow dog" contracts prohibiting membership in a union. The civil liberties of working people, particularly their First Amendment freedoms of speech, press, assembly, and protest, were violated with impunity in many parts of the country.

Government and employer violence against workers and unions was all too common during this period. In a report to the National Commission on the Causes and Prevention of Violence, historians Philip Taft and Philip Ross concluded that "the United States has experienced more frequent and bloody labor violence than any other industrial nation," with the bulk of it being initiated by employers.[12] This violence reached a crescendo in the late 1800s and early 1900s, when it fell disproportionately on unskilled workers, especially in mining. The Wobblies were smaller than the unions of the AFL, but the workers they did organize were found mostly in the unskilled trades facing this harsh repression.

It was in this context that the Wobblies came to focus exclusively on direct action, an approach they adopted from the revolutionary syndicalist unions of Europe. At the center of this direct action was the strike. More than simply the primary tactic of the Wobblies, the withdrawal of labor functioned as a synecdoche for their efforts to totally remove themselves from the existing economic and political order. Like their

European counterparts, the Wobblies believed that a general strike of all workers against the employer class and the state would be the means of ending what they called a system of wage slavery.

The preeminent theorist of revolutionary syndicalism, Georges Sorel, described the general strike in millenarian terms as a "myth" that should not be read or understood literally, but rather seen as the animating and mobilizing force in a grand historical "drama."[13] In a telling analogy, he compared it to the idea of the Second Coming of Christ, which he saw as the organizing myth of the early Christian Church.[14] Ruling out all reforms and all action within the existing political order as unacceptable compromises, Sorel put forward the general strike as the totality of change, as the revolution: it would institute a new order that placed "the forces of production in the hands of free men, i.e. of men who are capable of running the workshop created by capitalism without any need of masters."[15] The sentiments of solidarity engendered in a strike, which Sorel describes in sweeping poetic and romantic terms as the "noblest, the deepest and the most moving sentiments that (workers) possess," prefigure this new social order.[16] Central to this transformative moment is "proletarian violence," which Sorel praises at great length, telling his readers that when "carried on as a pure and simple manifestation of the sentiment of class war" this violence is "a very fine and heroic thing."[17] Tying together these different notions was Sorel's idea that a "militant minority" of syndicalist workers would provide the leadership for the general strike and proletarian violence.

The Wobblies embraced the vision of revolutionary syndicalism. (Together with other important texts of French syndicalism, Sorel's *Reflections on Violence* had been translated into English and widely circulated in the ranks of the IWW.[18]) Their opposition to the existing economic and political order was so uncompromising that they refused, as a matter of principle, to negotiate and administer contracts and collective bargaining agreements, making it next to impossible to sustain the gains won through strikes. Organizationally, the Wobblies were so suspicious that leadership might become autocratic they would resist the hiring of full-time staff for locals.

In a fight-fire-with-fire approach, the Wobblies responded to the widespread violence against labor at the turn of the twentieth century with their own counter-violence. In one high-profile case, IWW leaders

Bill ("Big Bill") Haywood and Charles Moyer were arrested and tried for the assassination of the former governor of Idaho, purportedly an act of retaliation for his declaration of martial law and use of federal troops to break a mine strike. The preponderance of evidence suggested some participation on their part, and many in labor circles thought they had been involved, but their prosecution was full of missteps, and the legendary Clarence Darrow won "not guilty" verdicts.[19]

The Wobblies openly advocated the use of sabotage, a term taken from the French syndicalists that explicitly included the violent destruction of property: it was, they argued, an act of self-defense in the "class war" that employers and the government waged against workers and their unions.[20] "The main concern to the revolutionist," wrote Wobbly Walker Smith, "is whether the use of sabotage will destroy the power of the masters."[21] In this respect, sabotage was a concept closely allied with the anarchist idea of "propaganda of the deed"—acts of violence that were designed to demonstrate that resistance to the system of wage slavery was possible.

The agent of these revolutionary acts was to be the Sorelian militant minority. "Our task is to develop the conscious, intelligent minority to the point," the Wobblies declared in the *Industrial Worker*, "where they will be capable of carrying the imperfectly expressed desires of the toiling millions" who are still "hopelessly stupid and stupidly hopeless."[22] Central to the IWW's vision of itself was its work as an organ of revolutionary propaganda.

Within the American labor movement, there was a strong critique of the anti-political stances of both the conservative pure and simple unionism of the AFL and the revolutionary syndicalism of the Wobblies. Henry Linville, the president of the New York City Teachers Union (he would later become president of the AFT), laid out the main grounds of how this criticism applied to the Wobblies in an unsigned opinion piece in *The American Teacher* (the AFT journal, of which he was editor).[23] In the labor movement, the Wobblies were seen as a "dual union" that divided and weakened workers through its competition with AFL unions, thus making it more difficult to win victories in battles with employers, but Linville still addressed them as fellow unionists. In the wake of the conviction of one hundred Wobblies for conspiracy to obstruct the war effort during World War I, Linville—a democratic socialist and a pacifist who was a friend of leading socialist Norman Thomas—expressed concerns that prejudice against the IWW had made it difficult for its members to obtain a fair trial. While they had been opponents of the war, as Linville himself had been, he saw no evidence that their antiwar propaganda had been pro-German or that their program had any "essential connection" with the Central Powers comprising Germany and the Austrian-Hungarian and Ottoman empires.

But a significant part of the problem the Wobblies faced, Linville wrote, was of their own making. Their opposition to all reform and electoral politics in their pursuit of "the millennium" was misguided utopianism that would leave the "current generation" with "no benefit." Many in the labor movement and among American radicals and liberals were critical of the Wobblies use of violent law breaking and sabotage, he noted, seeing such tactics as both unnecessary and counter-productive provocations. On these counts, the Wobblies had been obstinately closed to all criticism from others in the labor movement, leading to their isolation. (Five years earlier, Linville's Socialist Party had removed the IWW's Haywood from its leadership due to his continuous advocacy of violent tactics in defiance of party policy opposing them, at which point he and most IWW members had left the party.) Most importantly, while some political parties had been "disappointments," political action itself "has not proven a failure," Linville would insist.[24] There was insufficient reason to abandon efforts at winning reforms for working people through politics.

Tacit Syndicalism

In the post-World War I period, the Wobblies would fade as a force in the American labor movement. Part of the reason for their decline was intense government repression, as this was the era of the first Red Scare and the Palmer Raids. But the development of American Communism in the wake of the Russian Revolution also played a major role. In a way that has not been fully appreciated in the historical literature, the various strands of Communism in the United States drew much of their core leadership from the ranks of revolutionary syndicalism, sapping it of its vitality.[25] Top political leaders—including Bill Haywood, John Reed, William Z. Foster, James Cannon, Earl Browder, Ben Gitlow, and

Elizabeth Gurley Flynn—and leading trade unionists—including Harry Bridges of the International Longshoremen's and Warehousemen's Union, Mike Quill of the Transport Workers Union, Sasha Zimmerman of the International Ladies Garment Workers Union, Vincent Dunne of the Minneapolis Teamsters, and CIO staffer Len De Caux—were all revolutionary syndicalists who went on to embrace Communism.[26]

In the early years of American Communism, that transition was far easier than one might think. The Leninist doctrine that the liberation of workers could be achieved only through the revolutionary, violent overthrow of the existing state had many points of continuity with revolutionary syndicalism's notion of the general strike and its support of the use of violence. While American Communists of various stripes would become involved in reform struggles, it was with the idea that the struggle for particular reforms should serve as lessons in the need for revolution, not as positive ends in themselves. The syndicalist concept of the role of a militant minority in the labor movement shared many essential features with the Leninist concept of an elite vanguard political party that would direct the masses of working people.

Significantly, all of the strands of American Communism continued the syndicalist practice of refusing to contest elections in ways that would impact who held elected office and political power. Captive to a crude instrumentalist understanding of politics, government, and the state, they refused to endorse candidates of the major political parties, no matter how progressive, on the grounds that only an authentic revolutionary party of workers could be an acceptable vehicle for political and electoral action. Given the small numbers and marginality of American Leninists, this stance would postpone into the indefinite future interventions in elections that could actually contest for the power of government. Insofar as these parties participated in elections at all, it was to use their fringe candidacies as opportunities for the dissemination of revolutionary propaganda.[27] The main focus of their work was on direct action, primarily in the workplace.

The only significant break from revolutionary syndicalism to be found in the various strands of American Communism was with the idea that there should be "revolutionary" dual unions, opposed to the mainstream unions of the AFL. The position of William Z. Foster—that Communists should join the AFL unions and "bore from within" through opposition caucuses—eventually won out, but not until well over a decade after the founding of American Communism and after a politically disastrous period of isolation set into motion by Stalin's direction that revolutionary "red" unions be established as alternatives to the AFL unions.

This was a *tacit* syndicalism—one that, in the world of American Communism, dared not speak its name—but a syndicalism nonetheless. It continues to this day in such forms as the *rank-and-file* strategy, which understands itself as a vehicle for building a revolutionary socialist movement through work in the labor movement.[28] The development of a militant minority, organized through opposition caucuses within unions, is central to this approach. The goal is to win leadership positions and bring unions to a program defined by militant opposition to the existing economic and political order. The rank-and-file strategy not only prioritizes direct action in the workplace and strikes, but conceives of them in opposition to contesting elections by supporting major party candidates who can actually win office.[29]

When applied to the red states controlled by reactionary Republican governments that were the sites of the Teacher Spring strikes, the rank-and-file strategy dismisses such interventions as "electoralism" that falls "into the Democratic Party trap," and argues that this is an approach unions must "actively resist."[30] Public-sector unionists such as teachers, for whom the question of who holds elected office in state and local government is absolutely critical, are told that there is little that can or should be done about such matters until that future day when an authentic, independent party of workers can contest elections. For the teachers in the red Teacher Spring states of West Virginia, Oklahoma, Arizona, Kentucky, and North Carolina who went on strike because of the actions of their reactionary state governments, such syndicalist advice can only appear as a deluded take on their political reality.

The Syndicalism of A. J. Muste

Another tradition of syndicalism emerged from the early twentieth-century American labor movement, a tradition in which Bayard Rustin and the civil rights movement were located and one that provides important resources for the Teacher Insurgency today. This tradition owes more to A. J. Muste than to any other individual.[31] To understand Muste's distinctive contribution, it is necessary to situate him in the American labor movement and American left of the twentieth century. As World War I began, Muste was a young minister who had embraced the Social Gospel movement and identified as a religious pacifist and a socialist. In late 1917, his open opposition to the war would lead to the loss of his post as pastor of a Boston Congregationalist church. Muste then went to work for the American Civil Liberties Union, which had been founded during the war to defend the civil liberties of conscientious objectors, and he helped start a "Comradeship" ministry in Boston with a small group of clerics who shared his views on the moral imperative of social and economic justice.

In early 1919, a major strike broke out in nearby Lawrence, the largest textile manufacturing town in Massachusetts and the site of three of the four largest textile mills in the US.[32] Lawrence had already been the site of the famous "Bread and Roses" strike of 1912, which had involved Wobbly leaders Bill Haywood, Carlo Tresca, and Elizabeth Gurley Flynn. This strike was uncommon among IWW strikes for having actually won its main demands, but Wobbly doctrine prohibiting contracts and full-time union staff had left its Lawrence local vulnerable. Shortly after the end of Bread and Roses strike, the mill owners were able to break the union. During World War I, the mill workers had been able to use the combination of labor shortages and high demand for their product to wrest small concessions out of the owners, but once the war was over, the owners began laying off workers and reducing hours, and the workers struck in response, demanding higher wages with a shorter workweek.

When Muste and two of his fellow ministers went to Lawrence and offered their support, the strikers welcomed them into their committee. The strikers took warmly to Muste and one of his comrades after they were arrested and severely beaten by the police, only to reappear on the picket line as soon as they were released from jail. With valuable communication skills as an educated speaker of English among an immigrant workforce, a willingness to learn what he did not know, and a proven commitment to the striking workers, Muste was soon elected the general secretary of the strike committee—in effect, its primary leader. After a long and bitter 107 days on the picket line, through some of the coldest days of winter, the strike was won with a major pay raise of 15 percent for the textile workers.

The 1919 strike committee was filled with veterans of the Bread and Roses strike who were well versed in the syndicalist techniques of organizing a strike, but also conscious that Wobbly dogma prohibiting contracts and full-time staff had contributed to the demise of its Lawrence local. Reeling from government repression, the IWW itself was disorganized and in no position to play any meaningful role in the 1919 strike, even if the Lawrence workers had wanted their presence—which is questionable. But during the course of the strike, Sidney Hillman's young and growing Amalgamated Clothing Workers (ACWA) made contact with the strikers and provided vital material and organizing support.

The ACWA was committed to industrial unionism and a progressive political agenda, and after the successful strike in Lawrence, as well as strikes that had taken place in early 1919 in the New Jersey cities of Passaic and Patterson, two textile centers with a history of Wobbly strikes, it saw an opportunity to create a sister textile union along industrial lines. With ACWA assistance, locals from New England, New Jersey, and New York came together to establish the new Amalgamated Textile Workers (ATWA). Based on his leadership role in the Lawrence strike, Muste was elected its president, and a cohort of young socialist and pacifist intellectuals were hired as staff.

The initial ATWA organizing was successful—by the fall of 1919, it had fifty thousand members. But that momentum would not last for very long. A combination of negative factors—the 1920–1921 depression; ethnic conflict between immigrant workers; local government bans on union speeches, demonstrations, and meetings; sniping from the remnants of Wobbly support, and worker suspicions of its intellectual staff—would all converge to make it more and more difficult to sustain the ATWA. The ACWA began to pull back its support. By the end of 1921, the union was in disarray and retreat, and Muste had to move on.

Muste came out of the experience of the Lawrence strike and ATWA a seasoned trade unionist, strongly committed to the labor movement in which he would spend the better part of the next two decades. His brand of unionism was very much in a syndicalist vein: he was an advocate of strikes and other workplace actions, and he saw politics and involvement in elections as ineffective means for securing change. While his vision of a future society would be best described as democratic socialist, Muste would not join the Socialist Party because of its focus on electoral activity. But compared with the Wobblies and the various strands of Communism, Muste's brand of syndicalism was sober and practical: he found the IWW antipathy toward organization and its apocalyptic utopianism disastrous, and he had no brief for the sectarian warfare brought to the left by the supporters of the Russian Revolution who founded American Communism.

Muste and Brookwood Labor College

Muste soon found a home for these views as director of the newly established Brookwood Labor College, which under his leadership became the foremost American institution in the workers' education movement that took shape during the 1920s and 1930s.[33] From the start, Muste set out to make Brookwood into a vibrant institutional center of the progressive wing of the American labor movement. He assembled an activist board that included prominent union leaders who identified as democratic socialists—John Brophy of the Mineworkers, Fannia Cohn of the ILGWU, John Fitzpatrick of the Chicago Federation of Labor, Abe Lefkowitz of the New York City Teachers Union and the AFT, James Maurer of the Pennsylvania Federation of Labor, and Rose Schneiderman of the Women's Trade Union League. The Brookwood faculty brought together leading labor intellectuals and union educators such as Josephine Colby, Katherine Pollak Ellickson, David Saposs, Joel Seidman, Tucker Smith, and Mark Starr. This heady mix of left-wing labor intellectuals and trade union leaders, organizers, and activists quickly made Brookwood into an unrivaled center of discussion and debate on the strategic direction of the American labor movement and the future of working people in the United States. Under Muste's guiding hand, Brookwood was never narrow or provincial in this focus: it drew connections between the labor movement and other causes such as the African American freedom struggle and that of women workers.

Despite a relatively short life, Brookwood's influence was far-reaching. Its extension program and faculty were involved in all of the major worker education programs of its generation, and its courses and curriculum were often copied in other institutions. Its graduates included many who were central to the emergence of the Congress of Industrial Organizations (CIO) in the later 1930s, most famously Walter and Roy Reuther of the United Auto Workers (UAW), as well as leading civil rights organizers and activists such as Ella Baker and Pauli Murray. (The Reuther brothers, particularly Roy, later served as Brookwood instructors.)

During his time at Brookwood, Muste's closest allies in the labor movement were from the AFT. The staff of Brookwood was a local of the AFT, and Muste himself was elected a vice president of the national union, where he helped shape its vision and work. Muste worked closely with the New York City Teachers Union on an experimental K–12 school—Manumit School for Workers' Children—which employed the progressive pedagogy of John Dewey in the education of working-class students.[34] Muste considered himself a philosophical pragmatist in the vein of John Dewey, the best-known member of the AFT, and embraced Dewey's progressive pedagogy at Brookwood and in Manumit.

As Brookwood's influence grew, the conservative leadership of the AFL began to see it—and its ties to the progressive wing of the labor movement—as a threat. AFL leaders mounted an attack that portrayed the school as a hotbed of revolutionary propaganda and proselytization, and they called for the AFL member unions to cease all support for the college. The AFT led the defense of Brookwood inside the AFL and mobilized prominent educator members such as John Dewey and George Counts to defend it publicly. Dewey would take to the pages of the *New Republic* in that cause, noting that the school described its educational mission as "to teach students how to think, not to tell them what to think," and that the vibrant, free-wheeling discussions to which the AFL objected were a necessary component of learning how to think.[35] The refusal of the AFL leadership to provide Brookwood with the opportunity to defend itself in a hearing, Dewey concluded, was a "scholastic lynching." But the backing of the AFT and the support of Brookwood's friends and alumni within the labor movement was not enough to turn the tide against a leadership intent on ramming through measures designed to harm the school, and it would lose that critical fight. Over the coming years, the combination of the Great Depression and the loss of a good portion of its union participation would economically cripple the school and eventually force its closure.

As this fight was being waged and then lost, Muste concluded that there was a need for an organizational base independent of Brookwood to carry on the struggle for progressive trade unionism within the AFL. In 1929, he founded the Conference for Progressive Labor Action (CPLA), with a core leadership that included long time Brookwood board members Maurer and Lefkowitz; leading socialists such as Norman Thomas, Frank Crosswaith, and James Oneal; and a substantial cohort of prominent socialists in the labor movement. CPLA would differentiate itself from both the AFL leadership and the Communist Party, which was in a particularly sectarian period where it attacked progressive organizations across the left as "social fascists."[36] (Muste, Brookwood, and the CPLA all came in for their share of abuse at the hands of the Communists.) As the Great Depression hit, the CPLA would immerse itself in support of textile and mining strikes around the US, and it played a leading role in the organization of the unemployed, using direct-action tactics against evictions and mobilizing the unemployed in support of strikes.

In the early 1930s, Muste was swept away by the times, embarking on an ideological binge (he would later call it a "detour") that would undo much of what he had accomplished in the labor movement over the previous decade. When the Brookwood board and many on the faculty expressed concerns that his single-minded focus on the CPLA was leading him to neglect the school and put its future at risk, Muste resigned from the college, fueling its downward trajectory and eventual closure. He then took the CPLA to the hard left, transforming it into the American Workers Party (AWP). Seen in the most positive light, the AWP was an experiment in a revolutionary Marxism that was more open and unorthodox, more American in inspiration and language, than the political ideologies found in the parties of the various strands of Communism. But many of Muste's closest friends and trade union and political allies saw the AWP as a path to sectarian marginality and irrelevance, and long-standing relationships, including those with his AFT colleagues, were ruptured. Nonetheless, in 1934, Muste and the AWP would play a crucial leadership role in one of the most important labor battles of the 1930s—the bitter and violent Toledo Auto Lite strike.[37] The hard-won union victory in this battle set the stage for the unionization of Toledo and the auto industry as a whole. But whatever organizational momentum the AWP should have garnered from this important work was squandered when Muste was convinced by New York intellectuals Sidney Hook and James Burnham to combine the AWP with the thin ranks of American Trotskyism, a move that led to the loss of yet even more of his once-close political allies.[38] When the Trotskyists broke their word to Muste and took the merged organization into the Socialist Party for the purpose of gathering new recruits and splitting the Socialists, Muste finally reached the end of his "detour." That move was a violation of "working class ethics" that he could not abide. Politically isolated as a result of his own decisions, a chastened Muste found himself in a midlife ideological crisis that forced him to reassess his choices and life direction. He would leave the Trotskyists and find his way back to his religious faith and to a pacifism and socialism rooted in that faith. With his organizing talent and experience, he would soon find himself at the helm of the Fellowship of Reconciliation (FOR), the leading organization of religious pacifists in the United States.

Mustean Nonviolent Direct Action

Muste brought to the FOR a fervent conviction that American pacifism could not be defined by its opposition to violence and war alone, but must become "a mass movement for achieving social change by nonviolence."[39] This emphasis meant an orientation toward working with "oppressed and minority groups such as Negroes, share-croppers, (and) industrial workers."[40] No project better defined this Mustean approach than FOR's sponsorship of the Congress of Racial Equality (CORE), founded in 1942 as an organizational vehicle for mounting campaigns against Jim Crow racial segregation.[41] In the early 1940s, Muste hired a trio of young socialists and pacifists—Bayard Rustin, James Farmer Jr. and George Houser—as FOR staff to work on issues of race. With Muste's support, all three would play pivotal roles in the formation of CORE.

Before the birth of CORE, the concept of direct action had been generally associated with revolutionary syndicalism and its use of violence. The term would first appear in African American protests, however, as a doctrine of "nonviolent direct action" through the work of CORE.[42] Muste was central to the elaboration of this doctrine through his pacifist reimagining of syndicalism, and he would inculcate Rustin, Farmer, and Houser in its precepts and discipline. In Muste's hands, the syndicalist use of sabotage and violence to fight back against vicious employers and repressive states was transformed into nonviolent resistance and civil disobedience against unjust laws and governments; the strike was not only reconceived as nonviolent, but situated among a number of other tactics and techniques of nonviolent disruption and non-cooperation such as boycotts and sit-ins; the violent "propaganda of the deed" was remade into nonviolent acts of moral witness that would prove far more effective in engendering resistance to oppression; and the idea that direct action should prefigure a new, more just society became far more convincing when that action was nonviolent, recognizing the humanity of one's opponents and expressing a moral vision in which the means reflected the ends. There were others in American pacifism who sought to remake violent concepts of protest into a nonviolent movement—the refashioning of anarchism by the Catholic Worker movement of Dorothy Day and Peter Maurin is one such example—but Muste's project was distinguished by his insistence that pacifism must become a *mass movement* for nonviolent change. He never lost the instincts of the union organizer.

Over the course of the 1940s and early 1950s, CORE would use this Mustean vision to pioneer the tactics of nonviolent direct action that would be embraced by the civil rights movement of the later 1950s and early 1960s. One illuminating example is the 1961 freedom rides that would galvanize the nation and compel the integration of interstate buses and trains. These drew their inspiration from the earlier Journey of Reconciliation that CORE organized in 1947. Bayard Rustin would be arrested in one such early freedom ride in late 1947, which would result in his spending thirty days on a North Carolina chain gang.

Muste's work set the stage for the civil rights movement's emergence as a nonviolent protest movement: by reimagining syndicalism as nonviolent direct action, Muste made the wide adoption of direct action in the African American community possible; by giving nonviolent direct action a religious and moral foundation, Muste made it possible for many in the African American church to embrace that doctrine as part of their own prophetic Christianity, and to play a pivotal role in the civil rights movement; and by opening up the field of protest to many different types of nonviolent actions, Muste established the basis for the wide repertoire of direct actions the civil rights movement would develop, a repertoire that provided it with a crucial tactical flexibility and maneuverability in its battles with the Jim Crow regime.

With the civil rights movement's success in ending the de jure racial segregation of Jim Crow, the entire historical trajectory of American protest movements was transformed. Every significant protest movement in the US since 1960—the public-sector labor movement and the farmworker and domestic labor movements; the peace movement; the movements for Latino, Asian American, and Native American rights; second-wave feminism; the LGBTQ movement; the environmental movement; and the immigration rights movement—has borrowed significant parts of their language, their techniques, their tactics and their strategic approach from the civil rights movement. With its use of strikes and nonviolent civil disobedience, the Teacher Insurgency continues in that tradition.

Muste's Blind Spots

Yet for all of Muste's powerful vision of nonviolent direct action, he inherited two major blind spots from syndicalism that he never overcame. With echoes of the revolutionary syndicalist idea of a militant minority, Muste saw pacifists as a minority, small in number and likely to remain so into the foreseeable future, who constituted the vanguard of a "nonviolent revolution."[43] He would advocate that the FOR adopt an organizational infrastructure of disciplined cells, akin to that of Communist parties, in the pursuit of that revolution.[44] To be clear, Muste had become an unequivocal critic of all forms of Leninism after his experience with Trotskyism. Yet his criticisms focused single-mindedly on the Leninist advocacy of violence, treating it as an original sin from which all of its anti-democratic practices emerged.[45] The narrowness of this analysis blinded him to other sources of Leninist antipathy to democracy, including intellectual currents in which he himself continued to swim. As Michael Walzer has shown in *The Revolution of the*

Saints, the idea of a revolution led by an ascetic and disciplined minority that understands itself to be a moral "elect," anointed with the historical task of liberating the larger society, has origins that go back well before the Russian Revolution into Puritanism.[46] A similar strain of the ascetic purism of a minority elect also ran through another major influence on Muste, Gandhian nonviolence. In these traditions, as in Leninism, the elect conceives of itself as the bearer of moral absolutes, always the prophet and never the sinner. Essential democratic virtues—tolerance, civic humility, and above all, respect for the demos, the people, with all of its imperfections—are all too easily lost.

It is important to be precise about the nature of the problem here. A fundamental precept of any system of democratic governance is the right of dissenting minorities to advocate for politics and policies that differ from those of the majority and the government. However, this right carries with it the responsibility to respect the rule of the *demos*; that is, the right of the majority to form the government and enact policy. The minority can and should seek to convert the majority to its view, but it must not seek to substitute itself for the majority. This respect for the rule of the *demos* is why the classic doctrine of civil disobedience combines the nonviolent violation of an unjust law with the acceptance of the punishment that comes with breaking the law. To assert an unfettered individual right to disobey laws that does not recognize the right of the majority to make them is to replace democratic rule with anarchy.

Muste recognized the potential problem of individualist anarchy in civil disobedience, but his answer was to invoke the "higher law" of religious scriptures as the basis for disobeying civil law.[47] Religious teachings can provide a valid basis for why an individual decides to disobey a particular law, but it is not a substitute for recognizing the right of the people, through the majority, to rule—and Muste did not explicitly acknowledge that right in his discussion of civil disobedience. The larger democratic ethos in which the idea of civil disobedience must be embedded was a pale, faded background when set against the brightly colored moral absolutes Muste emphasized. This Mustean vision of nonviolent revolution worked reasonably well for experienced activists such as the veterans of CORE, but it had insufficient guardrails for the next generation of activists, the movements of the 1960s. For too many in its ranks, righteousness in the civil rights and anti-Vietnam war struggles evolved into self-righteous rage at the American people, precipitating a descent into violence and nihilism in such forms as the Weather Underground—the very sort that Muste abhorred. The ideals of participatory democracy and the "beloved community" were remade into farcical invocations of totalitarianism.

Muste's failure to recognize the dangers of acting as a minority vanguard was connected to a second blind spot—his dismissal of electoral politics. It is through democratic elections, after all, that citizens give their consent to be governed and the majority of the people choose the government. Muste's theory of nonviolent revolution, rooted in his syndicalist conviction that elections and politics were incapable of producing what he considered to be real change, found its corollary in a political theory that focused on the agency of a minority vanguard and afforded only occasional recognition to the majority rule of the people. In this respect, Bayard Rustin's argument in "From Protest to Politics" was not only a major change of his own strategic thinking: it marked a significant break from the views of his mentor, A. J. Muste.

PROTEST AND POLITICS IN THE TEACHER INSURGENCY

The main thrust of Rustin's argument, that engagement with electoral politics is required to enact meaningful change, was clearly correct—and not just for the civil rights movement in 1965. It has much wider applicability to the labor movement and to the wider world of democratic protest movements. Most important for the purposes of this book, the necessity of engagement with electoral politics is clearly the case for the Teacher Insurgency. The issues that motivated the strikes of 2018 and 2019 cannot be fully and successfully addressed without political and legislative action. The underfunding of public schools and its broad impact on teaching and learning—endangered teacher livelihoods; deteriorating school facilities; oversized classes; outdated textbooks and technology; curricula stripped of the arts, music, foreign languages, and physical education; and loss of such essential services as librarians, guidance counselors, school psychologists and social workers—cannot be fully and successfully addressed without legislative action that brings full, equitable funding. The issues of teacher professionalism—especially the use of standardized tests for school accountability, teacher evaluation, and student graduation and promotion—cannot be fully and successfully addressed without legislative action and without elected representatives appointing education officials committed to professionalism. Market-based reforms that undermine public education, such as vouchers and the effects of charter school expansion on public schools, cannot be fully and successfully addressed without legislative action. The social justice issues taken up by the strikes of the Teacher Insurgency—supports for homeless students to ensure the continuity of their education and protections for undocumented students from Immigration and Customs Enforcement (ICE) raids—cannot be fully and successfully addressed without legislative action. Of necessity, the strikes of the Teacher Insurgency have been political strikes, and their demands have been achieved to the extent that teachers and their unions have been able to use them, together with political action, to move a legislative agenda.

While Rustin's argument was an essential corrective to syndicalist notions of nonviolent direct action, there are points where his essay went too far in "bending the branch back." The title "From Protest to Politics," for example, suggests that politics should supplant protest. This one-sided view, an inversion of syndicalism, does not reflect the full richness of Rustin's thinking, but it has led many to read the essay in that vein. In using Rustin, we must be careful to insist on the dynamic tension between protest and politics, and on a dialectical approach in which each element, when properly deployed in combination with the other, makes a distinctive contribution to meaningful change that neither can accomplish on their own.

Our strategy needs therefore to be two-pronged, employing both protest and direct action, including strikes and civil disobedience on the one hand, and politics and electoral action that contests for the power of government on the other. Protest and direct action are forces that disrupt the status quo, and they play an important role in shifting the existing balance of power, much as the strikes of the Teacher Insurgency have done. They are the ground on which a visionary critique of the existing order is best made, and the form in which teachers and other working people assert their unwillingness to march forward under the influence of the powerful, at the expense of their schools, their students, and themselves. But for meaningful, lasting change to be made—for there to be not simply a compelling critique of decades of market-driven education reform and the damage they have done to public schools, students and teachers, but real change—the political power to govern must be contested and won. Direct action without the contest for political power provides a moral critique that is incapable of transforming law or government policy; electoral politics without direct action are reduced to transactions within the established political and economic order. Only together can protest and politics bring the change we want and need.

CHAPTER 6

The Teacher Strike

Conditions for Success

AT THE CENTER OF THE TEACHER INSURGENCY is one particular form of direct action—the strike. The strike occupies a distinctive place in the popular consciousness of teachers and working people more generally, primarily because of its extraordinary visibility, leverage, and power as a tactic but also because of the mythology and romance that is often associated with it. In this chapter, I begin by delving into the history of teacher strikes in the US, and showing why, despite their success in establishing public-sector unionism and collective bargaining (including teacher unionism) in the 1960s, they became increasingly ineffective by the mid-1970s and 1980s and had dwindled to a mere handful by the start of the twenty-first century. My objective is to identify the conditions in which a strike is likely to achieve the goals of teachers and their unions, and to delineate the strategic approach and the organizing that must be done for a strike to be successful and have maximum impact. I finish by laying out the strategic orientations that provide strikes with the greatest prospect of success, with examinations of the interface of strike organization and mobilization, the place of strikes in the larger repertoire of direct-action tactics, the political character of the strike, and the relationship of strikes and unions to the communities served by the schools The success of the Teacher Insurgency in reestablishing the strike as a powerful tactic is a welcome development, but to maintain and build on that success, we need to be acutely aware of the approaches that best situate teacher strikes to win.

THE HISTORY OF TEACHER STRIKES IN THE UNITED STATES

For much of their early history, both the American Federation of Teachers (AFT) and the National Education Association (NEA) had official no-strike policies.[1] Negative public reaction to the 1919 Boston police strike had generated major political and legislative setbacks for public-sector union organizing, including the destruction of all existing police unions.[2] The thinking of the young AFT was that a no-strike policy was necessary for its survival. The two public-sector unions formed in the 1930s—the American Federation of State, Council and Municipal Employees (AFSCME) and the American Federation of Government Employees (AFGE)—would also adopt no-strike pledges.

Despite these policies, there was a small flurry of teacher strikes after World War II, punctuated by high-visibility walkouts organized by AFT locals in St. Paul, Minnesota, and Buffalo, New York.[3] During the war, real teacher salaries had fallen by 20 percent, while the pay of industrial workers had increased by 80 percent; in 1946, the average teacher was earning less than the average autoworker and the average meatpacker.[4] These conditions led to increased militancy by teachers, including a limited number of strikes. Yet when a number of state legislatures responded with draconian legislation that imposed heavy penalties for striking, such as New York State's Condon-Wadlin Act, the strikes petered out, leaving no lasting effects.

The 1960 strike for collective bargaining by New York City's United Federation of Teachers (UFT) would prove to be a decisive turning point in this history, both in terms of the use of the strike as a tactic and in the success of strikes in winning their objectives. In the decade and a half that followed the UFT strike, teachers would seize on its example: there were more than a thousand teacher strikes across the US, involving hundreds of thousands of teachers.[5] The great preponderance of those strikes focused on demands for union recognition and collective bargaining and for salary increases and benefits enhancements through first contracts, and they were successful on both counts.[6] By the end of the 1970s, nearly three-quarters of all American public school teachers were covered by a collective bargaining agreement, and in one significant measure of accomplishment, teacher salaries had increased dramatically—both in absolute terms and in relation to other professions that required similar levels of education.[7]

This explosion in the number of teacher strikes was part of a larger public-sector strike wave, with dramatic increases in strikes across all types of government employment. It also drove that wave, as teacher strikes accounted for close to half of all public-sector strikes during the 1960s.[8] The late 1960s and early 1970s would also see strikes spread to the private sector, which experienced its own strike wave.[9] Just as the strikes of the 1930s and 1940s had played a pivotal role in establishing industrial unionism in the US, the strikes of the 1960s and 1970s would be central to establishing public-sector unionism. And teachers were the catalyst: "The vanguard place in union militancy," wrote former union organizer and labor academic Jack Barbash, "goes to the teachers."[10]

Yet this period of teacher strike potency would not last. Even during the late 1960s, the first signs of trouble had appeared with long and bitter strikes in New York City and Newark, which generated deep racial divisions and left lasting wounds in the civic fabric of those cities.[11] By the mid-1970s, a major unraveling in the power of the teacher strike had begun. Just as the 1960 UFT strike had marked the beginning of an era, the 1975 UFT strike marked its closing and the advent of a new period.

In 1973, the US economy entered into its deepest and longest recession since the end of World War II, with a devastating combination of rising unemployment and inflation that had not been experienced in previous economic downturns. New York City was experiencing its highest levels of unemployment since the Great Depression, largely due to the loss of manufacturing jobs. By 1975, the revenues of state and local governments across the US had plummeted, and many were experiencing major fiscal crises.

As the opening of school approached for the 1975–1976 school year, New York City announced many thousands of teacher and educator layoffs, massive increases in class sizes, and a freeze on salaries. In response, the UFT went on strike.[12] But in these circumstances, its leverage was limited; after a week on strike, a divided union unhappily swallowed an agreement that fell well short of satisfactorily addressing the devastating cuts to the schools and their teachers. It was another month before even this deal was secure, guaranteed only after teachers' pension funds were invested in bonds that would keep the city from going into bankruptcy. It would be decades before New York City's schools and teachers could make up the ground lost in 1975.

As Jon Shelton's *Teacher Strike!* details, the dismal results of the 1975 UFT strike fit a pattern that was repeated across the country, as teachers and their unions unsuccessfully employed increasingly unpopular strikes in attempts to stem the tide of government austerity policies that followed in the wake of the state and local fiscal crises of the mid-1970s.[13] As the efficacy of strikes diminished, their number fell: strikes were already in decline in both the public and private sectors by 1981, when President Ronald Reagan broke the high-profile strike of the Professional Air Traffic Controllers Organization (PATCO).[14] Reagan's destruction of PATCO would dramatically accelerate the fall in the number of strikes; and by the first decade of the twenty-first century, strikes of all types—teacher strikes, public-sector strikes, and private-sector strikes—had faded to a mere handful in the US.[15]

In what surely is an encouraging development, the strikes of the Teacher Insurgency are the first positive signs in a long time that the strike could be reinvigorated as a powerful direct-action tactic for teachers and other working people in the US.[16] If these trends are sustained and spread to the private sector, it will not be the first time that teachers blazed the path for the American labor movement in a strike wave. Yet the history of teacher strikes also stands as an object lesson for those who insist that militancy and strikes alone are sufficient for teacher unions and other unions to make progress. The successful use of the teacher strike requires more than a willingness to fight and demands more than acts of political will; it requires a thoughtful strategic approach that has grasped and incorporated the lessons of the history of the strike, that understands how and why teacher strikes could swell in number and efficacy and then ebb in power and dwindle to a precious few. Strikes have historical and political contexts.

The Declining Power of Labor

In 1960, New York City was a bastion of union power. The political and financial support of the city's unions would prove critical in converting the momentum generated by the UFT's strike into a victory for collective bargaining for teachers.[17] This prototype repeated itself across the nation—teacher unions and other public-sector unions were first established and became most potent in places where the labor movement was already strong. Legislation enabling public-sector collective bargaining was first and most fully enacted in states where the labor movement had a powerful political presence. Conversely, teacher unions found it more difficult to acquire a foothold in states, mostly in the South, where the labor movement was weak; the same states that had adopted "right to work" laws to forestall the unionization of private-sector workers would pass legislation prohibiting collective bargaining for public-sector labor.[18]

At the start of the 1960s, the American labor movement was near the high point of its economic and political power. The percentage of union members in the workforce stood at 31.4 percent, still close to its all-time high in the mid-1950s, and the absolute numbers of union members was still growing.[19] The labor-liberal political coalition that had been the basis for the New Deal remained politically hegemonic, anchored by the labor movement and progressive industrial unions such as the United Auto Workers (UAW).[20] Starting in the late 1930s and 1940s, and continuing well into the 1960s, the economic and political power of unions had produced an era that the economist Paul Krugman has called the "Great Compression," as income inequality in the US was dramatically reduced.[21] Union political power would provide much of the muscle behind the civil rights legislation and the liberal programs of the Great Society during the 1960s, including the War on Poverty, and made it possible for Bayard Rustin, A. Philip Randolph, and Martin Luther King to think that the broad social democratic agenda of the Freedom Budget discussed in chapter 6 could be enacted. Teacher unions and other public-sector unions benefited immensely from the political power of unions during this decade.

Over the course of the 1960s, however, the membership rolls and density of the industrial unions began to decay, a product of employment lost to technological change, of corporate-dominated globalization that sent industrial jobs to countries with authoritarian governments that suppressed labor and kept it cheap, and of an increasing resort to harsh anti-union measures by American businesses. By the 1970s, the growing loss of members had begun to impact the political power of these unions. The effect on the larger labor movement and labor-left political coalition was initially masked by the growth of public-sector unions during the 1960s and 1970s, but it began to take an increasingly visible toll. By the late 1970s, the American labor movement was in retreat and the labor-liberal coalition was coming apart. In the subsequent decades, the decline of the economic and political power of unions led to an explosion in income inequality, returning it to the Gilded Age levels of extreme wealth and poverty we are now experiencing.[22]

The recession and fiscal crises of the mid-1970s gave New York City's financial elite formidable leverage, much as they did across the country. The city's major financial institutions had become global operations, and their bottom lines were no longer closely tied to its economic fortunes. When they stopped purchasing the bonds of a city in increasingly desperate financial straits and when the federal government held back on providing financial aid, it raised the specter of the city defaulting on its obligations, including payroll for municipal employees, and entering into bankruptcy. With default and bankruptcy, the city would lose control over its economic affairs, creating severe hardships for the city's working-class and poor who relied on its services, and making it possible to tear up union contracts with the city. The financial elite was able to leverage this threat to have New York State establish a shadow city government in the form of an Emergency Finance Control Board (EFCB), which held what amounted to veto power over the city's budgetary decisions. The EFCB's imposition of severe austerity would cut deeply into the very muscle and bone of the public sector, including public education. Many of the policies and public-sector programs that had made New York City into a social democratic oasis since the days of Mayor Fiorello La Guardia and the New Deal, such as the free public college education at the City University that produced so many of the famous "New York intellectuals," were either eliminated or transformed into faded facsimiles of once-robust public goods and services.[23] The financial elite forced changes in the city's very social and economic fabric, introducing an era of extreme economic inequality: failed strikes carry real costs.

The 1975 UFT strike and the other teacher strikes of the mid-1970s were swimming upstream against powerful currents. Arguably, even the most strategically sound strikes would have had real difficulty achieving any measure of success under these circumstances. Yet the strike strategy of teacher unions in this period had major weaknesses, as the unions failed to grasp how the changing world required a retooling of what had worked so well only a decade earlier. It is important to learn how to avoid replicating these weaknesses, if the Teacher Insurgency is to be sustained.

The lessons of the history of teacher union strikes center on four key themes to which I will now turn: the organization and mobilization of strikes; the relationship of strikes to other direct-action tactics; the relationship of strikes to politics and government; and the relationship of strikes and unions to the communities served by the schools.

ORGANIZING AND MOBILIZING STRIKES

Strikes are not spontaneously born, the natural and inevitable expression of "an ardent sentiment of revolt, always present in the soul of the worker," as the syndicalists would have it.[24] Nor is it "misleaders" of workers, acting out of timidity and narrow bureaucratic interests or constrained by organizational structures and organizational conservatism, who have kept American workers from acting on this "sentiment of revolt" in recent decades.[25] Those are romantic conceptions, better suited for paeans to lost causes and dead heroes than to an understanding of the real world of strikes.

Strikes are a form of collective action and, like all collective action, they must be organized and mobilized. As a protest and a direct action, strikes can gather energy and acquire momentum from the general tenor of the times. In a period of mass protests such as the 1960s and early 1970s and again in more recent years, teachers and other working people are inspired by witnessing and participating in nonviolent direct action against the exercise of illegitimate and arbitrary authority, as such protests make clear that resistance is possible. But inspiration is the start, not the finish, of effective collective action, and is no replacement for organization.

Strikes are complex operations, involving a multiplicity of critical tasks that must be coordinated—picket lines, rallies, internal union communications, union meetings, media relations, community relations, and negotiations. The better organized the strike and the more fully these tasks are accomplished, the greater its chance of success. In this respect, the 2012 and 2019 Chicago strikes and the 2019 Los Angeles strike, with their careful and thorough school-by-school and teacher-by-teacher organizing and years of preparing the ground for the actual strike mobilization, stand as exemplars that should be emulated in the Teacher Insurgency.

The most essential organizational task is winning and keeping the allegiance of teachers to the strike. Teachers are knowledgeable and discerning political actors. They understand full well that strikes are a high-intensity and high-risk tactic, with the potential both to deliver advances and victories that could not be otherwise obtained and to end in major setbacks and defeats. The risk side of this equation is particularly acute in the three-quarters of all states where teacher strikes are illegal; in these states, striking becomes an act of civil disobedience and can result in severe penalties to teachers and their unions.

To be willing to go on strike and stay out until a settlement is won, therefore, teachers need to be convinced on a number of different counts: first, that they are fighting for important, worthwhile objectives; second, that those objectives cannot be achieved through other means that are not as high-intensity and high-risk as a strike; third, that the strike has reasonable prospects of success, and they are not joining a "Charge of the Light Brigade" for a noble cause that is doomed to failure; fourth, that the strike objectives have strong support in the community; and last, that the solidarity among teachers, which is essential to a strike's success, is strong and will hold. In significant measure, the last of these points is dependent not simply on the organization and mobilization of the strike, but also on the four antecedent conditions. If teachers become doubtful on any of these points, it will become difficult to mount or sustain a successful strike. While we are focused on teachers and strikes, there is a broader application of these conditions: in general, workers need to be convinced on similar counts to go on strike and stay out until concessions are won from the employer.

Given the high-intensity and high-risk nature of strikes, what political reasoning do teachers employ to make the difficult decision to strike? It is necessary here to go beyond the issues that have generated a particular strike and examine how teachers think in general about using the strike tactic. One useful window into the nature of teacher political agency vis-à-vis the strike can be found in the ways in which the strike was understood and practiced by previous generations of working people in the US, as these traditions played a formative role in the development of teacher unionism.

The Strike and the Civic Republican Traditions of Labor

Adapting the precepts of the civic republicanism expounded by Thomas Jefferson and Abraham Lincoln, among others, the nineteenth-century American labor movement saw the strike as a fundamental right of citizenship.[26] According to this perspective, the strike was not simply an expression of the collective power of working people, but also a manifestation of the republican liberty of free labor—an assertion of the freedom from domination that is the necessary foundation for the self-rule of the citizenry in a republic.[27] Workers must be able and willing to withdraw their labor through a strike, nineteenth-century unionists contended, or they will no longer be their own masters, but powerless subjects in a system of wage slavery. Much as elections and voting were understood to be the means for the civic reenactment and renewal of the social compact on which the republican government was based, strikes were viewed as public declarations of the republican liberty of working people, public affirmations of the dignity and civic worth of the citizen-worker. The often-elaborate pageantry of nineteenth-century strikes—the marches, demonstrations, rallies, and picket lines; the songs and dramatic performances; and the banners, garb and regalia of the unions—would symbolically stake this public claim on a republican citizenship for working people.

While this civic republican understanding of the strike as a declaration of the rights of citizenship is more often sublimated than explicit in the US strikes of the twentieth and twenty-first centuries, its continuing presence is powerfully captured in such moments as the 1968 Memphis sanitation workers' strike, which became well-known when Martin Luther King was assassinated while in Memphis to support the strikers.[28] The "I am a man" picket sign held by the African American workers in that 1968 strike has become an iconic emblem of the strikes of

American labor with its demand for the recognition of the rights of citizenship. Successful teacher strikes often highlight an analogous theme of the dignity and civic worth of teachers and the value of the work they do—that they are fighting for important, worthwhile objectives—and that powerful symbolic statement is one of the less appreciated motivations for teachers when they go on strike. It has been a theme in the strikes of the Teacher Insurgency.

If this discussion of the republican liberty of working people seems like an exercise in antiquarian history and political philosophy that is unconnected to contemporary reality, it is worthwhile to consider that under current American labor law, a worker surrenders most of her rights of citizenship—her freedoms of speech, press, of peaceful assembly and the right to petition to seek redress of her grievances; her right to due process; her right to fair and equal treatment—at the door of a non-unionized workplace. The legal protections for workers organizing a union have been whittled away over seven decades, and they are now very weak and mostly unenforced by government.[29] American law allows non-union workplaces to be "private governments," or what philosopher Elizabeth Anderson calls "dictatorships in our midst."[30] Under the doctrine of at-will employment that governs such workplaces, workers can be fired for any reason or no reason at all, save those instances where a firing involves documentable discrimination against a member of a protected class under civil rights law. In jurisdictions with incomplete civil rights protections, a worker can be fired for nothing more than her sexual orientation or gender identity—only twenty-two states provide full employment protection for LGBTQ employees. If a worker in a non-union workplace wears a button supporting a candidate for public office opposed by her employer or has a bumper sticker on her car supporting a cause opposed by her employer, she can be fired with no remedy in law.

As Alexander Hertel-Fernandez has thoroughly documented, US employers in non-union settings use their unchecked power over their workplace to compel political action on behalf of candidates, legislation and causes that promote the interests of the business and its owners.[31] When economic domination is turned into political coercion in these ways, it collides directly with the foundational republican idea of the self-rule of citizens. This is why the founding slogan of the

AFT—"Education in Democracy, Democracy for Education"—focused on the vital connection unionists saw between teachers being able to exercise the rights of citizenship inside the educational workplace on the one hand, and the work of teachers to promote democracy through their teaching on the other.

Civic republicanism was the source of another central concept in American labor's understanding of the nineteenth-century strike—the duty of solidarity. The first truly national labor union in the US, the Knights of Labor, articulated a labor republican vision of the future society it sought to establish, the cooperative commonwealth. At the center of that vision was the classical republican idea that government should promote the common good: "The best government (is one) in which an injury to one is the concern of all."[32] For the Knights of Labor, this principle of seeking the common good—what classical republicans called *civic virtue*—not only defined how government and society should function, but also how working people themselves should act with respect to each other.[33] Contemporary American unionists will recognize the Knights of Labor formulation as an early version of an axiom of labor solidarity that has continued to this day: "An injury to one is an injury to all."

At the heart of republican citizenship and civic virtue is the willingness to make personal sacrifices: citizens in a republic exercise civic virtue through a myriad of sacrifices, great and small, from putting their lives at risk to defend their nation from attack to paying taxes that support government goods and services that do not personally benefit them. As Danielle Allen makes clear in her discussion of sacrifice and citizenship in the context of the civil rights movement, some citizens are called to make greater sacrifices than others.[34] The African American families who sent their young children to integrate schools in Little Rock and to demonstrate in downtown Birmingham, with the full knowledge that they would face vicious racist harassment and violence, made sacrifices that no white families were ever called upon to make. But they judged that the value of those acts for the common good—of the African American community and of the society as a whole—made those difficult sacrifices worth performing.

Going on strike and practicing solidarity entails sacrifices, ranging from the loss of one's income for a period of the strike to the loss of one's job. As noted above, when strikes are prohibited by law, going on strike is an act of civil disobedience, and can incur fines for rank-and-file unionists and jail for union leaders. Yet American teachers have demonstrated again and again that they are prepared to make such sacrifices if going on strike means that they can secure a better future not only for themselves and their families, but also for the students they teach and nurture, the schools in which they work, and the communities they serve. By their very choice of vocation, entering an occupation with modest pay and benefits in order to be able to make differences in the lives of young people, teachers have demonstrated that they are prepared to make sacrifices for a greater good. So it should not be a cause for surprise that they would assume the sacrifices of a strike, provided that they know its objectives are important, that they cannot be achieved through other means, that the strike is winnable, that community support is strong, and that teacher solidarity will hold.

THE STRIKE AS DIRECT ACTION

"The strike is the only weapon labor has."[35] So said Harry Bridges, leader of the 1934 San Francisco general strike and longtime president of the International Longshore and Warehouse Union, on the occasion of his retirement from the union. Still deeply embedded in the syndicalism of his youth, Bridges minced no words: the strike was not *a* weapon, or even the *primary* weapon, of labor—it was the "*only* weapon."

Today, there are advocates of this single-minded focus on the strike within the labor movement; it is fetishized as a magical cure for more than a half-century of long-term secular decline in union power. No one has made that case with more force and consistency than Joe Burns, a one-time union organizer, local leader, and labor lawyer who has dedicated two books to the subject of "reviving the strike."[36] For Burns, the strike is the only means for rebuilding the American labor movement; he explicitly discounts the positive contributions of other direct-action tactics, organizing the unorganized, building strong relationships with community, social unionism, and labor law reform. Others make similar points. Eric Blanc, author of *Red State Revolt*, a book chronicling the Teacher Spring strikes of 2018, argues that the labor movement's long decline was a result of a focus on engaging in electoral politics—what he characterizes as "simply lobbying the Democrats"—as opposed to "building power by striking."[37]

But the decline in the use of the strike has been as much an effect of the decline of the power of the American labor movement as it has been a cause. A successful strategy for the revitalization of US unions must be more multifaceted and more dialectical than a simple focus on mounting strikes.

The irony here is that reliance exclusively on the strike creates the very conditions for weakening it as a tactic, making it less powerful and less effective. One of the reasons why teacher strikes went from being formidable tools for improving the lives of teachers in the 1960s and early 1970s to becoming ineffective and at times counterproductive by the late 1970s and 1980s was the fact that teacher unions had become wholly dependent on it, and did not increase the repertoire of direct-action tactics in their arsenals through tactical innovation and experimentation. When the only direct-action tactic a union has its toolbox is the hammer of the strike, it treats every strategic challenge as a nail, even when it poses a different problem that could be better addressed by a different direct-action tool or by political action.

The problem of becoming dependent on a single direct-action tactic is not restricted to unions: there are many examples of other protest movements that found themselves at considerable disadvantage for the same reason. The Occupy movement was mobilized around the single tactic of occupying public space; when it was forced out of this space, it lost momentum and public attention, and soon dissolved as an organized force.

By contrast, at its height during the 1960s, the civil rights movement engaged in constant tactical innovation and experimentation, with the insurgency peaking again and again as new forms of direct action were introduced.

As Doug McAdam explains in his study of the "Black insurgency," this tactical creativity was key in keeping the Jim Crow regime off guard and off balance; no sooner did white supremacist authorities adjust to one tactic, finding ways to respond to and check it, then they would find themselves confronted with a new strategy.[38]

There is no reason why unions—especially teacher unions—could not do the same. At the height of its influence in the late 1960s and early

1970s, the United Farm Workers (UFW) employed a strategy along these lines, surrounding the strike with other tactics of civil disobedience and nonviolent direct action, such as boycotts, sit-ins, and public fasts; the struggle of farmworkers to unionize and win a better life was framed as a civil rights struggle and a struggle for citizenship rights by a workforce of people of color, and wedded to community organizing.[39] A strategy that was entirely dependent on the strike would never have achieved the victories won by the UFW in those years.

The point here is not to retreat from the use of direct action, with its capacity to disrupt the existing balance of political forces, but to expand its use—to not become dependent on just one tactic, even a tactic as potentially powerful and important as the strike. To the extent that teachers and their unions have a wide repertoire of direct-action tactics, every action in that repertoire—including the strike—will be more effective.

STRIKES AND POLITICAL ACTION

Even among labor movement thinkers who recognize the value of different tactics of direct action, there are still those who counterpose the strike to political action. Labor organizer Jane McAlevey's book *No Shortcuts* provides an insightful analysis of different direct-action approaches in both union organizing and community organizing, but she still embraces a syndicalism dismissive of electoral politics when she concludes, "Ultimately, I don't think there's any way out of the crisis we're in this country right now unless we start having more strikes."[40] This is a revealing formulation, given the obvious challenge that it avoids discussing—the fact that in the US and many other nations, the executive and therefore the national machinery of the government are now in the hands of authoritarian, racist populists of the far right. The electoral defeat of those forces would certainly not end the global "crisis of democracy" in which we find ourselves, as that crisis did not begin with their election. But it is impossible to conceive of a realistic scenario where it is not a necessary first step in that process. Without any explanation of how "more strikes" would translate into electoral victories over these forces, the strike becomes a totem for addressing a crisis that, if unchecked, could lead to the consolidation of an authoritarian regime that has been unequivocally hostile to unions, among its many other anti-democratic postures.[41]

There is a fundamental problem with this counterposing of strikes and politics. In the US, politics have always been central to the outcomes of strikes, both in victory and defeat. The refusal of President Franklin Roosevelt and Michigan Governor Frank Murphy to use troops to suppress the 1936–1937 Flint sit-down strike was decisive in forcing General Motors to recognize and negotiate with the United Auto Workers, thus generating the breakthrough of industrial unionism in the US that followed the unionization of the largest corporation of its era.[42] As I have already noted, the willingness of President Reagan to break the 1981 air traffic controllers' strike destroyed their union and was a significant factor in the decline of strikes as a direct-action tactic of unions in the following decades.[43] Different elected officials with different relationships to labor would most likely have produced different outcomes in both cases. Erik Loomis's *A History of America in Ten Strikes* makes the telling point that politics and government involvement runs through these consequential strikes like a bright red thread.[44]

What is true of strikes in general is doubly true of teacher strikes and other public-sector strikes, as the employer is the government. By their very nature, these strikes are political. The 2018 Teacher Spring strike in West Virginia had the most success of the strikes that year precisely because the unions in that state were well established, with strong union density and a real and active political force; they were able to use their political capacity to move the state legislature and governor to act on those demands. The Los Angeles 2019 strike brought to public attention the question of how charter school expansion had had a negative impact on district schools, but it still required the organized political presence of the state's teacher unions to pass legislation that reformed, for the very first time, the process by which new charter schools were authorized. A reliance on the strike alone would not have achieved either of these victories.

The counterposing of strikes and politics can blind even perceptive observers to important political dynamics. Jane McAlevey's account of the 2012 Chicago strike focuses entirely on the union's impressive internal organizing and activation of its membership, which was indeed an absolutely crucial factor in winning that strike.[45] Maintaining solidarity is the sine qua non of every strike. But one searches in vain for a discussion of the relationships the Chicago Teachers Union (CTU) had built with the communities served by their schools, which created powerful public support for the strike and was also pivotal in its success. Nor is there any discussion of the CTU leadership's skillful use of political leverage—scheduling the strike for the heat of the 2012 presidential campaign, when maximum pressure could be brought to bear on Mayor Rahm Emanuel, President Obama's former chief of staff, to settle a high-profile strike in Obama's hometown. It was the combination of internal organizing and building relationships with community, the synergy of the direct action of the strike and politics, that led to victory in this important, pathbreaking strike.

THE STRIKE AND RELATIONSHIPS TO COMMUNITY

This understanding of strikes as part of a broader strategic approach is especially important when one considers a critical factor in the decline of the potency of teacher union strikes in the late 1970s and 1980s—the divisions that had opened up between the unions and the communities they served. The austerity conservatism that emerged out of the fiscal crises of the mid-1970s—known as Reaganism in the US—had as its primary objectives the gutting of the public sector and the evisceration of the social welfare safety net. It thus set its sights both on the workers and the unions that provided public goods and services on the one hand, and on the working-class and poor communities, disproportionately of color, that relied on those public good and services on the other. Attacks on public-sector employees as lazy, incompetent, and overcompensated were matched with attacks on racialized "welfare queens" and the "undeserving" poor, and both were condemned as "parasitical" on the "taxpayer."

To have had any realistic hope of blunting the assault of this austerity conservatism, it would have been necessary to develop a common front between the workers who provided public goods and services and the communities that relied on them. Like any political alliance, this front would have to be actively built and organized. But as much as the logic of joint opposition to attacks on the public services and goods was clear, there were also deep-seated suspicion and distrust on each side. The long and bitter Ocean Hill-Brownsville and Newark strikes had been on the order of epic Greek tragedies: out of a mutual failure to grasp the larger dynamics at work, the main characters fell into mortal combat that brought down both sides. Teacher unions had concluded that these strikes were existential struggles for survival; many in the Ocean Hill-Brownsville and Newark communities and beyond had concluded that unions were standing in the way of good schools for poor children of color. That accusations of racism and anti-Semitism pervaded these perceptions made them all the more intractable. These differences proved to be too great to overcome; neither teacher unions nor the communities they served saw each other as potential political partners at this critical moment. As a result, the strikes were politically isolated and unpopular, and a conservative politics of austerity won the day, to the detriment of both teachers and the communities.

One of the most positive aspects of the strikes of the Teacher Insurgency has been the strong support the teachers and their unions have received from the communities. That support did not appear ex nihilo, like Athena bursting forth full-grown from the head of Zeus. It was the product of a decade and a half of work on the part of teacher unions to build deep, long-lasting ties to communities. Contrary to the suggestion that building these ties was a diversion from the work of organizing strikes, it had been essential to their reemergence. In chapter 7, I will examine this work in detail.

Far too much of what passes for thinking about strikes in the US—including teacher strikes—rests on a "field of dreams" theory: Call it, and they will come. In this chapter, I have sought to go beyond such romantic notions, which are recipes for disaster. In their place, I have laid out the different conditions and approaches that have led teacher strikes to victory and defeat, with the objective of identifying a way forward that will continue the success of the strikes of the Teacher Insurgency.

CHAPTER 7

Organizing with Community

Bargaining for the Common Good

THE WIDE AND DEEP PUBLIC SUPPORT for the Teacher Insurgency strikes of 2018 and 2019 was unprecedented, and unforeseen even by astute observers of education politics. National, state, and local public opinion polls have consistently shown solid majorities in support of the strikes, with levels of support most often ranging between 75 percent and 80 percent of those polled.[1] This degree of support is remarkable not only because it runs counter to the previous history of teacher strikes, but also because teacher strikes are unquestionably a major inconvenience for families with school-age children. To attain such vigorous public backing, with the families of public school students providing the highest levels of support, there had to be a strong feeling that the teachers were fighting for something more than just themselves, that the strikes were also on behalf of the public schools and the students who were educated in them—that, in a phrase, the strikes were for and with the community.

Part of the loyalty of community was won by how the teachers and their unions have conducted the strikes of the Teacher Insurgency. When West Virginia and Oklahoma teachers organized to make sure that students who relied on schools for breakfast and lunch would still be fed during their strikes, they demonstrated a commitment to the welfare of their students that belied the right-wing attacks on the strikes and won the heart of their communities.[2] But the support of the community has deeper roots that extend back before the strikes. The groundswell of public support for the teacher strikes is intimately connected to the changing landscape of education politics.

In this chapter, I will discuss how the strategies employed in the Teacher Insurgency—and in particular, their adoption of the idea of bargaining for the common good—contributed to these high levels of community support for the strikes. The strategies grew out of an approach to relationships with community that teachers and their unions have been developing for a decade and a half. But it has important antecedents in the work of teacher unionists' work from the turn of the twentieth century, and I will discuss two of them—the first full community school in East Harlem and the first effort at bringing community schools to New York City. I will conclude this chapter by examining why this approach is bearing fruit today by examining a community-building project of the AFT in West Virginia and the approach of the United Teachers of Los Angeles in its 2019 strike.

BARGAINING FOR THE COMMON GOOD

"Bargaining for the common good" is shorthand for an approach to the negotiation demands of the union that does not limit itself to what are commonly viewed as traditional union issues, such as salaries and benefits, but also includes considerations about quality of the services that schools provide, with a particular focus on the education students need and deserve.[3] The Teacher Spring strikes of 2018 are illustrative of this approach, as they were fought as much over the effects of underinvestment in public education on the conditions of teaching and learning as over teacher salaries, pension, and health insurance. The Teacher Insurgency strikes of 2019 have extended this approach beyond the general issue of underinvestment by raising a variety of issues, including large class sizes; inadequate numbers of student support staff such as nurses, counselors, and librarians; excessive standardized testing; punitive student discipline practices; inadequate protections for undocumented and immigrant students; too few services to address the challenges faced by homeless students; and the problems created by unfettered charter school expansion. Increasingly, these strikes have drawn attention to the revenues used to support education—whether the wealthy and corporations are paying their fair share in taxes, and whether states and cities are investing in important public goods and services such as education or spending their budgets on economic development that benefits private interests.

"Bargaining for the common good" evokes the language of the labor republicanism of nineteenth-century American unions, with its focus on the good of the community and the welfare of all. One of the reasons why public support for the Teacher Insurgency strikes has proved so strong is that the community sees teachers as exercising the civic virtue of labor republicanism, sacrificing their income by striking in an effort to win educational essentials for their students. The teacher union slogan from the 1960s—"Teachers want what students need"—has been given a new power.

It is important to be precise about the new ground being broken with this approach. Since the beginning of the collective bargaining era, teacher unions have raised negotiation and strike demands that address the quality of education provided to their students. For example, in the negotiations for its first contract, New York City's United Federation of Teachers (UFT) demanded reductions in class sizes, proposed a teacher apprenticeship program in which novice teachers would be paired with accomplished veterans to support them in developing their craft, and put forward a comprehensive program to attract and retain experienced teachers in high-poverty schools that featured class sizes below the contractual limit, proven curricular programs, and literacy specialists.[4] The challenge that the UFT faced—and that every teacher union that has negotiated educational issues since the start of the collective bargaining era has faced—is that school districts often view such educational proposals as impinging on their "management prerogatives"; that is, the idea that management should be able to set the policies of schools and districts without regard for the educational thinking and experience of teachers. (In some states, the law even prohibits bargaining over educational issues, although this restriction has proved very hard to enforce.) Progress on educational issues can be a hard road to travel in the face of such attitudes, but there is still a real and substantial history of teacher unions successfully integrating educational issues into their contract demands to positive effect. Such efforts have produced important innovative educational initiatives such as peer assistance and review programs, the National Board for Professional Teaching Standards process (which certifies teachers who have demonstrated excellence in their craft), and programs that provide additional supports and resources to schools serving communities with high concentrations of poverty.[5] When teachers and their unions take up educational issues today, they are following a path blazed by their predecessors over the last six decades.

What distinguishes bargaining for the common good from the prior efforts of teacher unions, therefore, is not that the union makes demands on educational issues that impact the education of their students. The difference is more nuanced; it lies in the ways in which those educational demands are generated and framed and the nature of the fight conducted on their behalf. Mary Cathryn Ricker, past president of the St. Paul Federation of Teachers which pioneered this approach (and who now serves as Minnesota Commissioner of Education), described it as "teacher-community unionism."[6] This term signifies a bargaining process in which the union has invited the active participation of representatives of the community, leading to a partnership. In line with this approach, educational issues are framed as social justice issues.

To understand how and why this approach to partnership with community developed, it is useful to start with an examination of two little appreciated chapters of teacher union history: (1) the story of the first urban community school, East Harlem's Benjamin Franklin High School, and (2) the 1960s More Effective Schools program of the United Federation of Teachers (UFT), which sought to implement the community school model in all of New York City's high-poverty schools.

The Community School and Teacher Unionism

During the early days of the American republic, schools developed organically from the communities they served. However, by the second half of the nineteenth century, relationships between urban public schools and communities had become increasingly attenuated. Large, impersonal, and bureaucratized urban school districts emerged, largely in response to the extraordinary growth of the urban population and the massive increases in the numbers of students that came with the establishment of universal elementary school education. Urban communities—and especially working-class and poor communities, which are disproportionately composed of immigrants and people of color—were often alienated from the schools their youth attended.

It was in response to this developing alienation that the idea of "the school as social center"—what we would today call a *community school*—was first elaborated by John Dewey, the leading educator and philosopher of his day in the US and arguably the most prominent member of the American Federation of Teachers (AFT) in its first decades.[7] While at the University of Chicago, Dewey worked closely with Jane Addams and her Hull House, the first major settlement house in America; his notion of a community school was deeply influenced by Addams' philosophy that the settlement house needed to be rooted in the community in order to provide educational and social services.[8] For Dewey, the community school was "a center of life for all ages and classes . . . a thoroughly socialized affair in contact at all points with the flow of community life."[9] It would function as a "social center" of learning, with both formal and informal education for youth and adults, all centered on the goal of "bringing people together, of doing away with barriers of caste, or class, or race, or type of experience that people from real communion with each other."[10]

This Deweyan conception of a community school would find its first fullest expression in Benjamin Franklin High School, an East Harlem public school established in New York City during the Great Depression. Under the leadership of educator and sociologist Leonard Covello, Benjamin Franklin blazed a trail that made the school into the dynamic center of the community through a far-reaching conception of education into democratic citizenship.[11] Covello was a lifelong teacher unionist and democratic socialist; given Benjamin Franklin's mission and exceptional work, faculty with similar educational and political philosophies flocked to teach there. Central to the school's citizenship work were teacher union leaders Layle Lane, who served as an AFT vice president and led the national union's civil rights work, and Si Beagle, who would go on to play a pivotal role in the development of the UFT's More Effective Schools program.

Having grown up in an immigrant, working-class Italian-American family, Covello was keenly aware of the ways in which schools could be alienating institutions, driving wedges between students and their families and communities. In Benjamin Franklin, he set out to create a school in which students found their familial and communal ties and their heritage cultures affirmed, not denigrated and undermined. The school was fully integrated into the life and fabric of the community, at one point establishing centers in empty storefronts throughout East Harlem to facilitate this incorporation. From these centers as well as the main school buildings, Benjamin Franklin organized and provided adult education, citizenship naturalization services, an East Harlem community newspaper (published in English, Italian, and Spanish), social welfare and student aid services for students and families living in poverty, a housing committee, a health committee (which linked students and families in need with community health services), student tutoring, and juvenile delinquency prevention interventions.[12] The centers also organized cultural heritage festivals and events to ensure closer ties to the community.

In a foreshadowing of what is today called "community service learning" and "action civics," Benjamin Franklin's students were actively engaged in community improvement projects, from a sanitation project that cleaned up empty and abandoned lots that blighted East Harlem to the establishment of playgrounds. In this work, the school used to great positive effect Youthbuilders, a civics education program based on the premise that experience *in* democracy is the best education *for* democracy.[13] While most service learning focuses only on providing services to the community, Benjamin Franklin had its students take on the work of democratic citizenship, of advocacy for the common good of the community—from the construction of new facilities to house the school itself, to the successful erection of public housing to replace slum tenements, to an unsuccessful campaign to build a hospital in East Harlem.[14] Benjamin Franklin High School was "education as if citizenship mattered"—an education into democratic citizenship conceived as active, public work.[15]

Benjamin Franklin High School was distinguished from other community school experiments of the 1930s and 1940s in that it was a cosmopolitan urban school, with different ethnic groups and races in its student body. From the late nineteenth century through the mid-twentieth century, the demographic landscape of East Harlem had been transformed by successive waves of immigrants: first Irish and European Jewish immigrants, then Italian immigrants, and finally, Puerto Rican and southern African American migrants.[16] In a poor and working-class community, these transitions produced great battles over neighborhood turf. The battles were particularly severe during the late 1920s and 1930s, the period of the founding of Benjamin Franklin, as anger over the discriminatory treatment of African Americans by Italian and other white-owned Harlem businesses was intensified by the rise of fascism in Italy and the Italian invasion of Ethiopia. Harlem would experience major race riots in 1935 and in 1943.[17]

Benjamin Franklin faced this challenge head-on with a series of school programs that, when taken together, comprised arguably the most developed anti-racist, multicultural education of this era. Leonard Covello's papers and other sources include a number of course syllabi and accounts of teaching that demonstrate how real engagement with issues of race and class were integrated into many different subjects.[18]

Benjamin Franklin was the first school to incorporate into its instruction Rachel Davis DuBois's "cultural gifts" program, the earliest effort at developing systematic anti-racist education.[19] In the 1934–1935 school year, when the school first opened its doors, it worked with DuBois in putting on schoolwide assemblies and follow-up class lessons on different ethnic groups with the goals of reducing tensions and building positive self-images among the two student groups that had the most contentious relationships at that point, Italian-Americans and Puerto Ricans.[20] Another important component of this work was the development of a "human relations" film series, undertaken from 1937 to 1955 in conjunction with educator Alice Keliher and the Progressive Education Association.[21] Far from being isolated or superficial events, the cultural gifts assemblies and the film series were expressions of the school's approach to infusing anti-racist, multicultural themes throughout its curriculum.

Tragically, with the retirement of Leonard Covello, Layle Lane, and the founding generation of its educators in the mid-1950s, Benjamin Franklin lost its sense of mission and the distinctive programs that made it into a "community school" in the fullest sense of that term. But one of Franklin's educators, Si Beagle, went on to incorporate a number of the ideas that had been pioneered at Franklin into a UFT program that sought to develop community schools across the New York City public school system.

More Effective Schools: The 1960s Community School Experiment

The 1954 *Brown v. Board of Education* ruling that "separate educational facilities are inherently unequal" had a resonance that went beyond the efforts to end de jure racial segregation in the Jim Crow South. African American and other communities of color in the North saw this axiom as no less applicable to the de facto segregated schools that educated their children in urban centers such as New York City. Campaigns to end racial segregation in public schools began to develop in the wake of *Brown*.[22] Among union locals, few rivaled the UFT in its active support of the civil rights struggle in the South, and it (and its predecessor organization, the Teachers Guild) was similarly engaged in the emerging efforts to integrate New York City public schools.[23] To the frustration of the UFT and other advocates of school integration, New York City public schools became more segregated over the course of the 1950s and early 1960s, a product of "white flight" from the city to the suburbs, coupled with increasing migration of southern African Americans and Puerto Ricans into the city.[24]

Led by democratic socialists and social democrats closely allied with A. Philip Randolph, Bayard Rustin, and Martin Luther King, the UFT brought an analysis of the class dimension of racism to the problem of de facto school segregation. In this perspective, segregated schools were not only separate, but—just as important—unequal; that is, racial segregation and class inequality were fused together. As a consequence, racial segregation of schools could not be successfully undone without taking on their class inequalities. Establishing equity in teaching and learning conditions across *all* schools was seen as indispensable in ending racial separation.

There was much to recommend this approach as a matter of general principle, but it also spoke to the particular quandary that had arisen in efforts to end this segregation. Racial integration would prove to be a very short and Pyrrhic victory if the white student population left the public school system altogether, as had taken place in a number of different school districts, northern as well as southern.[25] Such an exodus was a real danger in New York City. Even without the racial integration of schools, there had already been "white flight" from New York City to the surrounding suburbs during the 1950s. If integration took place in a school system that remained fundamentally unequal, poor students of color who were left in the inner-city schools would experience little improvement in their education, and most parents of middle-class students, who were predominantly white, would look for ways to remove them from the increasingly inadequate public schools.

For racial integration efforts in New York City public schools to be successful, the UFT leadership believed that these efforts must include an extensive endeavor to improve the teaching and learning conditions in the segregated schools that served the low-income African American and Puerto Rican communities. In short, an educational initiative of the same ambition and scope as the Freedom Budget (see chapter 5) was required.[26]

With this understanding, in 1963 the UFT developed a program for racial integration that addressed the inequalities in New York City schools through what came to be known as the More Effective Schools (MES) initiative.[27] The MES agenda called for smaller schools, smaller classes, and team teaching, all to support teachers in providing individualized instruction and attention to students and in addressing each student's particular needs. MES schools would have a longer school day, and their curriculum would be enriched with art and music classes. Elementary schools in the MES program would provide free pre-K classes (which were extraordinarily rare in high-poverty schools during the 1960s) and would use heterogeneous and multi-grade groupings in their classes. Clusters of classes would have additional teachers assigned as academic intervention specialists; for example, reading teachers who would provide special instruction for students who were lagging behind in the acquisition of essential reading and writing skills.

MES schools would also become Deweyan social centers, open to all students and their families from 8 a.m. to 6 p.m., including weekends and summer months. They would provide a comprehensive array of social and health (medical, dental, and eye care) services to students and their families. Working closely with city's Department of Housing,

Department of Welfare, and other social services, MES schools would minimize the many disruptions in the education of students living in poverty that were due to transience and homelessness.[28] MES schools would have a full complement of guidance services; a full-time nurse or health counselor; a full-time social worker, attendance teacher, or school psychologist; and a community relations expert to facilitate school-community and school-family relations. In the days before special education services, MES schools would have special provisions for the education and care of emotionally disturbed students.

Meaningful professional development time and experiences were provided for supervisors and teachers, with a focus on introducing new pedagogical strategies and techniques and partnerships with post-secondary educational institutions. Teachers were given time to have grade-level and cluster planning meetings, and additional secretaries and aides were hired to free supervisors and teachers from non-instructional duties and allow them to focus on teaching and learning. MES schools were provided additional contingency funds to be used on programs they provided and supplies they needed, and they were given special latitude to organize their school in nontraditional ways to meet student needs, with school supervisors and teachers collaborating on those experiments.

Within the UFT, the leaders who came out of the socialist movement and saw themselves as part of a democratic left—Si Beagle, Richard Parrish, George Altomare, and Al Shanker, among others—were the strongest advocates of the MES program. AFT President Dave Selden, a democratic socialist who had been the UFT's main organizer in the battle for collective organizing, was a strong backer of the MES program, and with his support, the AFT made an effort to expand the MES model to other large urban school districts through a national initiative headed up by Beagle. It is not hard to hear echoes of the MES program in the demands of the Teacher Insurgency strikes, although it is unlikely that many striking teachers and union leaders know of the historical antecedents of their current struggles.

During the few short years that the MES project was funded, there was solid evidence of its educational success. Among other things, the schools attracted and retained experienced and accomplished teachers, and brought in middle-class families, especially educator families, who had been convinced that their children would receive a quality education in integrated schools.[29] But there are also lessons to be learned: MES schools that lacked cultures of collaboration among the educators were not able to use the additional supports and resources to full positive effect, and a more developed academic program that addressed the educational challenges faced by children living in poverty was needed. In what was to prove a significant shortcoming, during the few short years they were funded, MES schools were not able to sink the deep roots into the community that had defined Benjamin Franklin High School. In this respect, the MES program was particularly hampered by the relative absence of the voices of families and the community in important school decisions.

The UFT fought hard for the MES program, with a goal of expanding it to all racially segregated New York City public schools serving high-poverty communities. In 1967, the union would go on strike for two weeks, staying out well after it had reached agreement over salary increases that would make teachers into what the *New York Times* called "the best paid in the country" in order to win a promise for funds to expand the MES program.[30] The board of education and the city had grudgingly accepted the MES program: in their view, the union was telling them how to manage the schools, and this made them quite resentful. Moreover, with all of the academic enhancements, intervention supports, and social services it provided, the MES program cost approximately twice what the board had been previously spending on its racially segregated, high-poverty schools; the UFT's demand to increase the numbers of MES schools from twenty-one to three hundred would have required an additional expenditure of $150 million—$1.15 billion in 2020 dollars. A price ticket of this magnitude meant either that the city would have to increase its funding of schools by raising taxes, or that there would be less money for other parts of the budget that the city's political and economic elite would rather fund. A number of predominantly white middle-class communities, which had traditionally received the lion's share of education resources, began to express anger at the possibility of growing funding equity if MES began to expand beyond a handful of pilot schools with the UFT's support.

Despite its accomplishments, the MES ship would break up on the rocky crags of the late 1960s battles over community control. At the inception of New York City's community control experiment, the UFT was a supportive participant in advocating for and helping to launch a "demonstration district" in Ocean Hill-Brownsville, with civil rights movement veteran Sandy Feldman assigned to work as point person on the project. From the union's perspective, the students and schools of Ocean Hill-Brownsville would benefit immensely from the community school services and resources provided by MES, and the union actively sought the support of the district's board. But city officials looking for ways to stem the expansion of the MES program also sought the board's support, and they had the power to cede administrative authority to the board and give it more control over its schools.[31] In a fateful decision, the Ocean Hill-Brownsville board decided that more could be gained by allying themselves with the city's power elite than the UFT and turned down the MES program for their district. Supporters of the decision demagogically denounced the program as a "racist" form of "compensatory education," and refused the UFT request for their support during the 1967 strike in which the expansion of MES was a major demand.

The 1967 strike had the vocal support of the A. Philip Randolph, Bayard Rustin, and Martin Luther King, who, as democratic socialists, well understood that the racial integration of schools could be achieved only in tandem with ending the inequities between them. "I enthusiastically endorse the efforts of the teachers of NYC to improve their living and working conditions, and the quality of the education they dispense," King wrote in a telegram sent to the UFT for publication.[32] But many of the leaders of the Ocean Hill-Brownsville district had a much more constricted vision, one that ignored the class dimension of racial oppression in favor of a narrow nationalism. Foreshadowing the twenty-first century's market-driven education reformers, the district's leaders and its supporters would argue that public schools were "the primary cause of poverty," and teachers were the cause of the inadequate education in schools with high concentrations of poverty—thus, the solution was to replace them with "better" teachers who believed in their students.[33] During the 1967 strike, the district organized strikebreaking to keep its schools open, even as the schools across the rest of the city were closed. (One of the major organizers of this strikebreaking, then CORE leader and Black Power advocate Floyd McKissick, quickly went on to promote "black capitalism" on behalf of President Richard Nixon.)

In the wake of the 1967 strike, the Ocean Hill-Brownsville board identified a group of white UFT teachers who had been strike leaders and participants and acted to remove them as "hostile" to the district. It was the UFT's adamant and unbending opposition to this removal, which had been taken without any semblance of due process, that led to the lengthy and racially bitter 1968 strike and to the deep fissures between union and community that would persist for a generation. In the wake of the 1968 strike, the writing was on the wall for the MES schools; the initiative could not survive shrinking budgets and an antagonistic political atmosphere. A promising effort to create community schools across the nation's largest school district would end tragically, a victim to divisions between community on the one side and teachers and their unions on the other—to the detriment of both. Today, New York City's schools are among the most racially and economically segregated in the nation.[34]

TWENTY-FIRST-CENTURY APPROACHES TO COMMUNITY-UNION PARTNERSHIPS

It was not until a fresh generation of leadership had emerged that relationships of trust between local communities and the unions could be reestablished and partnerships forged anew. In 2001, New York City Mayor Rudy Giuliani attempted to turn five struggling public schools serving high-poverty neighborhoods over to Edison Schools, a for-profit education management corporation. In response, the community organization ACORN and the NAACP came together in common cause with the UFT, then led by Randi Weingarten, to defeat the effort.[35] Shortly thereafter, CC9 (Community Collaborative to Improve the Schools of District 9), a group of South Bronx community organizations, began an intensive engagement with the UFT that would lead to a common campaign to establish a "lead teacher" position in the District 9 schools, and in so doing, establish an ongoing partnership.[36] By 2007, when Mayor Michael Bloomberg and Chancellor Joel Klein proposed privatizing major management functions of the New York City public school system, a broad union-community coalition would fight against these changes and force revisions under the banner of "Put the Public Back in Public Education."[37] When Randi Weingarten was elected to the presidency of the AFT in 2008, she brought to the national union a new focus on organizing in partnership with communities and added an entire cohort of organizers dedicated to this work onto the AFT staff. These organizers have worked closely with AFT locals pursuing the strategy of bargaining for the common good.

Reconnecting McDowell

While increasing attention has been paid to this strategy in the wake of the Teacher Insurgency strikes, the groundwork of organizing in tandem with communities has been a long-term approach of teacher unions that was under way for a decade and a half before the strikes began. The power of these union-community efforts is illustrated by an AFT project in the crucible of the Teacher Insurgency—West Virginia.

In February 2018, the strikes of the Teacher Insurgency began with countywide walkouts in southern West Virginia, where traditions of militant unionism, originating in that region's coal mines, ran deep. The southernmost and poorest of the fifty-five counties in West Virginia, itself the fifth-poorest state in the union, is McDowell County. In better days, coal mining had been the county's economic backbone; but as technological changes in the industry and shifts to renewable and cleaner energy took a heavy toll on mining jobs, McDowell had fallen into a downward economic spiral.

Seven years before the Teacher Spring strikes began, the AFT organized Reconnecting McDowell, a major community-building project, to revitalize the county's public schools and in the process to help rebuild its economy.[38] The project was the brainchild of AFT President Randi Weingarten, developed in response to a request for help from Gayle Manchin, member of the state board of education and wife of West Virginia's then governor. At its start, the AFT recruited forty partners—community-based organizations, other unions, nonprofit groups, churches, public agencies, and private businesses—to this project; as a result of the work of project manager Leah Daughtry and others, today the number of partners stands at 125, and together they have contributed millions of dollars to McDowell's schools for new programs, needed services, and additional resources.

As part of its work, Reconnecting McDowell has brought tens of thousands of books to student and adult literacy centers; created mobile libraries on the school buses in this rural county; introduced broadband internet access to the county; and initiated a large-scale mentoring program for struggling students. Since the county lacks basic health-care facilities and access to health-care professionals, health clinics were established in two of the high schools, and mobile dental offices were established to periodically visit the schools. Reconnecting McDowell has introduced wraparound social services to all of the county's schools, and two have become full community schools, with programs and afterschool activities designed to engage students' families. And because the paucity of housing has forced most of its educators to live outside of the county and take on long commutes, Reconnecting McDowell has started the construction of a housing development for teachers to make it possible for the county to attract and retain accomplished teachers.

With all of these interventions, over the first five years of the program, the high school graduation rate rose fourteen percentage points and the postsecondary attendance rate rose fifteen percentage points. Reconnecting McDowell has created a model of an educational initiative that can be at the center of a comprehensive approach to overcoming rural poverty. An initiative like McDowell cannot do it all—major government investment in economic infrastructure and public works is necessary to truly turn around rural poverty—but it points to what can be done, if the political will to do it is there.

Trust between the McDowell community and the AFT has been built and strengthened over time, especially as it became apparent that the union had dug in for the long haul, rather than parachuted in and out of the county for the photo-ops and press releases that are the stock in trade of all too many elected officials. So when the Teacher Spring strikes first broke out in southern West Virginia in February of 2018, they had the complete and unflagging support of the community. Support of this nature does not arise spontaneously, and it does not take shape on social media. It is the product of deep, long-lasting relationships between labor and the community, forged out of work on behalf of the common good.

Organizing with Community in the 2019 Los Angeles Strike

When the United Teachers of Los Angeles (UTLA) went on strike in January of 2019, they published a "bargaining for the common good" platform, a broad set of negotiation demands that they had developed with their community partners.[39] A number of those demands—supports for immigrant students under attack by the Trump administration; reductions in standardized testing; and opposition to the further expansion of charter schools—were clearly the product of the historical moment. But other demands—smaller class sizes; more nurses, counselors, and librarians; funding for community schools; improvements in pre-K education—could have been taken straight out of the More Effective Schools program the UFT had fought for a half-century before.

The fact that the 1967 and 2019 strikes both centered on so many of the same demands allows for an interesting thought experiment, one in which we can compare the efficacy of the approaches used by the two unions in fighting for those demands. I want to be clear that there are some real limits to comparisons across significant intervals of time and space; most importantly, the historical and political contexts can be quite different. The 2019 UTLA strike took place at a time when both the union and the community had learned some very hard lessons of what happens when they are divided against each other. There had been decades of the underfunding of the Los Angeles public schools following Proposition 13, accentuated by the effects of the Great Recession of 2008. "Education reform" policies had sidelined both teacher and community voices in important educational decisions over public schools, and in proportion to the diminishment of teacher and community voice, the business interests that had captured the large Los Angeles charter school sector seized an ever greater role for themselves. In 2019, it was abundantly clear that the only way for union and community to defend and improve their public schools and to secure a real voice in their future was to unite and act together. By contrast, in 1967, both the UFT and the community had just experienced real growth in power and influence, and the schools were experiencing the first major influx of federal funds as a result of the Great Society. The imperative of a community-union partnership on behalf of public schools could be overlooked.

That said, there are still instructive differences in the approach of UTLA in 2019 and the UFT in 1967. Nearly five years before the 2019 strike, UTLA began a process of intensive community engagement, with the support of both national teacher unions and their California state affiliates. (UTLA is a joint local of both the AFT and the NEA.) At the center of this engagement process, and providing its organizational infrastructure, was Reclaim Our Schools Los Angeles (ROSLA). ROSLA was formed as a coalition of UTLA and three other core organizations: a California-based community organizing network known as the Alliance of Californians for Community Empowerment (ACCE); a Los Angeles–based advocacy organization dedicated to promoting progressive economic policies through strategic alliances, the Los Angeles Alliance for a New Economy (LAANE); and a youth empowerment organization, Students Deserve. As a sign of its commitment to this work, UTLA provided programmatic support to ROSLA and its core organizations.

The four core organizations engaged in far-reaching conversations designed to build a shared understanding of the experiences of each group's members with Los Angeles public schools. It was important, for example, for the three non-student organizations to understand just how students experienced the random searches that the Los Angeles school district conducted in the name of school safety. The objective of this process was to develop a common understanding of what needed to be done to make Los Angeles schools places where students would thrive and an agreed-upon strategy for achieving this goal. Two years before the 2019 strike, ROSLA published "A Vision to Support Every Student," in which it laid out this understanding.[40] The common good demands of the 2019 strike were drawn from this document and this process, as well as from UTLA's engagement with its own members.

In the lead-up to the 2019 strike, the base of support established through ROSLA was expanded to a wider array of community organizations. During the course of the strike, the fruits of the labor-community partnership became apparent in the massive public support for Los Angeles teachers and their demands. This support was key in the successful conclusion of the strike, with its major wins on both common good demands and improvements in teacher compensation.

Heading into the 1967 strike, the UFT had strong, long-standing relationships with Martin Luther King, A. Philip Randolph, and Bayard Rustin, born out of the union's prodigious work on behalf of the civil rights movement. Those relationships were a substantial resource in its fight to expand the MES, as King, Randolph, and Rustin were not only deeply committed to substantive programmatic approaches to overcoming poverty, but also prepared to publicly defend that commitment at a real political cost to themselves. Their public support for the UFT and MES was pivotal in the 1967 strike.[41]

But the support of prominent national figures was not a substitute for organic relationships with local communities in New York City, and on this count, the UFT was vulnerable. MES had been developed entirely by teachers and their union, without active community involvement. It had been formulated with the best of intentions and was based on the best thinking in education on how to overcome the obstacles poverty placed in the way of education. But given that it had not been a partner in that process, the community felt no investment in its product. And this failure created an opening for those who sought to drive a wedge between the union and the community. If there is one lesson we can learn by comparing the strikes of 1967 and 2019, it is the vital importance of building a strong community-union partnership that rests on common understandings and shared strategies.

PART THREE

Organizing Teachers, Teachers Organizing

CHAPTER 8

Teacher Organizing and Collective Identity

"POWER DERIVES FROM ORGANIZATION." Those are the words of A. Philip Randolph in the passage that provides the epigraph to this book. As his decades of work in the labor and civil rights movements demonstrate, Randolph did not conceive of organization as a static and fixed framework: one cannot build organization the way one builds a house, erecting a complete structure that is then fit for inhabitation for many years. Enduring organization does, of course, require an edifice—the established structures of representation and democratic decision-making, and the apparatuses that carry out the organizational mission. But seen through the lens of building and exercising power, the vitality of organization lies in more than its formal structure—it is found in the web of relationships established within and through that structure. Without this connective tissue, a formal organizational structure is an ossified skeleton. Organizing is the ongoing work of creating, growing, and strengthening these relationships that make it possible for individuals to come together in collective action on behalf of a common cause. Out of this work grows a *we*—a collective identity that is capable of exercising political agency and of wielding power, as Randolph understood so well.

Most of the literature on organizing sidesteps the construction of the collective *we*. Instead, it emphasizes the identification of issues that are of concern to those organizing, and the mastery of techniques used to mobilize around these issues and establish a formal organization.

That is certainly the focus, for example, of the classic treatise on community organizing, Saul Alinsky's *Rules for Radicals*.[1] It is also the focus of the organizing manual of the leading development center of contemporary community organizing, the Midwest Academy.[2] And it is the focus of handbooks of labor organizing, including texts written by those who understand themselves to be union insurgents.[3] There is no question that issues provide the raw material of organizing, and that a good grasp of techniques such as how to identify and cultivate organic leaders and how to map a workplace is essential to organizing. I will not address either of these matters in this book, because a number of published works already discuss them—and do it well. But there is something fundamental to organizing that is missing in accounts that address only issues and techniques, and it is this fundamental element—the process of forming the collective *we*—that I will address here.

I begin with a few observations on the nature of organizing, arguing that it is in the main a learning process. On this basis, I draw a close parallel between democratic organizing and progressive education in the Deweyan tradition, in both of which conversation and dialogue are at the center of the process. This connection allows us to see how good organizing involves the profoundly democratic practice of "talking to strangers," to borrow Danielle Allen's turn of phrase. In her organizing conversations, an accomplished organizer looks to understand not just the issues that have precipitated the particular organizing project, but also the reasons why those issues are important to those who are organizing. To understand these motivations, I argue, it is necessary to plumb the deep wellsprings of identity—in our case, the identity of *teacher*—that are constituted in discourses. Following these prefatory points, I will be able to turn to an analysis of the four discursive themes that I see as central to the formation of the collective identity of *teacher*, and thus to the organizing of teachers in the subsequent chapters of this section.

DIALOGUE AND THE ORGANIZING PROCESS

At the heart of good organizing is meaningful, purposeful dialogue. It is only through a multitude of organizing conversations that the members of a group develop a widely shared, explicit understanding of the objectives they share and the collective action they will employ to accomplish them. As I noted in chapter 4, the solidarity that is indispensable for collective action is not a natural state of being—it must be actively built out of the relationships working people have with each other. To withstand the challenges from the powerful that it will inevitably confront, an organizing endeavor needs a formidable sense of solidarity, and such solidarity is best built with a foundation that rests on the bedrock of group members' strong feelings and genuine connections to each other. These sentiments and ties will become apparent only through serious conversations.

The centrality of conversation to organizing is why I would contend that an organizer's most important skill is listening, as paradoxical and counterintuitive as that might appear to someone who has never been engaged in that work. For an organizing dialogue to take place, an organizer needs to learn about more than the immediate issues animating the effort, which should be obvious enough. She needs to understand why those issues are important to the members of the group—how they fit into their understandings of themselves, the labor they perform, the people with whom they work and for whom they care, and their aspirations for themselves and for others in their lives. This can be learned only by active listening and the dialogue ensuing from it.

In describing this organizing process, I have been deliberate in my choice of words. The title of this section of the book, "Organizing Teachers, Teachers Organizing," is designed to signify a break with an all-too-common conception of organizing, one in which the organizer or the militant minority is the subject and protagonist of the organizing process—the actor with the knowledge of what is to be done and the skills to do it—and the group being organized is reduced to an "Amen" chorus. Teachers will recognize that this organizing model closely parallels didactic, top-down conceptions of education, in which the educator alone possesses all of the relevant knowledge to be taught and the skills to teach it and students are the largely passive recipients of that knowledge—so much raw material to be shaped and so many *tabulae rasae* for others to write on. The parallels between organizer-centered organizing and teacher-centered education are so strong because organizing is in significant measure a learning process, one in which those who are organizing learn about their collective power and how it can be built, strengthened, and exercised. Both organizer-centered organizing and teacher-centered education share a fundamental misunderstanding of how we learn, a misunderstanding in which those who are doing the organizing and learning are seen as largely passive, the objects of the process. And when the organizer and the teacher are conceived as the sole custodians of the important knowledge and the sole authors and protagonists of the process, the privileged status given to their authority renders these models anti-democratic.

Against this didactic, top-down understanding of organizing, I want to pose an organizing model articulated through the language of progressive education, drawing especially on the work of John Dewey, who understood well the nexus of power, organization, and learning. Dewey's understanding of education as "the process of coming to share in the social consciousness," and his insistence that learning takes place through doing—by the active engagement of the learner with what is to be learned—provide a solid template for effective, good organizing.[4]

Contrary to a common misperception of progressive education, active learning on the part of the student does not occur spontaneously, with the teacher playing little or no role.[5] Rather, in Dewey's pedagogy, the teacher needs to be far more skilled in her presence than if she were engaged in didactic instruction; she is guiding her students through a process of inquiry, posing carefully crafted questions that help students clarify both the subject material and their own thinking; providing resources, especially those with divergent views and evidence, for her students to consider and engage with; and identifying dilemmas in and obstacles to their plans of action. Teacher and students are in constant dialogue and in this respect are active partners in the learning process.

This Deweyan philosophy of education embodies a conception of democratic leadership and accountable authority. Similarly, a Deweyan model of organizing requires a skilled and democratic organizer who is in constant dialogue with those organizing, asking the questions and posing the alternatives that allow them to be the authors of their own organizing—learning their power by actively building and using it. Just as good progressive education imparts to students the skills of logical reasoning, critical thinking, historical analysis, and problem solving that can be applied in other circumstances they face, good progressive organizing provides an understanding of collective power and the democratic methods through which it can be built and exercised that serves those organizing well into the future. "Organizing teachers" and "teachers organizing" should be one and the same process.

The Democratic Character of Union Organizing

An appreciation of organizing as an exercise in democratic learning, rooted in dialogue and conversation designed to build mutual understanding and collective action, shares important common ground with conceptions of democracy envisioned as building solidarity among citizens. Danielle Allen's argument on behalf of a democracy that is rooted in "talking to strangers"—the process of building trust and political friendship among citizens through conversation and joint action on matters of civic significance—is a particularly relevant formulation in this regard.[6] The task of organizing coworkers across differences of race, sex, sexual and gender identity, religion, and immigration status—coworkers with different life experiences, different ways of seeing the world, and different predispositions on how to act—involves the same fundamental challenges as uniting citizens in all of their diversity to act politically. Indeed, both union organizing and democracy conceived as "talking to strangers" are political projects that do not attempt to subsume these differences in a purported unanimity of views or in a language of abstract universality. Instead, they acknowledge and address differences as a necessary predicate to building broad agreement on shared purpose, and to moving to common action even with the inevitable dissenting views on what should be done.

In this respect, it is significant that Allen begins her reflections on citizenship and democracy with a meditation on the famous photograph of the young African American student Elizabeth Eckford being cursed and taunted by white student Hazel Bryan for seeking to enter and racially integrate Little Rock Central High School. That photo rendered visible the contours of a Jim Crow public space founded on the exclusion of African Americans and enforced through violence; in so doing, it became a pivotal symbol of a nation finding itself forced to confront that reality. To find a path to democratic solidarity in that context, the differences between Bryan and Eckford—between the citizenship, manifest in the power of ownership over the public sphere, granted to Bryan, and the denial of that same citizenship to Eckford—had to be addressed. The elision of those differences of access to citizenship in the name of a universal, such as the "one nation, indivisible" affirmed in the Pledge of Allegiance, empty the democratic project of its meaning and promise and render it impotent.

The same principle is true in organizing a union. The different experiences of working people, on the job and in their communities, cannot be put to the side to focus only on what those groups have in common, to be ignored in the name of a universal working class. Such formulations erase the ways in which forces such as racism and sexism function in the lives of different workers. It is essential for the building of solidarity that unions take on such questions directly, engaging in common action to oppose individual and institutionalized prejudice and discrimination. Organizing must address *both* what we have in common and how we differ.

In her discussion of citizenship, Allen highlights the role of sacrifice, pointing to the unequal burdens assumed by African Americans in the quest for a citizenship and democratic order that included Americans of all races. In chapter 6, I discussed this theme in the context of the willingness of teachers to take on the sacrifices of striking, with the potential for fines and the loss of pay—even the possible loss of their jobs—in order to promote "common good" demands that benefit their students and their education. There I argued that sacrifices such as these were at the center of the labor republicanism that shaped the worldview of nineteenth-century American unions. The idea of sacrifice is perhaps even more important in the context of building union solidarity. If trust among citizens is built, as Allen argues, by "a willingness to sacrifice some of one's own power for the sake of common agreement," what could be a more powerful path to trust and solidarity among coworkers than the willingness of those in the position of relative power—white workers, male workers, straight and cisgender workers, native-born workers, and workers from majority faith traditions—to renounce the power of that position and take up the struggle against prejudice and discrimination as their very own?[7]

One historian of the American labor movement has described unions as "schools of democracy."[8] This characterization is apt in a number of different respects. First, in governing themselves in their unions, working people learn the fundamentals of representative democracy, such as how to run a meeting that engages in democratic deliberation and decision-making and how to run a democratic election. Second, there is ample evidence that unions in general—and teacher unions especially—increase the participation of their members in the political process and electoral politics.[9] This enhanced participation is seen not just in voting, but also in campaigning in elections, communicating with elected officials and engaging in public discourse on matters of civic import, and involving themselves in protests and other forms of public political declarations. Indeed, it is precisely because teacher unions increase the civic participation and efficacy of their members that they are targeted by those who want to minimize citizen participation in the political process: the advocates of "voter suppression" are invariably the partisans of "union suppression." And finally, a view of organizing as "talking to strangers," as building trust and political friendship through conversation and dialogue, allows us to understand just how fundamental democracy is to unions: the very generation of solidarity that creates and sustain unions is at the core of democratic self-rule—of identifying shared objectives and deciding on common action.[10]

ORGANIZING AND DISCOURSES

Just as a teacher needs a solid understanding of her students to successfully engage them in their learning, an organizer must have a robust understanding of the people with whom she is working to lead a democratic organizing process. For the organizer of teachers, this understanding requires a full appreciation of their motivations to organize. As I noted, such an appreciation is developed by going beneath the immediate precipitating issues of an organizing project to the deep wellsprings of their identities as teachers—how they understand themselves and the labor they undertake, how they feel about the people with whom they work and for whom they teach and care, and their aspirations for themselves and their significant others. These wellsprings emerge from what I will call *discourses*—ensembles of thinking, communicating, and acting in ways that enact socially significant identities.[11] It is from discourses that we construct narratives of our own being and give meaning to our lives, and it is in shared narratives that we create a basis for collective action.[12] Power relations between teachers and others are constituted and given expression in discourse. For teachers, I argue in the following chapters, there are four primary discourses used for developing our narratives—teaching as nurturance, teaching as a profession, teaching as labor and craft, and teaching as a vocation of democratic intellectual work.

Why do I propose that we turn to discourses to find a basis for forming the narratives of collective teacher identity in our organizing? Here it is necessary to understand why the question receives so little attention in the dominant approaches to organizing. In significant measure, it is because they rely on a set of largely unexamined assumptions that suppose an almost natural development of such an identity, along these general lines: all working people have in common "objective" interests of an economic nature, and from those common interests a "subjective" consciousness of their affinity with other working people—a *class consciousness*—will, under the right conditions, develop. The substance of the *we* of the organizing process, this consciousness of a collective identity, is thus inscribed in the workings of the economy and is logically derived from them. All that remains is the development of a mass consciousness of this pre-given *we* and that happens organically, emerging out of struggle, without any special attention paid to this aspect of the organizing process.[13]

I argue that this set of assumptions misunderstands how collective identities are formed and transformed, and does so in reductionist ways that misinform our organizing work.[14] The formation of a *we*—including the formation of the collective identity *teacher*—is a more complex process, with a much greater need for organizing and political interventions. Following Laclau and Mouffe, I reject the view that the discourses of teacher identity are purely subjective, and that they emerge—in the classic Marxian trope of building construction—as superstructural floors that rest on an objective economic foundation.[15] Instead, discourses of teacher identity are constitutive of a material world of social institutions in which teachers work and live, such as the school, and of social practices in which they enact their identity as teachers, such as engaging students in their learning. In such a world, teachers are both the subject and object of discourses of teacher identity, simultaneously shaping and being shaped by them.

This point becomes clearer when we examine a particular discourse, such as that of teaching as nurturance. A teacher's use of the language of nurturing cannot be meaningfully separated from the actual relationships she has with her students or from the institution of the school that both influences the teacher-student relationships within it and, in turn, is influenced by them. Consequently, when a teacher talks about her "care" for "her kids," to take one of the simplest forms of a nurturing language, she is describing how she understands her relationships with her students, an understanding that shapes how she interacts with them and how she acts as an intermediary between them and the larger world, starting with the institution of the school and radiating out. In these actions and interactions, she and her fellow teachers participate in the evolutionary trajectory of that discourse of nurturance. Of particular importance for our purposes, these teachers will determine whether—and if yes, how—that discourse of nurturance can become a basis for collective action among them. A consideration of the language of teacher nurturance in a disembodied form, separate and apart from this material world in which it is embedded, is thus not only radically incomplete, but essentially misleading. Indeed, a proper understanding of discourse in the organizing process sees it as more than communication narrowly conceived, restricted to conversations and speech interactions. Since discourses are embedded in material practices and institutions, they carry implications for how those practices should be conducted and how those institutions should be organized. For example, in chapter 9, I demonstrate how the discourse of nurturance has implications for how schools should be organized to support teachers in their caring for their students. That is why a substantial portion of my discussion of discourses of teacher identity will examine institutional and programmatic issues.

Discourses and Identities

Four important corollaries follow from this understanding of discourse in general, and discourses of teacher identity in particular: (1) emotions are central to the formation of collective identities and thus to good organizing; (2) collective identities, including teacher identities, are plural and contingent in nature, and not expressions of an inner "essence";

(3) an analysis of collective identities should start from their particular expressions, and not assume that it is the expression of some underlying universal form; and (4) the discourses of teacher collective identities are contested, with competing conceptions of what teaching is and what it should be at work.

To address the first of these corollaries, the assumption that collective identities are derived from objective interests and rationally determined by them leads organizers to push to the margins the powerful emotional content—the passions—of organizing. None of the most widely known and used texts on organizing—not Alinsky's *Rules for Radicals*, not the Midwest Academy's *Organizing for Change*, not Labor Notes' *Troublemakers Handbook*—explicitly address this emotional dimension of organizing because they all assume that collective identity is a fundamentally rational project, a consciousness of common objective economic interests. While there is now a substantial scholarly literature on the role of emotions in social movements, there is scant evidence that the important insights of that literature have been incorporated into organizing work, especially in the labor movement.[16] Since the emotions of organizing are present and active even when they are not explicitly recognized, organizers end up addressing them in intuitive ways that often fall short of what is needed. Individual organizers with better emotional and interpersonal skills will achieve better results in intuitive interactions, but even their skills will not be used to best effect.

One important consequence of this "rationalist" view of identity formation is a narrow and unhelpful understanding of such phenomena as racism, which is understood and fought as an "irrational" form of "false consciousness"—nothing more than a divide-and-conquer tool of the elite to blind working people to their true interests. But racism is not a misunderstanding of true interests; it is itself a material discourse that shapes collective identities and, as such, it is embedded in social practices and institutional forms that provide tangible benefits to those in the dominant position in the racial hierarchy. This material reality of racism must be addressed if organizing across racial identities is to be successful.

An understanding of collective identity as rooted in discourses such as those I analyze in this section puts the emotional dimension front and center in the organizing process, making it possible for organizers to think systematically about the role of such passions as anger, love, shame, guilt, fear, and hope in their work and to execute strategies designed to build and maintain strong affective bonds among the organizing.[17] Solidarity is far more than a consciousness of common interests: it is an emotional commitment of those organizing to each other, and it is the strength of that emotional commitment—not the intellectual understanding of interests—that will steel an organizing project when it is tested.[18]

Second, the assumption that collective identity is determined by objective economic interests means that it can take only one "true" form, one essential identity that is logically derived from those interests. In this thinking, a single collective teacher identity—whether it be one of the four discourses I examine in the following chapters or something else entirely—is designated as *the* authentic expression of teaching and teachers. Against this one-dimensional view, I argue that collective teacher identity is constructed on a field where a number of discourses of teaching are in play, and that different combinations of these discourses produce different inflections of teacher identity. Individual teachers may well draw on one more than another in their understandings of themselves as teachers; nonetheless, it is generally the case that teachers draw on a number of them in their understanding of themselves as teachers. Further, our identities as teachers are not segregated from other parts of our personal identities: for example, the discourse of teaching as nurturance is particularly important for so many teachers of color precisely because they entered teaching out of a desire to teach students of color, with whom they identify.[19] Organizing that relies on a monolithic conception of teacher collective identity effectively abandons the remainder of the discursive field, leaving it wide open for opponents of the organizing project.

Third, following from the previous point, our analysis of collective identities should not begin with a general theory—that is, with abstract and undifferentiated categories that are assumed to be universal, such as *worker* and *citizen*, out of the premise that particular collective identities such as teacher are logically derivative of these categories. Rather, we should start with the particular identity—in our case, the *teacher*. There will be points of commonality between different particular identities—what I have to say about teacher collective identity will be particularly resonant, for example, with the collective identities of nurses—but there will also be divergences. Unity of these different identities cannot be assumed in a general theory: it must be painstakingly built in practice.

Fourth, the discourses of teaching are themselves contested, with contending understandings of what teaching is and what it should be. Political scientists describe certain fundamental political concepts, such as democracy and republicanism, as fundamentally contested, with politics taking the form of an agonistic struggle over which meaning will dominate at any given point in time.[20] In the same way, discourses such as teaching as a profession and teacher as labor and craft are also fundamentally contested, with quite different conceptions of what it means to be part of a profession or part of labor in contention. To the extent that a single meaning is attributed to a given discourse of teaching, it misreads the contested nature of that discourse, and ill informs organizing work. For example, it is not uncommon on the left to view teacher identity as a contest between the discourses of teaching as labor and craft and teaching as a profession: the identity of labor and craft is portrayed as form of a class consciousness that embraces solidarity beyond teachers, and the identity of the professional is cast as the "elitist" alternative that eschews solidarity with others.[21] In ignoring the existence of democratic conceptions of teacher professionalism, such arguments have the effect of abandoning the field of discourse to the very elitism they oppose; in eliding tendencies within discourses of labor and craft that are not consistent with their view of a broad solidaristic vision, they ill prepare us to fight against such negative conceptions of teacher as labor and craft.

What I have sought to do in this chapter is to provide an overview of the complex political terrain on which the collective teacher identity—the *we* of teacher organizing—is constructed. It should now be clear that assumptions that a collective teacher identity will emerge organically out of objective economic interests are misguided. Such assumptions fail to address the centrality of emotions to organizing and the importance of consciously building a collective identity; they thus place a much heavier burden on organizing issues and techniques for the success of an organizing project. In viewing these discourses as having a single meaning, these assumptions ossify what is in reality a field defined by its dynamic character and fluidity, with a considerable capacity for change. While the complexity of this terrain may at first appear daunting, it is in fact an extraordinary opportunity—an understanding of teacher collective identity as rooted in these discourses opens up a whole range of interventions that were before only partially understood, in isolation from each other. The task of constructing a collective *we* can now be seen not only as interventions in contested discourses of teaching, but as the task of weaving together these different discourses into one coherent collective teacher identity: to the extent that discourses of teaching as nurturance, as a profession, as labor and craft, and as a vocation of democratic intellectual work are bound together as part of a democratic organizing project conceived in Deweyan terms, they combine the most progressive and forward-thinking, the most solidaristic and democratic conceptions of each discourse. It is to that task that I now turn.

CHAPTER 9

The Discourse of Teaching as Nurturance

IN THE US, K–12 TEACHING has historically been an occupation dominated by women, especially at the elementary school level.[1] This dominance was intertwined with the common perception that teaching, like other female-dominated occupations such as nursing, was a "caring" profession. The discourse of teaching as nurturance thus had its origins in the gendered nature of teaching and in the traditional gendered social division of labor: women were assigned the "private" emotional and reproductive labor of the domestic sphere—the work of caring—while men performed the "public" work of production and civil society.

Given the gendered origins of the discourse of nurturance, I will begin this chapter by bringing the insights of feminist and queer theory to bear on it, exploring the political dimensions of caring practices that are commonly seen as personal. Education guided by an individual "ethic of care" is insufficient, I contend; it must be complemented by a collective "politics of care," extending a teacher's "care" for her own students to "care" for all students. A politics of caring contains within it, I argue, an immanent critique of how schools are organized in ways that make teacher caring for students difficult and ineffective, and in some contexts, next to impossible. Consequently, these politics point to a set of policies that support teacher caring in their classrooms and schools. Many of these policies, such as school-based social services and small class sizes, have been the focus of the "bargaining for the common good" that emerged from the Teacher Insurgency. It is counterproductive for teachers to attempt to assume the entire burden of caring for their students as individuals: the social side of schools—their organization and their culture—has a very powerful impact on the quality of the relationships within them. To care for their students in the fullest and most effective ways, teachers need to be organized for collective action, focused on a politics of caring.

GENDER AND CARING

The gendered quality of the discourse of nurturance appears in a telling difference with the other discourses of teaching discussed here. While the other three discourses are paradigmatically public in nature, the stuff of ongoing civic contention and political debate, the discourse of nurturance appears initially in subterranean, private language. It finds its first expressions in direct conversations between teacher and student, as well as in the teacher-to-teacher discussions of students that occur in the lunchroom and the copying room. Insofar as this discourse appears in the languages and dicta of educational bureaucracies, the news media and the government, it is only in the most refracted ways—most often in the form of diffuse and unfocused complaints that teachers "no longer care" about their students. The discourse of nurturance, with its implicit frame of teacher as surrogate parent, would thus appear to be a clear expression of the personal in education.

But can we simply accept these binary oppositions associated with the traditional gender roles—the masculine and the feminine, the rational and the emotional, the political and the personal, the public and the private—as an unproblematic lens for understanding the discourse of nurturance? Here feminist and queer theory provide some valuable insights. In an age of the Me Too movement and the public reclaiming of stigmatized and marginalized sexual identities, it has become apparent that there are important political and public dimensions to matters once dismissed as personal and private. What is more, the erasure of issues such as workplace sexual harassment and spousal violence is now understood to be symptomatic of a particular set of gendered power relations. What appears at first to be personal, and therefore apolitical, stands revealed upon analysis as having a significant political aspect. The discourse of teaching as nurturance can also acquire a political dimension; I contend that the task of organizing is to draw out that political dimension, making the connection between it and the personal discourse of caring. Moreover, given the intensity of the emotional bonds that come with nurturing relationships, a politics based on a discourse of nurturance can be an extraordinarily powerful force in organizing.

There is a scholarly literature—the feminist ethic-of-care approach to education developed by Nel Noddings, among others—that can help us think about how we might fashion discursive interventions that could lead to a politics of nurturing.[2] This literature takes as its starting point the foundational work of Carol Gilligan.[3] Gilligan argued that the dominant school of moral philosophy and psychology had incorporated into its model of moral deliberation only those attributes associated with the traditional gender roles of men, as it had postulated that the development of abstract and universal moral principles was the highest stage of moral reasoning. In so doing, it had excluded the "different voice" of women, who more often thought of morality in terms of an emotionally rich commitment to care for others in particular relationships.[4] This idea of an ethic of care captures an important aspect of the morality of the discourse of nurturance used by teachers, both women and men, with its focus on their particular relationships with their students.

Insofar as Gilligan's work pointed to the false universality and implicit gender bias of the dominant paradigm, it performed a valuable intellectual service. However, as a number of feminist critics have argued, Gilligan and others of her school retain the model of moral orientations polarized along the line of traditional gender socialization; she simply reversed the valorization of two elements, so the ethic of care associated with women's "different voice" was now the moral philosophy of choice.[5] If we were to adopt this view uncritically, we would be left with a personal ethic of care that was limited to the particular relationships a teacher has with her students.

THE POLITICS OF CARE

What is needed is a discursive bridge between a teacher's ethic of care for her own students and a political project that advocates for the care of all students. For materials to construct this bridge, we might look to John Dewey's writing in *Schools and Society*: "What the best and wisest parent wants for his child, that must we want for all the children of the community. Anything less is unlovely, and left unchecked, destroys our democracy."[6] Within a discourse of nurturance centered on the metaphor of teacher as parent, we can employ Dewey's dictum to generalize from the ethic of care for particular students in a teacher's class to a more encompassing politics of care that incorporates larger and larger concentric circles of students—in the rest of the school, the rest of the community, and the rest of the nation.

Since teachers are already surrogate parents of other people's children, a discursive extension of the personal ethic of care into a politics of care for all children would appear to be an almost natural evolution. But we should not underestimate the transformations that take place with the development of a politics of care. Consider the emotional aspects of that development. In the women's traditional gender role, emotions are carefully policed: expressions of affection are considered appropriate feminine, part of women's nurturing nature, while expressions of anger are deemed to be characteristically masculine, and thus inappropriate for women. Given the historical makeup of the US teaching profession, these gendered rules of emotional expressiveness were part of the expectations of how teachers should act.[7]

Yet the idea of a politics of care is rooted as much in a deep anger at what is happening to one's students and to other students as it is in powerful feelings of affection for them; in important ways, it is a sublimation of that anger into public action, with the objective of winning power to change the conditions that are harmful to students. It is thus based on an assertiveness that breaks decisively with the traditional gendered expectations of passivity for a female-dominated occupation. A politics of care necessarily requires an expansion of the role of teacher as mediator between her students and the outside world, since she becomes an advocate for her students. In insisting on the political and public character of their personal care for their students, both women and men teachers articulate their care in decidedly feminist ways.

While a discourse of teaching as nurturance emerges from the institution of the school—as it is the school that brings teachers and students together—it also creates the basis for an immanent (or internal) critique of that institution: how its practices, culture, and organization can stand in the way of teacher caring being efficacious and making a difference in the lives of young people. In the face of factory-model schools that are not simply large, bureaucratic, and impersonal but also seem institutionally indifferent to the fate of the students put in their care, critiques based on a politics of care are quite powerful. Against government educational policy that can at times appear to embody the worst moments of a distant and callous state, the politics of care affirms the importance of the school as a place of nurture and the centrality of the teacher-student relation to education.

In this light, it is particularly interesting that the discourse of nurturance resonates deeply among committed teachers of children in inner-city schools, especially teachers of color. Powerful research demonstrates that African American students, especially boys, do academically better when they believe that their teacher genuinely cares about them and their success.[8] Conversely, there is evidence that students of color often drop out out of a feeling that no one in their school cares about what happens to them.[9] What is perhaps not as well understood is that these questions of caring among communities of color have deep historical roots. Metaphors of teacher as parent and class/school as family are compelling images in communities that have historically had their family ties torn asunder by oppressive institutions, from slavery onward, leaving them to painstakingly rebuild communities of nurturance for their young. This legacy of cultural resistance through caring found its way even into many of the African American schools of Jim Crow segregation, despite the onerous, suffocating restrictions of the system; one of the unintended consequences of ending de jure segregation was the loss of many of these real—albeit imperfect, given their context—communities of care.[10] Like the elders of the slave quarters, many of the teachers of the segregated African American school were immersed in the discourse of nurturance, framing their identity of teacher in terms of a parental responsibility to their students.[11]

This legacy continues today among many of those who teach students of color, as they live out the paradox that, as the Sweet Honey in the Rock song goes, "your children are not your children."[12] Here, note must be taken of the potential for conflict, too often actualized, between teachers and the families of their students.[13] There are aspects of a caring role that diminish the potential for conflict, but by no means eliminate it. Indeed, in some modalities, a caring relationship between student and teacher can spark rivalry and jealousy between teacher and parent. When the teacher-parent relationship is overlaid with differences of class and race, the potential for misunderstanding and miscommunication multiplies. While it is ultimately the teacher's responsibility to acquire a solid understanding of a student's heritage culture and to communicate with the student's family in the respectful manner of partnership, the school has an institutional duty to support this work, providing teachers with the resources, supports, and professional development that facilitates positive relationships with families. A focus on the politics of caring—on advocating for what students need to grow as healthy human beings and be successful in their education—is an important bridge in achieving mutual understanding between teachers and the families of students.

CREATING CARING SCHOOLS AND CLASSROOMS

How do we create schools and classrooms where the caring of teachers is not thwarted, but made efficacious?[14] Clear, unmistakable policy implications emerge from the immanent critique of the school in the discourse of nurturance. Consider, for example, a teacher in a large, comprehensive middle or high school. On the average, she will teach five different classes a day, with class registers of thirty and above; she will thus be interacting with 150 or more teenagers each school day. Moreover, in school districts that reorganize their secondary schools on a biannual basis, she could well be teaching in the range of three hundred different students over the course of a school year. At the very best, this teacher can provide close and meaningful, individual attention to a very small fraction of those students, no matter how many need her care. In under-resourced large schools serving high-poverty communities, where student need is the greatest, the American political and educational system has created overwhelmed systems of triage, haphazardly organized, that necessarily leave unattended many students who need personal care. Is it at all reasonable to blame a teacher in that school for not "caring enough" about those students, as elected officials who are responsible for these systems are wont to do? Moral agents are constrained by the conditions under which they act, teachers no less than the rest of humankind. (And who benefits from the fiction that if only the teachers cared enough, all of these students would receive the attention they need, even when the necessary supports and resources are so clearly missing? Certainly not the students in need of care.)

But it is possible to organize schools in ways that facilitate care for students. The movement toward the creation of small schools, in which educators can know all of their students well and provide them with individual instructional attention and guidance, clearly owes a debt to the discourse of nurturance.[15] The "extended family" scale of the school allows for personal attention to and engagement with each student, and makes it possible for the school to be governed democratically in a town meeting fashion. Moreover, the small school scale makes it much easier to establish the school building as a safe, welcoming environment—an absolute prerequisite to real, serious education. The push toward smaller class size and smaller teacher-student ratios, while operating within a more limited organizational horizon, produces similar effects. Smaller class sizes and teacher-student ratios are educationally beneficial not simply because they allow teachers to provide more attention to the learning of individual students; they also make it possible for more nurturing teacher-student relations to blossom, and this caring culture in and of itself improves education.

In this respect, the capture of the small school movement by philanthropy in the thrall of market-driven approaches to education (referenced in chapter 3) was a most unfortunate development.[16] Given the blinders of its market-oriented vision, this philanthropy never understood that small school size was important only because of what it made possible—a caring school culture; face-to-face democratic decision-making in the school; and strong school-community ties. These features all cut against the grain of a market-based vision of schooling, with its focus on competition and creating winners and losers, and consequently were pushed to the margins of this philanthropic intervention. When its fetishized and decontextualized understanding of school size produced what Michelle Fine has called "large schools in small school drag," and when these schools proved disappointing, this philanthropy was quickly off to the next magic bullet in its market-driven worldview, charter schools. But the original vision of small schools remains a compelling project for those who want to create caring schools.

There is not much in schools, from classroom pedagogy to out-of-control testing to the relationship between school culture and student conduct, that is not touched by the discourse of nurturance and whether it is organized in ways that support efficacious caring for students. Many of the demands raised by the bargaining for the common good of the Teacher Insurgency, such as the need for school-based social services and health care (which are central to the community schools discussed in chapter 7), are directly connected to a discourse of nurturance. A focus on the relationship between teacher and student, and on the quality of the interaction between teacher and student, can be educationally transformative. But only when it embraces a politics of care that understands that teacher-student relationships take place in institutional settings and cultural contexts that can either support or obstruct caring. When caring is understood to be the sole responsibility of the individual teacher, it leads to perverse conclusions. How often is the teacher's sense of parental responsibility to her children played off against the need for her professional development and for free time for professional work: "How can you leave your children with a stranger?" Missing from the exchange is any sense of how the improvement of a teacher's pedagogical skills and how time for lesson preparation, assessment, and other professional work with her colleagues is central to the education of her students. How often is the teacher's sense of parental responsibility to her children played off against the need for collective action by teachers: "How can you join in a job action/strike when it takes you away from your children, abandoning them and depriving them of their education?" But the very issues that demand collective action cannot be separated from the quality of the education those children and future children will receive. The conditions in which a teacher works are the same conditions in which her students learn.

An unbridled personal ethic of care can thus become its own worst enemy. Teaching is the type of work that is open-ended, and one can always find something more to do to help one's students.[17] Guilt about being a less-than-perfect parent, about not having done that last little extra something, can be a very powerful—and negative—passion in teachers. A teacher who makes the pursuit of an individual ethic of care her whole existence, turning herself into a martyr of caring, will inevitably burn out and find herself unable to continue to provide care.

This is a particularly severe problem among novice teachers, and it plays an important role in their high dropout rate from the profession. It is also a serious predicament in the establishment of new, small schools seeking to establish an ethic of care. Far too often, staff who are young and deeply committed spend the first years of the school in inordinately lengthy, time-consuming meetings that recreate the wheel out of a desire to do everything "right." This level of enthusiasm cannot be sustained over the long run, and a more balanced approach must be developed if the teachers—and thus, the school—are to sustain themselves.

Nowhere is this problem more acute, however, than in charter schools that demand their teachers work long days, work weekends and summers, and be available by cell phone in the evening—all in the name of care for students.[18] In my work with charter school teachers who were organizing into a union, I have seen how these demands are often a greater issue than matters of salary and benefits, which are typically inferior to those provided in district public schools.[19] It does not take long for teachers to understand not only that such a work life is unsustainable, but that it harms students. The inevitable burnout leads to a constant churn of novice teachers, who leave at the very point they have actually learned some of the fundamental skills of teaching, a process that generally takes a number of years. And students suffer as the teachers with whom they have established meaningful, trusting relationships are constantly leaving the school.

A balance between care for one's students and care for oneself is essential. Part of the danger in an unfettered individual ethic of care lies, therefore, in the nature of the discourse of nurturance: in framing the teacher as parent, it takes up a metaphor that is commonly understood in terms of individual responsibility, of an isolated agent (or two) acting separately from communal resources and supports. As important as individual action and responsibility are, there is no way that an individual teacher can make the necessary difference in the lives of young people solely by herself. Caring for one's students demands a politics of caring, and the discourse of teaching as nurturance needs to be sutured with the other discourses of teaching in a collective teacher identity.

CHAPTER 10

The Discourse of Teaching as a Profession

OF ALL THE DISCOURSES of teaching examined in this book, the discourse of professionalism is the one that most often appears in public discussions of teaching and education, where it is deployed from a number of different—even contradictory—vantage points. To sort out the different ways in which the idea of teacher professionalism is now employed and contested, I begin this chapter with an examination of its emergence at the turn of the twentieth century, when nascent teacher unions first elaborated it. I show that the efforts to professionalize teaching differed significantly from the earlier efforts to professionalize law and medicine. I then consider the "essentially contested" nature of teacher professionalism, showing why calls to avoid the discourse and to abandon efforts to define it in progressive ways would place us at a significant disadvantage in fighting against the deskilling and deprofessionalizing effects of market-driven education reform.

A progressive teacher professionalism must elaborate a positive vision of teaching. Referencing the work of teacher union around the National Board for Professional Teaching Standards and similar efforts, I tease out professional conceptions of accomplished teaching, of professional development of teacher expertise, and of participation in a professional community. I conclude the chapter with the elaboration of a model of democratic teacher professionalism, where teachers work in partnership with the community being served.

THE DIMENSIONS OF TEACHER PROFESSIONALISM: A HISTORICAL VIEW

What constitutes a profession? There is a sociological literature that identifies a number of characteristics of an ideal type of a profession, such as its distinctive knowledge base and education, its service orientation and self-regulation, and its prestige and status.[1] While this literature can be of use in understanding the discourse of teacher professionalism, it must be used critically, with a major caveat. To the extent that the early professions of law and medicine are used as a template for all professions, this literature loses sight of a major difference between those early professions and later professions such as teaching. The legal and medical professions were founded by men who understood themselves to be "gentlemen," with the aristocratic belonging and sensibility that terms applies; moreover, they were created in partnership with the state, which established a "sheltered market" for legal and medical services through a system of professional licensing. By contrast, teacher professionalism developed out of a female-dominated occupation that was largely middle- and working class in composition and was directly employed by the government; these characteristics led teachers to seek alliances with the labor movement and generated a much more complicated, and at times antagonistic, relationship to different apparatuses of the state.

The earliest expressions of teacher professionalism would emerge out of the complex, cross-cutting politics of the "rationalizing" and "centralizing" reforms of the Progressive Era.[2] The nascent teacher organizations and unions of this era were forcefully opposed to efforts to rationalize education and make it more efficient by applying to schools and teachers the scientific management principles that Frederick Winslow Taylor had formulated to organize the assembly lines of mass-production factories.[3] These efforts were most often promoted by superintendents and others at the center of the emerging education bureaucracies and their partners in the world of business, and teachers understood them as attempts to strip them of their skill and their authority over their work—in effect, as bids to reduce them to unskilled laborers. Taylor had famously written of how his scientific management could divide the labor process into unthinking, repetitive motions so simple that they could be performed on an assembly line by "an intelligent gorilla," so the introduction of this method into education was a particular affront to educated teachers.[4]

The movement to impose scientific management on schools made teachers suspicious of other reforms from these same quarters. This was especially the case with civil service reforms targeting political machines that used the hiring, promotion, and firing of public employees for patronage, since many incumbent teachers had been the beneficiaries of this patronage and the ethnic networks on which it was based. As the political machine was one of the few means of access to the public goods of the state that middle- and working-class communities had in the Progressive Era, teachers were far from convinced that hiring reforms that sidelined local ward politicians in favor of a central authority would work to their benefit.

But once they were on the job, teachers found that politicized promotions and firings could be a dicey matter, given the potential for changes in who held local elected office. To provide protections against the loss of their jobs for capricious or discriminatory reasons, teachers became advocates of the civil service practice of tenure, a due process right that required that the school district demonstrate good cause to fire a teacher. During the Progressive Era, teacher organizations and unions were successful in having most states adopt laws enacting teacher tenure. Furthermore, benefits such as improved salaries (pay was quite low, based on the notion that the mostly female teaching force were not family breadwinners) and pensions (which were first established in this era) could not be provided by local ward politicians; they could only come from state and large city governments. So rather than simply looking to the state to protect them from an unregulated market in an arm's-length partnership, as lawyers and doctors had done, teachers found themselves in close quarters with the state, at times caught up in a patron-client dynamic with local political machines, at other times in an adversarial stance that sought protection from government apparatuses. It was out of this complex, even contradictory, set of relations with the state that teacher professionalism took shape, with its strongest advocates found in the fledging teacher unions.

Over the course of the Progressive Era, many of those in education who were proponents of teacher professionalization allied themselves with elite reformers looking to clean up corrupt political machines. In places like New York City, this alliance resulted in the virtually simultaneous passage of tenure laws and the introduction of independent agencies for teaching licensure and hiring, such as the city's Board of Examiners; both were viewed as important steps in securing the professional autonomy of teaching from government and politics. (While the Board of Examiners did put an end to patronage in hiring, it would introduce its own discriminatory measures, such as oral exams that regularly failed candidates with "ethnic" accents.[5]) In the context of this alliance, teacher organizations were able to stalemate attempts to control teacher pedagogy through the imposition of scientific management; insofar as there were pedagogical deficiencies among teachers, they argued, they would be best addressed by developing postsecondary teacher education programs and in-service professional development. Yet the attempts to deskill teachers' work and micromanage the educational process were never fully defeated, and they continue to this day in ongoing struggles over who controls pedagogy and instruction, with teachers and their unions facing off against administrators, education bureaucrats, business interests, and elected officials.

Early teacher unions and allied advocates of teacher professionalism insisted that education, unlike the public services that could be provided by unskilled and uneducated labor, had to be a professional enterprise: to do their work well, teachers needed to have a mastery of teaching skills, a thorough knowledge of pedagogy, and a full comprehension of the subject matter being taught.[6] It followed that to acquire and maintain a professional teaching force, personnel decisions needed to be removed from political influence and made instead on the basis of professional qualifications and performance. In their alliance with the reformers of the Progressive Era, the advocates of teacher professionalism, including teacher unions, would seek to deny government officials the power to use public schools for political ends. The ultimate objective of this effort, always contested and never fully accomplished, was to carve out a semi-autonomous political space for public education, so it would be as much part of civil society as of the state.

In the first decades after their founding, teacher unions would test this developing idea of teacher professionalism in the battles they would fight over academic freedom. In New York City, teachers and teacher union activists were suspended, given punitive forced transfers, and fired for no other reasons than they had spoken out against discriminatory policies toward married woman teachers, were opposed to World War I, or were members of pacifist, civil libertarian and left-wing organizations. Well into the 1920s, leading teacher unionists were being denied promotions for some of the same reasons. It was not until the late 1920s that the unions, working with the American Civil Liberties Union (whose academic freedom work was led by teacher unionists), successfully overturned these political decisions. In this work, the unions looked to expand the idea of teacher professionalism to argue against all politically motivated personnel decisions.

These differences between the early professions of law and medicine and the later profession of teaching shed important light on the contending paradigms of professionalism in education today. Those who favor market models of education often offer a vision of an educational system in which teachers would no longer be unionized or have the protections of tenure, but nonetheless would have somehow become "more professional" in the mold of the early legal and medical professions.[7] In this view, unionization and tenure are posed as barriers to acquiring the levels of prestige, autonomy, and compensation enjoyed by doctors and lawyers. To be plausible, this argument requires that one: (1) disregard the actual history of teacher professionalism and the structural reasons why it did not take the same form as medicine and law; (2) ignore the radical changes of recent decades in law and medicine, where conglomeration and bureaucratization are leading to the rapid decline of independence and self-employment; (3) pay no attention to the role of institutionalized sexism in the low status and prestige of American teaching prior to unionization; and (4) elide the historic role that teacher unions have played in promoting teacher professionalism, starting with their very founding. Importantly, this argument requires that one ignore the reasons why teachers sought restrictions on the apparatuses of the government that employ them, and why they continue to need those protections.

THE CONTESTED NATURE OF TEACHER PROFESSIONALISM

The fact that appeals to teacher professionalism can be employed in retrogressive ways has led some to argue that teachers and their unions should eschew altogether professional discourses of teacher identity, and instead adopt in their place more progressive discourses of teaching as labor and craft, or "social justice" conceptions of unionism.[8] It is certainly true that appeals to professionalism have been used to oppose teacher collective action and unionism ("professionals don't organize and don't strike"), to support efforts to masculinize teaching (by unfavorably comparing the numbers of women in education to the male-dominated professions of law and medicine), and to encourage teacher identification with economic and social elites and disidentification with the communities they serve.[9] But to focus only on the negative uses of professionalism is to provide a very partial and skewed reading of the discursive terrain. A full examination demonstrates that teacher professionalism is an "essentially contested" idea, given contending and even contradictory meanings by those who adopt it, with those different meanings reflecting fundamentally different and even opposed political vantage points.[10] As much as there are retrogressive ways to deploy the discourse of professionalism, there are also progressive ways in which it is used, such as the idea of democratic professionalism I discuss later in this chapter. Whatever the intentions of those within the ranks of unions who argue that we should abandon the discourse of professionalism, the practical consequences of their stance is to withdraw from the fight to define the most commonly used discourse of teaching—a self-defeating abstentionism cedes that battle to our foes.

When one considers the material relationships and institutional settings from which the discourse of professionalism emerges and which it seeks in turn to shape—first, the relationship of teachers to each other in the professional community of teaching; second, the relationship of teachers and their professional community to educational administrators and bureaucrats, to schools of education in the academy, and to government departments of education and the regulations they produce; and third, the relationship of teachers to the communities they serve—it becomes apparent that leaving the field of battle would necessarily have ruinous effects on the overall struggle for democratic education and would make it much more difficult to mount effective teacher collective action.

This point is only accentuated when one considers the question of teacher professionalism in light of the last two decades of top-down, technocratic, and market-driven education reforms in the United States, from No Child Left Behind to Race to the Top. As I discussed in chapter 2, these reforms transformed—for the worse—the existing systems of school accountability, teacher evaluation, and student promotion and graduation by centering them on standardized exams. The use of standardized test scores to make high-stakes decisions about the future of students, teachers, and school had the effect of undermining and sidelining the professional judgment of educators and of reducing far too much of the educational process to debased test prep. These reforms have played a major role in the crisis of the teaching corps that American education now faces, and they were an important focus of the strikes of the Teacher Insurgency.

The market-based reforms that struck at the professional judgment of educators should be understood in their full political and economic contexts, which I discussed in chapter 3. Politically, these reforms were part of a movement to shift power and control over important educational decisions to sites where the elite could work its will with much greater ease—away from teachers to administrators, away from educators to bureaucrats and government officials, away from schools and communities to educational bureaucracies and government, and away from elected school boards to appointed executive branch officials insulated from popular discontent. Economically, their reforms sought to integrate K–12 education into a global knowledge economy increasingly bifurcated along the lines of the production and use of knowledge—between *educated, self-programmable labor* that produces new knowledge, with significant control over the labor process on the one hand, and *generic labor* that uses the knowledge created by others, executing decisions and engaging in a labor process over which it has little control, on the other—with the object of reducing American teachers to generic labor. The "teacher proof" pedagogy and instrumental curriculum of "no excuses" charter schools represents the logical conclusion of such reforms. No substantive knowledge of teaching methods or mastery of teaching skills is required to deliver the scripts, so virtually anyone with a postsecondary degree can "teach." (In this regard, the campaign of Success Academy's Eva Moskowitz to hire teachers who have no license and no meaningful preparation to teach is telling.[11]) A withdrawal from the fight to define the discourse of teacher professionalism at this moment—when the attacks on professional educational judgment carry such weight—can only have tragic outcomes.

A POSITIVE AGENDA FOR TEACHER PROFESSIONALISM

To be successful, a teacher professionalism agenda cannot be purely defensive. It must, of course, resist the efforts of non-educators—administrators with little or no classroom experience, educational bureaucrats, business interests, and elected officials—to take control of pedagogy and professional knowledge and, in so doing, reduce teachers to generic labor that executes decisions made by others. But without a positive vision of teacher professionalism to advance, defensive struggles against "hostile takeovers" by non-educators will take the form of a long and ultimately losing war of attrition. Only a compelling vision of teacher professionalism can rally teachers and convince the larger public of its importance. Such a vision must include four essential points: a professional conception of accomplished teaching, a focus on the development of the professional expertise of teachers, an understanding that professionalism requires participation in a professional community, and a model of democratic professionalism that works in partnership with the community being served. I will now address each of these points in turn.

One useful window into this vision can be found in the work that teacher unions have done to promote professionalism in their ranks. Perhaps the best (although by no means the only) illustration of this teacher professionalism agenda is the National Board for Professional Teaching Standards (NBPTS).[12] Originally conceived by the late AFT President Al Shanker and initiated by national teacher leaders and educators with the active counsel and support of both national teacher unions, NBPTS created a national system of voluntary board certification that recognizes teachers who demonstrate accomplished teaching.

To this end, it established rigorous, peer-reviewed standards and procedures for certification. While the details of these standards and procedures vary with different student developmental levels and subject areas, they all have the common foundation of five NBPTS core principles, which articulate a philosophy of educational professionalism. Accomplished teachers: (1) are committed to students and their learning, (2) know the subjects they teach and how to teach those subjects to students, (3) are responsible for managing and monitoring student learning, (4) think systematically about their practice and learn from experience, and (5) are members of learning communities. The NBPTS certification process itself involves ongoing professional collaboration and growth, with a focus on the creation of a portfolio that includes representative artifacts of teaching practice, such as videotapes of classroom instruction and examples of student work.

Many teacher union locals have integrated the NBPTS into their day-to-work. Their educational and professional development arms support teachers in the extensive certification process; in contract negotiations, many locals have obtained financial support for teachers applying for certification and salary differentials for board certified teachers. Governed and led by a twenty-nine-member board of directors, the majority of whom are themselves board-certified, active classroom teachers, the NBPTS established itself as a teacher-run entity, independent of the state. Given the origins of the teaching profession, this independence is key; as a practical matter, it has been essential in maintaining the professional integrity of the NBPTS process.

The teaching envisioned by the NBPTS standards is a complex and challenging undertaking, and it takes years for a teacher to truly master it. In a class, a teacher is called on to utilize and integrate three different knowledge sets—of pedagogy, of the subject material, and of the particular students she is teaching—in an interactive exercise that includes in-time monitoring of student engagement, understanding, and behavior and adjustments to her lesson plan based on that monitoring. Over time, this teacher reflects on how well her interventions—her lessons, the underlying methods she is employing, and her interactions with her students—are working, and she tests out different approaches and modifies her instruction to produce better results. Throughout this process, she is in dialogue with other teachers in her professional community, starting in the school and going beyond, on these new approaches—on refinements of established methods, on what works well with particular students, and on the state of the knowledge of the subject(s) she teaches. To be accomplished in all of this work, she must learn how to "think in action." The exemplary teacher becomes what Donald Schön calls a "reflective practitioner," integrating the theory and practice of teaching on a continuous process: she is not only the user, but also the active author, of professional knowledge.[13]

As a point of contrast, consider the practice of teachers who are required to use heavily scripted, "teacher-proof" lessons and curricula, such as those that are employed in many no-excuses charter schools. Doug Lemov's *Teach Like a Champion*, the handbook widely used and heralded in such schools, is instructive in this regard. In this handbook, teaching becomes a series of techniques, without any meaningful consideration of the ultimate ends of education.[14] The first technique it presents reads as if it were taken straight out of the time-and-motion studies that Taylor had used to break down the assembly-line process into discrete, mindless steps: the teacher is told how to train her students to hand in papers so that the task is accomplished with a minimal use of time—and to use a stopwatch to get students to do it in shorter and shorter periods of time. (Lest the reader think that such a stark example might be unfairly taken out of context, I would note that Lemov cites a prominent charter school leader as the source of this technique. And though he acknowledges that there will be skeptics, he justifies its prominence on the basis of the time he believes will be saved for instruction.[15])

Accomplished teaching does involve the use of particular techniques, albeit not ones fixated on mindless tasks such as handing in papers. But for the right techniques to be identified and used appropriately, they must be seen as tools for accomplishing the ultimate objectives of education, such as education into democratic citizenship. The teacher must be constantly evaluating the utility of particular methods and how she uses them in light of the progress her students make toward those objectives. For example, a teacher's mastery of questioning techniques is particularly important because good questioning is essential to eliciting and developing the thinking and communication skills of students—especially analytical reasoning, the use of supporting evidence, critical thinking, and problem solving.[16] Without constant reference to these ultimate objectives of education, the teacher becomes little more than a technician who executes a plan established by others—the very definition of generic labor. In the setting of no-excuses charter schools where student performance on standardized exams is given the highest priority, the exams become the de facto objective of education; essential skills that standardized tests do not and cannot begin to adequately capture, such as the skills developed by good questioning, are pushed to the side.

PROFESSIONAL AUTHORITY AND TIME FOR TEACHERS

Like the discourse of nurturance, the discourse of professionalism provides an immanent (or internal) critique of the contemporary organization of teaching and schools. For teacher professionalism to flourish, two issues in particular must be addressed—the professional pedagogical authority of teachers, and the professional non-instructional time during the workday for self-directed and collegial work, especially professional development.

In the era of twenty-first-century market-driven education reform, American teachers have increasingly experienced the imposition of rigid instructional formulas and standardized materials, the mandating of lock-step pacing calendars and particular formats for lesson plans, and a micromanagement that extends to such matters as the details of bulletin boards—all manifestations of a deskilling and deprofessionalization of teaching. Against this reality, a discourse of professionalism insists on the professional authority of teachers—the freedom to teach in ways that accord with what the body of professional educational knowledge tells us about how young people learn. To be clear, this authority is *not* license for individuals to do whatever they please in a classroom, regardless of its educational efficacy: for example, an individual teacher does not get to decide that she will use lectures to instruct adolescents, when all of the educational research and cognitive science demonstrates that it is the most ineffective means of educating young people. Rather, the freedom to teach is a professional authority, rooted in and based on the knowledge and standards of the professional community of teachers; it is collegial authority that is shared by all teachers. In their promotion of teacher professionalism, teacher unions should negotiate contractual protections for the professional authority of teachers, as many have done.

Establishing professional authority extends beyond the individual classroom to restoring professional educational judgment in such critical decisions as student promotion and graduation, teacher evaluation, and school accountability.[17] Testing data should inform, never substitute for, such judgment.

For teachers to grow professionally, they need the time and space to learn, with opportunities to work with and learn from each other: the workday of teachers needs to be organized with such learning as a central purpose. Examined in comparative international perspective against other OECD nations, American public education provides minimal amounts of non-instructional professional time for teachers. For example, despite a working day that is longer than the American average, Japanese teachers spend less time in direct classroom instruction—teaching twenty-two hours per week in elementary schools, seventeen hours per week in middle school schools, and fifteen hours per week in high schools. The remaining time is spent working with colleagues, visiting parents, counseling students, and pursuing learning in their field of specialization.[18]

Just as importantly, the teacher professional development that does occur in American schools under the direction of supervisors and school districts often ignores what educational research tells us about learning in general and teacher learning in particular.[19] Where professional development should be ongoing, with continuing support during the implementation of new approaches, too often it takes the form of one-shot workshops; where it should be job-embedded and focused on student learning, too often it is removed from the school and focused on administrative and district priorities; where it should concentrate on a specific curricular question, too often it is generic and diffuse; and where it should provide opportunities for teachers to work together, especially in grade or subject teams, too often it isolates teachers from each other. Most importantly, where teacher professional development should be intellectually engaging, with a regard for teachers as the authors of professional knowledge, too often it treats teachers as passive transmission belts for others' ideas and plans. In my many years as a teacher union organizer and leader, I have never been in a school that was an intellectually engaging place for students that was not also an intellectually engaging place for teachers, with high-quality professional development. The problem is that there are far too few such schools.

To promote teacher professionalism, teacher unions have negotiated contractual clauses for time and space for teachers to work professionally with each other and to include meaningful teacher voice in the planning and execution of professional development. Many teacher unions have organized their own educational and professional development arms—some quite extensive, with decades of work in the field—to deliver professional development that is high quality and not subject to the whims of changing district and state leadership.[20]

In sum, a progressive teacher professionalism requires a vision of accomplished teaching, of what teacher professional authority is and how it should be used, and of the ways in which teachers should be supported so they can become increasingly expert in their teaching.

DEMOCRATIC PROFESSIONALISM

The adage "Knowledge is power" points us to the inescapable power dimensions of the discourse of teacher professionalism. From its beginnings in the Progressive Era, this discourse as pursued by teacher unions has been a political project that sought to secure the knowledge and craft of teaching from interventions by non-practitioners that would have the effect of debasing and degrading it. To this end, it has developed a positive vision for the development of the teaching profession. In this moment, the discourse of teacher professionalism is a profoundly democratic movement, empowering the ranks of teachers by providing the means to master and practice their craft as it should be done.

But the command of specialized, expert knowledge that defines professionalization also raises another issue of power—the relations of power between the professional and the laypersons she serves. In schooling, this power is found in the relationship between educators on the one hand, and the students, families, and communities served by their schools on the other. One does not need to accept the entirety of Michael Lipsky's study of "street-level bureaucrats" or Michael Foucault's investigation of power and disciplinary knowledge (I do not) to recognize that on one crucial point they are correct: power is an intrinsic component of the relationship between a profession and the community it serves.[21]

It is not possible to elude or eliminate this dimension of professional power. The claims of critics such as Ivan Illich that professional knowledge is mostly the mystique of esoteric language, and that the little of expert knowledge that is of real value can be made easily accessible for lay populations, are deeply impractical and utopian in the worst sense of the word.[22] Insofar as we have a vision of schooling that empowers young people, it will necessarily require a foundation of skilled and knowledgeable educational professionals with a deep understanding and established practice of how to educate for democratic citizenship. These are not capacities that a layperson could acquire without substantial education, classroom experience, and participatory membership in a professional community. The issue is not whether educational expertise is indispensable for accomplished teaching and quality education, but whether that expertise can be democratic, exercised in partnership with fellow citizens, and employed on behalf of the common good of students and the larger community. Indeed, in an age of the deskilling and technocratic micromanagement of teaching, the very success of the professionalization project will rest in no small part on the ability of teachers and teacher unions to negotiate and maintain democratic forms of professional authority.

For a robust concept of democratic professionalism, we can turn once again to John Dewey and his debate with the journalist Walter Lippman. An ex-radical who had become disillusioned with American democracy and public opinion, Lippman believed that the general welfare was best secured when issues of public policy were treated as technical matters and decided by disinterested, neutral experts.[23] The public was simply too ill-informed and too self-interested to be trusted with decision-making power, Lippman argued, in a foreshadowing of recent arguments for eliminating elected school boards, marginalizing community and teacher voice in schooling, and handing decision-making over to remote executive branch bureaucrats. In *The Public and Its Problems*, Dewey responded that a "class of experts is inevitably so removed from common interests as to become a class with private interests and private knowledge, which in social matters is not knowledge at all. The man who wears the shoe knows best that it pinches and where it pinches, even if the expert shoemaker is the best judge of how the trouble is to be remedied."[24] If a reform project were to correctly identify and address the problem at hand, it would require input and partnership from both the professional and the community. Neither can produce the necessary change on its own.

Dewey's vision of democratic professionalism was rooted in the republicanism that had been so central to the nineteenth-century American labor movement.[25] He certainly acknowledged that power dynamics created by professional knowledge and skill are real. But he also acknowledged that there was a redemptive political equality in the republican tradition of citizens who share equally in the sovereignty of "we the people"—that, if it were properly recognized and embraced, would provide the basis of a partnership between professional and community.[26] This democratic professionalism was central to Dewey's vision of the school: it must be a place of democracy—including the different voices of teachers, students, families, and community in important decision-making—if it is to teach democracy.[27] The theme of schools as democratic communities has long held a place of prominence in teacher unions. I will return to it in my discussion of the fourth discourse of teaching as a vocation of democratic intellectual work, as this is one more area where are a suturing of the different discourses will prove essential in establishing a progressive collective teacher identity.

I do not want to understate the challenges in developing a democratic professionalism. The power dynamic between knowledgeable expert and layperson is rarely simply that; it is most often overlaid with other power differentials, especially those associated with class, race and ethnicity, and gender. As such, there will be times when democratic professionalism will require hard conversations. For our part, teachers will need to listen respectfully to and find ways to act on the insights of the families and community on where "the shoe is pinching," especially when they raise difficult issues such as whether a particular curriculum is adequately educating students of color and whether codes of conduct are unduly punitive and discriminatory.[28] Just as listening is the essential skill in organizing, it is central to a democratic professionalism.

CHAPTER 11

The Discourse of Teaching as Labor and Craft

AMONG MANY OTHER REASONS, teachers do what they do to earn a living for themselves and their families. For the most part, the schools they teach in are public schools, and their employer is an entity of the government, although its exact configuration varies from state to state. Smaller numbers of teachers work in charter schools and private schools, with employers that are non-governmental and private organizations. But all teachers work for an employer that pays them a salary, and with a very small number of exceptions, provides them with health insurance and a pension. In general, this employer sets the terms and conditions under which they labor, either through collective bargaining with unions or unilaterally where there is no union representation. In the most basic sense of the word, therefore, American teachers are labor, and have been such throughout American history.

Labor is often thought to be an economic category, separate and apart from the "consciousness" of economic status by those who fall into this category. But in viewing labor and craft as a discourse—an ensemble of thinking, communicating, and acting that plays out an identity and is materially embedded in social practices and institutions—I reject this separation. In this chapter, I will show how the discourse of teaching as labor and craft is rooted not only in the relationships teachers have with their employers—that teachers work to earn their living—but also in the relationships teachers have with each other in their common cause to win fair compensation and their participation in organizations and communities that protect and promote their craft. Teacher unions are, of course, the primary organization through which teachers act on behalf of each other and their craft. I examine the differences between craft unionism and industrial unionism to show what teacher unions should take from each tradition of union organization. In particular, I show how the idea of an *apprenticeship*—that one can best learn a craft through a mentorship with an accomplished practitioner—provides a model for addressing areas of critical weakness in the preparation, induction, and development for American teachers. In advocating for and sponsoring teacher education residencies, mentoring programs and peer assistance and review programs, teacher unions have developed the most promising approaches.

WHY TEACHERS ORGANIZE IN UNIONS

When American teachers began to organize themselves at the turn of the twentieth century, looking to collective action to address common issues, their employment status gave them good reason to see a strong affinity with organized labor—and therefore, to form teacher unions.[1] Those issues included the compensation they received for their labor. In some quarters, the fact that unions have always advocated for the bread-and-butter needs of teachers—most importantly, their salaries, pensions, and health insurance—is taken as proof that this is all unions do.

Teachers and their unions have no reason to apologize for such advocacy. As a matter of simple justice, the inadequate and inequitable compensation of American teachers must be addressed: a modest middle-class income, health insurance, and retirement security are certainly not too much to ask of a society for those who dedicate themselves to the education of young people. It is long past time that we corrected the historic wrong of the institutional sexism that penalized a predominantly female occupation. That in recent years teacher compensation has suffered and fallen further behind comparable occupations only compounds the historic wrong.

More is involved here than fairness. The treatment of teachers is reflective of the failure of American government and society to make the education and nurturance of its young—especially its poor youth and youth of color—a priority. In pursuing their own economic cause, teachers make teaching a more attractive option for other dedicated women and men, and thus contribute to the development of a high-quality system of public education that will serve American youth in a way befitting the richest nation in the history of the world. A discourse of teaching as labor will thus have as a central component advocacy for the bread-and-butter needs of teachers.

But the notion that teacher unions do nothing but advocate for their members' economic needs can only be sustained out of willful ignorance of both their history and contemporary reality, underscored by the Teacher Insurgency strikes. Teacher unions have incorporated their advocacy for those needs into a larger vision of what is important for their craft and for an economic democracy that serves working people as a whole. The discourse of teaching as labor thus includes an understanding of teaching as a craft and connections between that craft and labor more generally.

In employing the term *craft* to describe the labor of teachers, I adopt a language that American teachers themselves often use to characterize their work and to describe their adversarial relationships with employers that are far removed from the world of classrooms.[2] But the term also invokes the history of how American labor has organized itself into unions, and I am using it in ways that run against the grain of how many progressive historians and unionists understand that history, so a word of explanation is required.

CRAFT UNIONISM AND INDUSTRIAL UNIONISM

For the first half of the twentieth century, there were deep divisions in American labor over what was the best organizational form for unions, and these differences eventually broke out into open war in 1935, when a group of unions seceded from the American Federation of Labor (AFL) and formed the Congress of Industrial Organizations (CIO).[3] The AFL had been established in 1886 by craft unions that were organized on the basis of specific skilled trades, such as carpenters, painters, tailors, and cigar-makers. Before the AFL, national union organizations such as the Knights of Labor had been flashes in the pan, but the AFL and its craft unions had proven to have real staying power. Far too often, however, AFL craft unionism had based itself on exclusionary practices—barring from membership not only the unskilled, but also immigrants, people of color, and women.[4] Moreover, the craft unions of the AFL developed an outlook of "pure and simple" trade unionism that focused narrowly on the short-term interests of their particular segment of organized labor, avoiding any connection to larger struggles for social justice and democracy.[5] Finally, by insisting on their particular craft jurisdictions, AFL craft unions had hamstrung all efforts to organize mass production industries such as auto and steel, which combined a number of traditional crafts with unskilled, assembly-line labor. As these industries came to dominate the American economy in the early twentieth century, the AFL and its craft unions found themselves increasingly on the defensive, and by the 1920s, they were shrinking. It was only with the establishment of the CIO, which seized the organizing opportunity provided by the 1935 Wagner Act with a philosophy of industrial unionism, that those mass production industries were successfully unionized and that American labor unions regained the initiative that led to their most successful historical moment.[6]

The CIO unions were distinguished not simply by the fact they organized on an industrial basis, bringing all of the workers in an industry together into a single union where they could exercise the greatest leverage against the employer. As a general rule, they were also more progressive than the AFL craft unions—more inclusive in their willingness to build diverse organizations that included all workers, regardless of race, gender, and immigration status, and more likely to advocate for working people as a whole. Prominent leaders of the CIO such Walter Reuther of the United Auto Workers (UAW) and Sidney Hillman of the Amalgamated Clothing Workers (ACW) had come out of the socialist movement, and they promoted a social unionism that had a broad economic agenda and built a strong labor electoral presence in support of New Deal progressives. Given these historical differences, industrial unionism is generally seen as a progressive development in American labor, while craft unionism is commonly viewed as outdated and regressive.

This positive view of industrial unionism was largely held by the pioneering generation of teacher unionists who won collective bargaining in the 1960s and 1970s. In many ways, they modeled their union organization and their politics after Walter Reuther's UAW. For example, key leadership figures in the UFT's battle to win collective bargaining rights, such as Dave Selden and Ely Trachtenberg, had learned their unionism from participation in the UAW.[7] Reuther provided key financial aid to the UFT in that historic battle.

There are clearly aspects of industrial unionism that should be maintained and highlighted in a discourse of teaching as labor: today's teacher unions are industrial unions for education, organizing all but the supervisory and administrative staff in preK–12 schools and postsecondary institutions.[8] Teacher unions oppose all forms of discrimination and actively embrace and defend members who are immigrants, people of color, women, of minority religions and faiths, and LGBTQ in an era when the attacks on these groups have grown. And teacher unions increasingly put forward a broad agenda that unites union and community, and advocates for all working people.

But the industrial unionism of the UAW and the CIO provides precious few resources for organizing around the teaching craft in defense of teacher knowledge and teacher skill. Indeed, one of the most common understandings of industrial unionism was that it was possible because the workforce had been stripped of the skill and knowledge of the artisan workers of the pre-industrial economy—a development that, it was argued, homogenized the workforce and gave it an identity of interests.[9] In this perspective, craft unionism—and with it, a focus on workers' knowledge and skill—had been historically superseded by industrial unionism.

This deskilling of labor was the main theme of Harry Braverman's classic work on the "degradation of work," which he understood as a process rooted in the logic of capital accumulation, with workers largely reduced to the role of passive victims.[10] A number of education scholars have applied Braverman's analysis to education, arguing that teachers are being "proletarianized" by the deskilling of their work.[11] But as critics of Braverman have argued, control over knowledge and skill was in fact contested, as labor has historically resisted attempts to dominate it and degrade its work through deskilling.[12] This is certainly true of the history of teachers and their unions, as we have seen with respect to the attempts to impose the scientific management of Taylorism on schools, and it remains valid to this day.[13] Craft unionism, which has always had worker skill and knowledge at its center, was one of primary means of that resistance, although it was largely absent from Braverman's narrative. Rather than succumbing to the evolutionary schematics that always end with the deskilling of labor triumphant, might it be the right time to examine anew the nature of craft unionism, and see what resources it could provide us? Might we not consider the possibility that the form craft unionism took in the past was a historically contingent combination of different elements, and that there is no intrinsic or essential connection between a craft unionist focus on skill and knowledge and exclusionary (nativist, racist, and sexist) practices of membership, narrow conceptions of self-interest, or opposition to industrywide union organizations?

There are good reasons to take a fresh look at this question. "New labor history" studies of the early stages of working-class organization in different national contexts point to the central role not of unskilled manufacturing labor, but of skilled artisans.[14] Utilizing a new appreciation and analysis of the languages and cultures of labor, these studies have found the beginnings of unionism in the world of the artisan—the guilds and journeymen brotherhoods that took shape in the late Middle Ages and were transplanted from Europe to the Americas.[15] The labor republicanism that was central to nineteenth-century American unions, with its regulative ideals of the common good, citizenship, and civic virtue, had similar historical origins in the world of the artisan and provided a basis for nineteenth-century struggles against employer efforts to wrest control of the labor process from craft workers.[16] Studies of the industrial unionism of the CIO have shown that it was the skilled workers in the mass production industries, not unskilled assembly-line workers, who were the pivotal core of the unionization campaigns.[17] Rather than viewing American craft unionism as a prisoner of the historical circumstances from which it emerged, it makes more sense to understand its late nineteenth- and early twentieth-century form as the articulation of a number of different elements, some of which might be recovered for discourse of teaching as labor, others of which must be left behind.

THE CRAFT OF TEACHING

The craft union tradition brings to the discourses of teacher identity an important understanding of teaching as a skill. In sharp contrast to the debasement of teaching that emerged out of the last two decades of education reform, with the radical separation of the theory and practice that comes from the deskilling of teaching, the craft union model views teaching practice as inseparable from teaching knowledge: the accomplished teacher creatively integrates the performance and the knowledge of teaching, the artistic and the scientific aspects of her skilled labor.[18] Against conceptions of education that view the teacher as an atomistic actor, the discourse of teaching as labor and craft highlights the social and communal nature of education and teaching.[19] It sees teaching, like other crafts, as rooted in and dependent on the work and activities of organized communities of practitioners skilled in that craft. Far from being in necessary competition with the discourse of teaching as a profession, then, this discourse of teaching as labor and craft complements the more progressive and democratic versions of discourse of teaching as a profession. In combination, they produce a richer, more variegated vision of teaching.

The conceptual frame of craft unionism provides the means to address two central issues in the promotion of accomplished teaching—the education, preparation, and support of novice teachers and the continuing growth and refinement of skill among experienced teachers. In the institutional configuration of American education that developed over the twentieth century, these tasks were increasingly controlled by supervisory bureaucracies and education schools within the academy, with results that have fallen far short of what is needed. Today, it is generally recognized that the two of the greatest institutional shortcomings of American education lie precisely in these areas.

Study after study of American education has contained the almost commonplace observation that many American teacher education programs fail to produce graduates who are properly prepared to assume full-time teaching responsibilities, due in no small part to the inadequate attention those schools pay to the teacher practicum and the disjuncture between the theories of education prospective teachers are taught and the actual practice of teaching. A quarter-century ago, the report of the National Commission on Teaching and America's Future raised the alarm that American teacher education was "thin, uneven and poorly financed" in comparison with the education of other professions in the United States and to teacher education in other countries.

Today, too little has changed; the number of exemplary programs are few and far between.[20] Indeed, the last two decades of education reform have only exacerbated the problem, as programs like Teacher for America send novice teachers into the schools that have the greatest challenges with the most inadequate of preparations—five-week summer "boot camps."[21]

Moreover, in-service programs for the support of novice teachers generally share all of the problems of professional development that I discussed in chapter 10. Given the critical nature of the first years of teaching for a teacher's career and the often inadequate pre-service education they have received, these shortcomings have much greater negative effect on novice teachers. The numbers are telling: 42 percent of all new teachers in the United States are dropping out of teaching by their fifth year, with even higher rates of attrition in the schools serving high-poverty communities.[22] The American teaching corps has long been a leaky bucket, with teachers leaving as fast as they could be replaced—and now, with the dramatic decline in the numbers of graduates of teacher education programs in recent years, it will become harder and harder to even keep pace with the losses of existing teachers.

The apprenticeship programs central to the craft union tradition provide the basis for an alternative approach to teacher education, induction, and ongoing development—one in which the organized community of skilled teacher practitioners assumes responsibility for the crucial activities of learning and refining the craft. Apprenticeships operate on the premise that one learns a craft by a gradual immersion into its practice under the guidance and with the counseling of those who already mastered it, and that one improves one's skills by collaborative work with other practitioners. Seen in this light, the apprenticeship model provides the conceptual inspiration for a series of union-initiated and -supported programs—teacher education residency programs, mentoring of novice teachers, and peer assistance and review programs.

Teacher education residency programs are centered on a rigorous full-year classroom apprenticeship with an accomplished teacher mentor; the study of pedagogy and theories of education take the form of reflections on the learning of the teaching craft through the apprenticeship.[23] Since such programs typically provide financial support to their residents, they require an up-front investment in teacher education that only a few districts have been willing to make; for example, successful teacher internships undertaken by New Visions for Public Schools and the International Networks for Public Schools with the support of the United Federation of Teachers had to be abandoned because the New York City school district was unwilling to assume the cost once seed money from foundations was exhausted. This aversion to investing in good apprenticeship-based teacher education is shortsighted, as graduates of these programs have proven more likely to be successful in the classroom, and remain in education, simply because they enter teaching well-prepared. Over the long term, programs such as the teacher residencies actually produce a saving, as the continuing churn of novice teachers in the status quo carries a heavy educational cost and a financial burden of a constant, high-density induction program. Moreover, financial support for their residents allows these programs to address critical needs in teaching, such as the demand for more teachers of color, especially African American teachers.[24]

Given that most novice teachers enter the classroom without the benefit of a solid pre-service preparation, it is essential that they receive strong mentoring support from an accomplished veteran teacher, especially at the critical beginning of their teaching career. Education research is clear that quality mentoring makes a critical difference in the success and retention of novice teachers.[25] In a number of school districts around the country, this mentoring is an important component of peer assistance and review (PAR), in which experienced classroom teachers, selected with union approval, mentor and evaluate their peers, especially novice teachers.[26] Precisely because PAR embodies the craft union model of a community of practitioners regulating their own practice, it has been fought both by those who view it as a surrender of management prerogative and by those who view it as inconsistent with industrial unionism.[27] But after its implementation in different school districts around the country, it has demonstrated that the surest road to quality teaching is teachers assuming the power and responsibility for their own craft. The craft union tradition's unique blend of a focus on the wages and working conditions of its members with an emphasis on the integrity and quality of its craft is an especially felicitous combination in an era when the economic and educational concerns of teacher unions are more and more inextricably fused.

CHAPTER 12

The Discourse of Teaching as Democratic Work

NO ONE BECOMES A TEACHER IN THE UNITED STATES with expectations of becoming wealthy and powerful. Rather, most women and men who become teachers do so out of a vocation, a sense of a calling to their work. This vocation is sometimes expressed in general terms, as a desire to make a positive difference in the lives of young people; this iteration of a teacher's calling plays a major role in the discourses of teaching as nurturance and teaching as a profession I have examined in the preceding chapters. But the teacher's vocation is also often articulated in a more politically explicit fashion, as a commitment to *empowering* poor, working-class, and disadvantaged youth and to realizing the full democratic potential of public education. It is this second meaning of a teacher's calling that finds expression in the discourse of teaching as a vocation of democratic intellectual work.

In this chapter, I will inquire into the nature of this democratic vocation, which has defined teacher unionism from its very beginnings. I start with a discussion of how the work of teachers is intellectual in nature and how, as a consequence, teachers see themselves as public intellectuals in a practical sense of that term—as organizers and disseminators of educational practices that embody and promote civic principles. When teachers understand themselves as *democratic* public intellectuals, they organize their classrooms in ways that model democratic deliberation and prepare their students to be citizens capable of exercising self-rule in a republican government. Where they have opportunity to do so, teachers create schools that are organized along democratic principles and promote democracy in the world. Such an education requires a robust conception of democracy, I insist, and cannot be limited to a procedural understanding in which all that matters is the rule of a majority. In particular, two substantive principles—one based on liberty and one based on equality—must be at the core of democratic education. Finally, for public schools to realize their democratic mission, it is important to understand them as much part of civil society as the state.

TEACHERS AS DEMOCRATIC PUBLIC INTELLECTUALS

From their very beginnings, teacher unions have identified themselves with a notion of teaching as a democratic calling. In her landmark 1904 address to the NEA convention, "Why Teachers Should Organize," Chicago teacher union leader Margaret Haley succinctly described the parameters of this discourse of teaching as a vocation of democratic intellectual work: "It is the public school teachers whose special contribution to society is their own power to think, the moral courage to follow their convictions, and the training of citizens to think and to express thought in free and intelligent action."[1] This was no idle principle for Haley; well before the passage of the Nineteenth Amendment and the advent of women's suffrage, she was organizing women teachers as political and civic activists, challenging the wealthy and powerful on behalf of the teachers themselves and the students they taught.[2] Haley writes in her autobiography, "If our democracy is to continue, the teachers of this nation must teach the children of the nation the obligations of citizenship in a true democracy." These words have remarkable resonance in 2020, when the future of American democracy hangs in the balance.[3]

There is ample evidence that this vision of their vocation animated teachers as they first organized for collective action. It was captured in the earliest slogan of the American Federation of Teachers, "Democracy in Education, Education for Democracy." John Dewey, as the leading American theorist and proponent of democratic education, was given the place of distinction as the first member of the AFT precisely because of his influential work on this subject.[4] This was not an empty honorific; Dewey was an active member of the AFT and its New York City locals and played a significant role in the early struggles to build teacher unions.

The first generation of teacher unionists saw Dewey as one of themselves not just because he fought for their causes, but because they saw themselves as public intellectuals broadly conceived, with Dewey occupying the first rank of that social category and identity. By *public intellectual*, I do not mean the narrow understanding of that term that is now current, a usage that is restricted to "men and women of letters" who publish and speak on issues of public import to a broad audience.[5] Teacher unions certainly had intellectuals of this sort in their ranks—Dewey himself, Reinhold Niebuhr, George Counts, Ralph Bunche, Sidney Hook, Franz Boas, Bertram Wolfe, and A. J. Muste, to name just a few. And at a time when PhDs were a small fraction of their numbers (unlike today), many of the early teacher union leaders held doctorates. But teacher unionists had a more inclusive understanding of the term *intellectual* and their place within it, one akin to Antonio Gramsci's conception of those who—with their intellectual labor—create, disseminate, and implement culture broadly understood.[6] Public intellectuals were the subset of this category of intellectual whose cultural work is directly concerned with public life, its organization, and the issues associated with it.

If we employ a Deweyan understanding of education as a process of enculturation and socialization that introduces youth into their culture as active participants in it, teachers will be seen as paradigmatic public intellectuals in this more inclusive sense, as the elaborators of civic culture and the promulgators of public discourse. The teacher as public intellectual, what Gramsci would have called the "organic intellectual," is much more than an orator or preacher—an evangelist—of a given set of political and civic ideas. In her classroom and school, she is the "constructor (and) organizer" of educational practices that embody and thereby promote civic and political principles.[7] Significantly, the "common sense" perception most teachers have of their work insists on its practical-intellectual character, and on the importance of this practical-intellectual work to public culture and life.

When a teacher understands herself as a *democratic* public intellectual, there are important ramifications for her classroom practice. A democratic classroom is established as much by *how* the teacher teaches as by *what* she teaches, as much by the "hidden curriculum" of her classroom as by her subject matter and formal curriculum.[8] While students certainly need to understand the conceptual foundations and history of democratic governance, for example, how these subjects are taught makes all the difference. If they are taught in a didactic and lecturing manner, disconnected from current disputes and struggles, the main lesson for students will be that democracy is an empty idea that has little to do with them, and even less to do with their participation in the important decisions that impact their lives. The question of pedagogy, which can be more or less democratic in every subject classroom, is paramount; different modalities of teaching either strengthen or diminish, build up or tear down, the dispositions, skills, and knowledge of democratic citizenship.

A teacher who sees herself as a democratic public intellectual organizes her classroom in ways that model democratic deliberation and decision-making. She prioritizes the participation of all students, and her teaching ensures that dissenting voices and divergent thinking are respectfully heard. Every voice is valued in her classroom, with a special emphasis on including female students and students from marginalized and stigmatized communities in class activities and discussions. Classroom discourse is organized around the principle that interventions must be crafted to persuade, with judgments and conclusions that are not simply asserted, but supported with logical arguments and supporting evidence. Her class focuses on real-life problems and issues, and it does not shy away from controversy, which interests and motivates student in their learning. Debates and disagreements over ideas, and the ability to engage and negotiate those differences—what political philosophers call *agonistic pluralism*—are all seen as essential to a democratic classroom, just as they are essential to a democratic society.[9] These modalities of teaching are not particular to civics, history, and social studies classes, although they are especially important in those contexts, given the subject matter. Rather, they constitute a democratic pedagogy that can and should be employed in all of education. When students learn through a pedagogy of this order, they learn as much about their own potential power as citizens in a democracy, and how to exercise that power, as they do about the particular subject, whatever it may be.

The successful use of a democratic pedagogy does not exist in an educational or political vacuum. It requires more than the teacher's democratic intentions and aspirations; it demands a level of accomplished teaching that comes only from well-honed skills and real classroom experience. There is thus a necessary connection between the discourses of teaching as a profession and teaching as a craft on the one hand, and teaching as democratic intellectual work on the other. Participation in professional and craft-based communities, so important to the refinement of teaching skills, is connected to teaching as democratic intellectual work.

SCHOOLS THAT PROMOTE DEMOCRACY

The professional and craft-based communities that form among teachers in their schools have the greatest impact on teaching in general—and on teaching as democratic intellectual work. For Haley, Dewey, and other first-generation teacher unionists, the practical intellectual work of teaching had a critical purpose of creating, organizing, and operating schools that employed democratic practices to promote egalitarianism and democratic governance in the larger society. In their view, democratic educational practices in schools and classrooms were by no means automatic or inevitable, but with hard work, they could be achieved. George Counts, the leading mid-century American educator after Dewey, addressed this issue in a famous 1932 tract, *Dare the School Build A New Social Order?*[10] For Counts, who was elected AFT president in a battle for the future of the union between the democratic left, of which he was part, and the authoritarian left of the Communist Party, the question was not whether the school *could* have a critical, democratic function vis-à-vis the established powers, but whether it *dared* to do so.

Despite the generally lukewarm and even hostile responses of educational bureaucracies to experiments in democratic schooling, teacher unionists have always found ways to establish demonstration proofs of what could be done. These proofs took the form both of schools within the existing public school system—such as Benjamin Franklin High

School (discussed in chapter 7)—and independent schools outside of it—such as John Dewey's laboratory school at the University of Chicago and the Manumit School (see chapter 5).[11] These were schools premised on the idea of education "as if citizenship mattered."[12]

In recent years, a new generation of demonstration proofs of democratic schools have been established by teacher unionists and union-supportive educators such as Ann Cook, Deborah Meier, Peter Steinberg, and Claire Sylvan, among others; networks such as the Coalition of Essential Schools, New York's Performance Assessment Consortium, the Internationals Network for Public Schools, and the Bard Early College High Schools contain scores of these schools from across the country.[13] While democratic schools do not, of course, follow an identical pattern in pedagogy, curriculum, or organization, similar themes appear frequently, such as teaching students to think critically through inquiry learning and the "habits of mind" outlined in Meier's *The Power of Their Ideas*, building strong organic ties with community, and giving teachers real voice in educational decision-making.[14] Notably, these schools are all small schools dedicated to a politics of caring.

There are two distinct senses of the term *democratic* that could be used to characterize the schools described above—first, as a matter of their constitution, their internal decision-making, culture, and relationships are democratic; and second, as a matter of their relationship to the community and society, they are a democratic and democratizing presence. These two senses of democracy are frequently intertwined, and not just in this set of schools. As a practical matter, democratic habits and sensibilities are not easily contained within a particular domain of an institution or a society; they are of their very nature politically contagious, with a tendency to spread to broader and broader horizons. Those who have been excluded from ostensibly "universal" principles of democracy such as liberty, equality, and solidarity demand that they be applied to them. Over time, they have had a measure of success—never complete and never irreversible, but still real success—in achieving those demands in education, as in other parts of society. Yet it is still useful to draw a distinction between these two senses of a democratic school in order to pay particular attention to the second sense of the term. As I have noted, the quality of the relationships between a school and its teachers on the one hand, and its students, their families, and their community on the other is at the core of establishing a democratic professionalism, and of building partnership with community. A discourse of teaching as democratic intellectual work must pay particular attention to them.

In chapter 6, I showed how these matters were at the center of a particularly trying moment in the history of teacher unions during the 1970s, when the mutual alienation of community and union was at its height, to the detriment of both sides. In more recent decades, relationships between unions and communities have been rebuilt and strengthened through common work and solidaristic support of each other's campaigns and issues, a process that over time establishes and reinforces trust. It is the community engagement work of the AFT and teacher unions around the country—the bargaining for the common good and the work with community groups and civil rights organizations—that has rebuilt community-union ties. While an intellectual analysis of the underlying issues is no substitute for that on-the-ground relationship building, it can shed light on what led to conflict and what can be done to ensure that it does not recur. It is particularly important because it lays out a normative basis for how public education in a democratic society should function, rather than simply criticizing the shortcomings in its current governance. Such a vision is an important part of a discourse of teaching as democratic intellectual work.

The intellectual crux of the problem lies in the thin and poorly conceived concept of democracy—as majoritarian, or purely procedural—that is too often employed in education. In this view, a particular group—educators, parents, local communities, or elected officials and their appointees—is understood as possessing the right to govern public education, and all decision-making power is vested in the representatives of that group, with the expectation that they speak for its majority. A series of defective approaches to education are produced—syndicalist (educator control), paternalist (parental control), populist (local community control), and bureaucratic statist (control by elected officials through their appointees, such as mayoral control of schools). Generally speaking, this is more a question of how educational governance is approached in practice, rather than an explicit political statement, which would be widely viewed as a power grab, and so is avoided. Consequently, it is in practice that these approaches invariably come into conflict with each other, as much because of what they share—the idea that decision-making power should be vested solely in representatives of a chosen group—as because of how they differ—which group should have that power. The story of the divisive Ocean Hill-Brownsville and Newark strikes of the late 1960s and early 1970s is in no small part the story of competing claims in this vein on effective control of the public schools.

The shortcomings of these approaches extend well beyond their common unwillingness to recognize the legitimate claims of other stakeholders to a voice in the educational decision-making process. A fully democratic system of governance for education cannot consist solely in the sharing of decision-making power, as important and necessary as that sharing is. A more robust vision is required, one that starts with the acknowledgment that democracy has a substantive and normative content—the establishment and maintenance of a political society in which all citizens ("we the people") share in ruling.

For citizens to share in ruling, the political and governmental structures, including education, must enable them to do so. The denial of the rights and duties of citizenship to some Americans and the suppression of free inquiry, expression, and association are anathema to democracy, even when they are authorized by a particular majority at a particular time. Such practices strike at the very core of a society in which all citizens share in decision-making, either by excluding significant segments of the citizenry from that rule or by restricting the ability of citizens to communicate freely and engage in meaningful deliberation. For example, in this normative vision of a democracy, laws that restrict the ability of some citizens to vote and have an equal voice in establishing the government are understood as fundamentally anti-democratic and illegitimate, regardless of the procedures employed to enact them. Stated in an affirmative form, democracy has as part of its necessary foundation what I call an *equality principle* (full rights and duties for all citizens) and a *liberty principle* (freedom of inquiry, expression, and association for all citizens). Without these two principles, the citizenry cannot rule in a meaningful way.

Public schools must be designed to nurture citizens' capacity for democratic self-rule. In the words of New York State's highest court in the Campaign for Fiscal Equity case, public school students should be educated, at a minimum, with the knowledge and skills necessary for them to function "as civic participants capable of voting and serving on a jury."[15] Given this primary function, public schools must also be constrained by the same substantive principles as democratic government. In her study *Democratic Education*, Amy Gutmann puts the issue in these useful terms: Public schools should be limited by tenets of non-discrimination (the equality principle) and non-repression (the liberty principle). "The principle of non-repression prevents the state, and any group within it, from using education to restrict rational deliberation of competing conceptions of the good life and good society," Gutmann maintains, and the principle of non-discrimination demands that "all educable children must be educated."[16]

No stakeholder can violate these principles, I contend, and still claim to be operating within the terms of a fully democratic conception of education. This truth of this maxim quickly becomes apparent when one considers what would appear to be the strongest case for unequivocal majoritarian control of educational policy, the one put forward by the state itself—that is, by the elected officials who are the representatives of the public that finances public education. It was this claim that undergirded the top-down mandates of No Child Left Behind and Race to the Top and the moves toward mayoral control and state takeovers in the "education reforms" of the last two decades. The rapprochement between teacher unions and communities over the last two decades was accelerated by their common recognition that the policies that led to growing state power in public education were excluding both groups of stakeholders from a meaningful voice in education decision-making. To understand the fallacious nature of the claim that direct governmental control is democratic education, it is necessary to examine the place of public education in a modern democratic order.

PUBLIC SCHOOLS IN CIVIL SOCIETY

One of the defining characteristics of democratic government is the separation of the state from civil society—the civic associations and networks that are independent of direct state control. These civic bodies range from unions, churches, political organizations, and social movements to cooperatives, neighborhood associations, and, I argue, public schools.[17] Since the individual citizen in isolation is powerless against the powerful modern state, these civic bodies—citizens in combination—are the primary means of significantly checking the power of that state, curbing its tendencies toward authoritarian rule, and mobilizing democratic power to control it. Where the modern state must of necessity possess and use the power of coercion, civil society is much more the realm of the consensus.[18] Consequently, a primary indicator of the authoritarianism of a state is the extent to which it undermines the independence of civil society, endeavoring to bring these civic bodies under its direct command and coercive power.

Civil society is the foundation of a robust and vibrant public life. As I noted in chapter 10, from their earliest days, teacher unions have sought to carve out a political space for public education that is as much a part of civil society, with a significant degree of autonomy from direct control of the government, as it is part of the state. As the place where future citizens first learn the civic knowledge, skills, and dispositions that make their participation in public life and in the democratic rule of the state possible, the public school needs that relative autonomy. Since young people must learn "not just to behave in accordance with authority, but to think critically about authority if they are to live up to the democratic ideal of sharing political sovereignty as citizens," direct state interventions that reach down into the very constitution of the school with the objective of controlling teaching and learning endanger the democratic mission of the public school.[19]

It follows that the state must accept the constraints of the equality and liberty principles in educational policy making, and that it must allow a significant degree of authority for professional educators in concert with parents and community members to determine pedagogical and curricular matters, with decisions being made as close to schools and classrooms—to the students—as practicable. While their professional expertise gives educators a leading role in this process, there must be a meaningful voice for parents and the community in these decisions. When the state violates the equality and liberty principles, democratic education is fundamentally compromised. When it ventures into the substance and detail of pedagogical and curricular decisions, it provides poor educational direction, with rigid, top-down formulas and policy more in tune with superficial fads and shifting public opinion than educational needs. At its worst, it produces educational policy designed to thwart critical thinking about authority.

Advocates of school privatization often invoke the perils of state control of education, with misleading talk of public schools as "government schools." In an American political order where four decades of austerity, deregulation, and privatization policies have increasingly given rise to a laissez-faire economy, it is private businesses and corporations—in which power is increasingly unchecked—that are among the most authoritarian entities; and the people who work for them have the fewest rights. The undermining of private-sector unions, the one institution of civil society with the capacity to introduce a measure of economic democracy into the workplace, is a particularly telling indication of this development. That school privatization advocates promote the evisceration of teacher unions as a primary benefit of their policies speaks volumes about their intentions. Yet the freedom of association for teachers and the voice of teachers, parents, and community in decision-making would not be the only targets of school privatization. While the equality and liberty principles are a subject of ongoing contention in public schools, they are an endangered species in private schools. The movement to establish private school vouchers in the United States was developed as part of efforts to resist the mandate of *Brown v. Board of Education* to end de jure racial segregation in public schools.[20] The democratic mission of schools to educate students into democratic citizenship is best delivered from a public space within civil society.

It would be a serious mistake, however, to downplay the ongoing struggle over the democratic character of public education. As a practical matter, American public schools are often governed in ways that violate the principles of equality and liberty. To cite the most troubling example, the maintenance of public schools and school districts that are de facto segregated by race and class—with inferior funding, resources, and supports provided to the schools serving communities of color and high-poverty communities—clearly contravenes the equality principle. For America's public schools, the normative vision of democratic education remains as much aspiration as it is reality. But for teachers acting as democratic public intellectuals and for their unions, that aspiration provides a North Star that guides our work.

CONCLUSION

The Power of Teacher Collective Action

THIS BOOK HAS EXAMINED the Teacher Insurgency through the lens of the strategic challenges confronting it and the discourses of collective identity we as teachers use to understand ourselves and act in the world. The purpose of this examination was to plot a way forward for American teachers and our unions, laying out a path that addresses both the immediate issues that gave rise to the Teacher Insurgency and the contested future of teaching and public education that underlies those issues. Given this focus, teacher agency—the power of teacher collective action—has been at the heart of this study.

The strategic challenges posed by the Teacher Insurgency are questions of what we teachers should collectively do to build our power, especially through our unions, so we can change our schools and our society for the better. What is the work of mobilization and the work of organization, and in what ways are both forms of work central to collective action? What is the relationship between mobilization and organization, and what role does social media play in that relationship? What is the relationship between protest and politics? How and when should we use the two different forms of collective action—direct action and electoral politics? What does each form of action accomplish, and how can synergy between them optimized? How should we organize our strikes to maximize their success? And how should we work in partnerships with community? These are the strategic challenges we face, and each requires choices on the political roads we will take.

Drawing back to a wider lens, the discourses of teacher identity are the primary social media through which we understand ourselves as teachers, and through which we then act as teachers in our classrooms, our schools, and the world, both individually and collectively. As teachers, we are both the subject and the object, the producer and the product of these discourses. When we organize for collective action, we use these discourses to bring ourselves together and accomplish important purposes we share. At the same time, we seek to change for the better the material practices, such as teaching, and the institutions, such as schools, in which these discourses are embedded. The work of teachers organizing is in no small measure the suturing together of these discourses of nurturance, of professionalism, of labor and craft, and of a vocation of democratic intellectual work, melding them into a single collective teacher identity that draws on the solidaristic and democratic components of each discourse.

In the course of this examination, I have drawn on a rich history of teacher organizing and teacher collective action, with illustrative examples of how teachers have worked to realize that original slogan of the AFT—"Education in Democracy, Democracy for Education." It is not a simple narrative; there have been setbacks as well as advances, and the best of intentions have not always produced positive results. But there are important lessons to be learned both from defeat as well as victory.

Notwithstanding the powerful evidence of this work and more, teacher agency is often missing in scholarly writing on teachers and schools, even among those who imagine themselves as the authors of radical critiques of American education. There are those who insist that schools and teachers inevitably reproduce the inequalities of the existing political and economic order. During the 1960s and 1970s, an age of educational ferment, the leading "radical" account of "schooling in capitalist America"—still widely read and cited today—insisted that schools necessarily reproduce the capitalist system by preparing working class students for a life of subordination in factory jobs.[1] It was an analysis as much structural functionalist, bereft of actual social conflict, as it was Marxian.[2] In this same vein, revisionist histories of American education read its historical trajectory, from the mid-1800s promise of free and universal public education forward, as "ironic" and "illusory," serving the interests of the economically powerful behind a façade of concern for the working class and poor.[3] (The unions of the nineteenth century fought hard for free and universal public education and the abolition of child labor, linking the two as essential democratic reforms, but insofar as these unions appear in revisionist narratives, it is in passing, as unwitting tools of the wealthy.) More recently, a Foucauldian lens has been employed to see schools as "total institutions" operating under the same logic as prisons and psychiatric asylums, with teachers employing discipline and intrusive surveillance to shape students into "docile bodies."[4]

What these accounts have in common is a radical gloss on a fundamentally conservative denial of teacher agency, a disavowal of the capacity of teachers to engage in collective action for progressive and democratic ends.[5] Like all social actors, as teachers, we are constrained by the conditions under which we act. We can dare to engage in democratic teaching and create schools for a democratic order, but that work is at many times difficult precisely because it often cuts against the grain of the larger society, especially in an age of an authoritarian populism fueled by racism. Only those who have never actually tried to reform student conduct practices, and to end the discriminatory and punitive policies of zero tolerance, for example, can imagine that such democratic changes in the culture of schooling are easy work, especially when they call into question the social mores that have fueled decades of mass incarceration. Edicts delivered from on high do none of the hard work that must take place in schools, and they can even be counterproductive when they provide none of the supports or resources necessary for such change. Real democratic change in education is demanding, but possible when teachers take the lead and engage in collective action. That is the most important lesson of the Teacher Insurgency, and it is the one I now leave with the reader.

Notes

CHAPTER 1

1. On the fight against Scott Walker's anti-union laws in Wisconsin, see *We Are Wisconsin: The Wisconsin Uprising in the Words of the Activists, Writers, and Everyday Wisconsinites Who Made It Happen*, ed. Erica Sagrans (Minneapolis: Tasora Books, 2011); and John Nichols, *Uprising: How Wisconsin Renewed the Politics of Protest, from Madison to Wall Street* (New York: Nation Books, 2012).
2. Noam Scheiber and Kenneth P. Vogel, "Behind a Key Anti-Labor Case, a Web of Conservative Donors," *New York Times*, February 25, 2018, www.nytimes.com/2018/02/25/business/economy/labor-court-conservatives.html; Celine McNicholas and Zane Mokhiber, "Who's Behind the Janus Lawsuit?" *American Prospect*, February 26, 2018, prospect.org/justice/behind-janus-lawsuit/; Mary Bottari, "Behind Janus: Documents Reveal Decade-Long Plot to Kill Public-Sector Unions," *In These Times*, March 2018, inthesetimes.com/features/janus_supreme_court_unions_investigation.html.
3. Madeline Will, "See How Your State's Average Teacher Salary Compares," *Education Week*, April 24, 2018, blogs.edweek.org/edweek/teacherbeat/2018/04/teacher_pay_2017.html.
4. There are a number of published narratives of the West Virginia strike, often combined with the other strikes of the teacher spring. Steve Greenhouse's recent book *Beaten Down, Worked Up: The Past, Present, and Future of American Labor* (New York: Knopf, 2019) contains an informative chapter (chapter 20) on the subject. See also Diane Ravitch's *Slaying Goliath: The Passionate Resistance to Privatization and the Fight to Save America's Public Schools* (New York: Knopf, 2020), chapter 15. While it will become clear over the course of this book that I disagree with the theoretical framework that informs Eric Blanc's *Red State Revolt: The Teachers' Strike Wave and Working-Class Politics* (New York: Verso, 2019), his account of the strikes of the Teacher Spring should also be read. I have found particularly useful a collection of first-person accounts written by West Virginia teachers themselves: Elizabeth Catte, Emily Hilliard, and Jessica Salfia, ed., *55 Strong: Inside the West Virginia Teachers' Strike* (Cleveland, OH: Belt Publishing, 2018). The collection allows the reader to see the events from different teacher vantage points in different parts of the state, while many other published narratives are seen through the eyes of only a small number of teachers.

5. For national coverage, see Josh Delk, "Hundreds of Teachers Hold Walkout, Protest in West Virginia," *The Hill*, February 2, 2018, thehill.com/homenews/state-watch/371989-hundreds-of-teachers-hold-walkout-protest-in-west-virgina.
6. Jay O'Neal, in *55 Strong*, 22.
7. Personal communication with Bob Morgenstern, AFT Regional Representative with responsibility for West Virginia.
8. As quoted in Mitch Smith and Monica Davey, "Chicago Teachers' Strike, Longest in Decades, Ends," *New York Times*, October 31, 2019, www.nytimes.com/2019/10/31/us/chicago-cps-teachers-strike.html.

CHAPTER 2

1. State education spending has been calculated in slightly different ways, but the ratio between the state spending the most per student and the state spending the least in different measures is consistently in the vicinity of 3:1. A 2019 report of the Albert Shanker Institute and Rutgers Graduate School of Education explores this issue in depth; see Bruce Baker, Matt Di Carlo, and Mark Weber, "The Adequacy and Fairness of State School Finance Systems," www.shankerinstitute.org/resource/adequacy-and-fairness-state-school-finance-systems. Similarly, *Education Week* places Vermont at the top of a list of state funding for education at $20,795 and Utah at the bottom at $7207 ("Per Pupil Funding, State by State" in *Education Week*'s Quality Counts 2018, www.edweek.org/ew/collections/quality-counts-2018-state-finance/map-per-pupil-spending-state-by-state.html). There are a few states with smaller tax bases that punch above their weight in funding education and a few states with larger tax bases that do not fund education at their capacity; but as a general rule, the wealthier states provide more substantial funding for education.
2. Bruce Baker, *Educational Inequality and School Finance: Why Money Matters for America's Students* (Cambridge, MA: Harvard Education Press, 2018).
3. Kim Phillips-Fein, *Fear City: New York's Fiscal Crisis and the Rise of Austerity Politics* (New York: Henry Holt, 2017).
4. Vanessa Rancaño, "How Proposition 13 Transformed Neighborhood Public Schools Throughout California," KQED *California Dream* Report, Oct 25, 2018, www.kqed.org/news/11701044/how-proposition-13-transformed-neighborhood-public-schools-throughout-california.
5. William Evans, Robert Schwab, and Kathryn Wagner, "The Great Recession and Public Education," *Education Finance and Policy* 14, no. 2 (Spring 2019): 298–326: doi:10.1162/edfp_a_00245.
6. American Federation of Teachers, *A Decade of Neglect: Public Education Funding in the Aftermath of the Great Recession* (Washington, DC: AFT, July 2018), 4, www.aft.org/sites/default/files/decade-of-neglect-2018.pdf. Dollar figures are adjusted for inflation.
7. The best overview of these developments is found in AFT, *A Decade of Neglect*.
8. AFT, *A Decade of Neglect*, 5. Originally, 300,000 positions were lost; at the point that the Teacher Spring emerged, most of those positions had yet to be restored.
9. AFT, *A Decade of Neglect*, 5.

10. AFT, *A Decade of Neglect* (California and Oklahoma State Reports).
11. Alanna Fuschillo, "The Troubling Student-to-Counselor Ratio That Doesn't Add Up," *Education Week*, August 14, 2018, www.edweek.org/ew/articles/2018/08/14/the-troubling-student-to-counselor-ratio-that-doesnt-add.html; National Association for College Admission Counseling (NACAC) and the American School Counselor Association (ASCA), *State-By-State Student-to-Counselor Ratio Report*, n.d., www.schoolcounselor.org/asca/media/asca/Publications/ratioreport.pdf.
12. American Society of Civil Engineers, "2017 Infrastructure Report Card: Schools," www.infrastructurereportcard.org/wp-content/uploads/2017/01/Schools-Final.pdf.
13. Council of Great City Schools, "Reversing the Cycle of Deterioration in the Nation's Public School Buildings," October 2014, www.cgcs.org/cms/lib/DC00001581/Centricity/Domain/87/FacilitiesReport2014.pdf.
14. Kenneth Shores and Matthew Steinburg, "The Impact of the Great Recession on Student Achievement: Evidence from Population Data," Stanford Center for Education Policy Analysis, posted August 31, 2017, ssrn.com/abstract=3026151; C. Kirabo Jackson, Cora Wigger, and Heyu Xiong, "Do School Spending Cuts Matter? Evidence from the Great Recession," Working Paper no. 24203 (Washington, DC: National Bureau of Education Research, January 2018), www.nber.org/papers/w24203.
15. Lauren Camera, "Teacher Salaries Fell 4.5% Over the Last Decade," *US News and World Report*, April 29, 2019, www.usnews.com/news/education-news/articles/2019-04-29/teacher-salaries-fell-45-over-the-last-decade; AFT, *A Decade of Neglect*, 5.
16. Lisette Partelow and Abby Quirk, "Strikes Driving Change in States with Lowest-Paid Teachers," Policy Brief (Washington, DC: Center for American Progress, April 16, 2019), www.americanprogress.org/issues/education-k-12/news/2019/04/16/468000/strikes-driving-change-states-lowest-paid-teachers/.
17. Sylvia Allegretto and Lawrence Mishel, *The Teacher Weekly Wage Penalty Hit 21.4% in 2018, A Record High* (Washington DC: Economic Policy Institute, April 2019), www.epi.org/165729; Bruce D. Baker, Matthew Di Carlo, and Mark Weber, *School Finance and Teacher Pay Competitiveness*, Research Brief of the School Finance Indicators Database, a joint project of the Albert Shanker Institute and Rutgers University Graduate School of Education, Washington DC, July 2019), schoolfinancedata.org/wp-content/uploads/2019/07/SFID_TeacherWageBrief_July2019.pdf. The results of these studies are generally quite consistent; I have cited the estimate of the EPI report, since the EPI report is limited to public school teachers, while the School Finance Indicators Database brief includes both public and private school teachers in its calculations.
18. Emma Garcia and Elaine Weiss, "Low Relative Pay and High Incidence of Moonlighting Play a Role in Teacher Shortage," in *The Perfect Storm in the Teacher Labor Market* (part 3) (Washington DC: Economic Policy Institute, 2019), www.epi.org/161908; Jaime Lowe, "The Second Shift: What Teachers Do to Pay Their Bills," *New York Times Magazine*, September 9, 2018, www.nytimes.com/interactive/2018/09/06/magazine/teachers-america-second-jobs.html; Katie Reilly, "'I Work 3 Jobs and Donate Blood Plasma to Pay the Bills.' This Is What It's Like to Be a Teacher in America," *Time Magazine*, September 13, 2018, time.com/longform/teaching-in-america/.

19. Monique Morrissey, *Teachers and Schools Are Well Served by Teacher Pensions* (Washington DC: Economic Policy Institute, October 17, 2019), www.epi.org/136634.
20. Donna St. George, "Kentucky Teachers Shut Down Multiple School Systems in Uproar over Pension Bill," *Washington Post*, March 30, 2018, www.washingtonpost.com/local/education/kentucky-teachers-shut-down-multiple-school-systems-in-uproar-over-pension-bill/2018/03/30/00d8697e-3421-11e8-94fa-32d48460b955_story.html.
21. Leo Casey, "The Will to Quantify: The 'Bottom Line' in the Market Model of Education Reform," *Teachers College Record*, 115, no. 9 (2013): 1–7.
22. Shannon Ryan et al., "Leaving the Teaching Profession: The Role of Teacher Stress and Educational Accountability Policies on Turnover Intent," *Teaching and Teacher Education* 66 (August 2017): 1–11, doi:10.1016/j.tate.2017.03.016; Nathaniel von der Embse et al., "Teacher Stress, Teaching-Efficacy, and Job Satisfaction in Response to Test-Based Educational Accountability Policies," *Learning and Individual Differences* 50 (August 2016): 308–317, doi:10.1016/j.lindif.2016.08.001; Elina Saeki et al., "The Influence of Test-Based Accountability Policies on Early Elementary Teachers: School Climate, Environmental Stress, and Teacher Stress," *Psychology in the Schools* 55, no. 4 (February 2018): 492–502, doi:10.1002/pits.22112.
23. Frederick Winslow Taylor's system of "scientific management" undermined worker control of the labor process in craft manufacturing by breaking down the labor process into a series of discrete physical actions that could be continuously repeated on an assembly line. For an overview of the effort to introduce scientific management into early twentieth-century public schools, see Raymond Callahan's *Education and the Cult of Efficiency: A Study of the Social Forces That Have Shaped the Administration of the Public Schools* (Chicago: University of Chicago Press, 1962). An important account of how teachers responded to the imposition of factory model schooling can be found in Richard Altenbaugh, "Teachers and the Workplace" in *The Teacher's Voice: A Social History of Teaching in Twentieth-Century America*, ed. Richard J. Altenbaugh (London: Falmer Press, 1992, 155–169).
24. Margaret Haley, "Why Teachers Should Organize," *Journal of Education* 60, no. 13 (September 1904): 215–216, 222, doi:10.1177/002205740406001303.
25. For an overview of these issues, see Richard Ingersoll, *Who Controls Teachers' Work? Power and Accountability in America's Schools* (Cambridge, MA: Harvard University Press, 2003).
26. Manuel Castells, *Communication Power* (Oxford: Oxford University Press, 2013); and *The Rise of the Network Society* (Cambridge: Blackwell, 1996).
27. Castells, *Communication Power*, 30.
28. Emma Garcia and Elaine Weiss, *U.S. Schools Struggle to Hire and Retain Teachers: The Perfect Storm in the Teacher Labor Market* (part 2) (Washington, DC: Economic Policy Institute, 2019), 6–7, www.epi.org/164773.
29. Sam Fulwood III, "Teachers Quit Their Jobs in Record Numbers During 2018," *ThinkProgress*, December 30, 2018, thinkprogress.org/teachers-quit-their-jobs-in-record-numbers-during-2018-497f2162b3a6/; Bureau of Labor Statistics JOLTS (Job Openings and Labor Turnover Survey), www.bls.gov/jlt/jlt_table1_dec2018.txt.
30. International comparisons cannot be made with precision, given the absence of a single study employing the same definitions and measures of teacher attrition

across all OECD nations. But the magnitude of the different national estimates found in various studies is such that it must be noted. Richard M. Ingersoll et al., *Seven Trends: The Transformation of the Teaching Force* (Washington, DC: Consortium for Policy Research in Education Research Report, 2018:18–21, repository.upenn.edu/cpre_researchreports/108.; Elka Torpey, "Projections for Teachers: How Many Are Leaving the Occupation?," *Career Outlook*, U.S. Bureau of Labor Statistics, October 2018, www.bls.gov/careeroutlook/2018/data-on-display/how-many-teachers-are-leaving.htm; John Ainley and Ralph Carstens, *Teaching and Learning International Survey (TALIS) 2018 Conceptual Framework*, OECD Education Working Paper no. 187, 22, www.oecd.org/officialdocuments/publicdisplaydocumentpdf/?cote=EDU/WKP(2018)23&docLanguage=En.

31. Leib Sutcher, Linda Darling-Hammond, and Desiree Carver-Thomas, *A Coming Crisis in Teaching? Teacher Supply, Demand, and Shortages in the U.S.*, Learning Policy Institute Brief (September 2016), learningpolicyinstitute.org/sites/default/files/product-files/A_Coming_Crisis_in_Teaching_REPORT.pdf; *U.S. Schools Struggle to Hire and Retain Teachers.*
32. *Frustration in the Schools: Teachers Speak Out on Pay, Funding, and Feeling Valued*, 51st Annual PDK Poll of the Public's Attitudes toward the Public Schools (September 2019), pdkpoll.org/assets/downloads/2019pdkpoll51.pdf.

CHAPTER 3

1. What I say about millennials is also true of the subsequent Generation Z, but they are just starting to enter the teaching force and are not yet present in significant numbers (Noah Smith, "Why Millennials Are Sour on the Economy," *Bloomberg Opinion*, September 28, 2018, www.bloomberg.com/opinion/articles/2018-09-28/why-lots-of-americans-are-sour-on-the-economy). Unlike the high income mobility of the post-World War II baby boom generation, in which 90 percent of the cohort earned more than their parents, income mobility among millennials has fallen to 50 percent, with the decline largely attributable to the growth in income inequality over the last half-century (Raj Chetty et al., "The Fading American Dream: Trends in Absolute Income Mobility since 1940," *Science* 356, no. 6336 [April 2017]: 398–406, doi:10.1126/science.aal4617).
2. American Federation of Teachers, "The Student Debt Crisis," www.aft.org/highered/student-debt-crisis; Noah Smith, "Student-Loan Debt Is Crushing Millennials" *Bloomberg Opinion*, November 2, 2018, www.sltrib.com/opinion/commentary/2018/11/06/noah-smith-student-loan/.
3. Julie Margetta Morgan and Marshall Steinbaum, *The Student Debt Crisis, Labor Market Credentialization and Racial Inequality: How the Current Student Debt Debate Gets the Economics Wrong* (New York: Roosevelt Institute, 2018), rooseveltinstitute.org/wp-content/uploads/2018/10/The-Student-Debt-Crisis-and-Labor-Market-Credentialization-final-1.pdf.
4. Bilan Jama, "Unsustainable Trends in Teacher Debt and Teacher Pay," *Shanker Institute Blog*, February 5, 2019, www.shankerinstitute.org/blog/unsustainable-trends-teacher-debt-and-teacher-pay.

5. Sylvia Allegretto and Lawrence Mishel, *The Teacher Weekly Wage Penalty Hit 21.4% in 2018, A Record High* (Washington DC: Economic Policy Institute, April 2019), www.epi.org/165729.
6. Drew DeSilver, *Most Americans View Unions Favorably, Though Few Workers Belong to One* (Washington, DC: Pew Research Center, August 30, 2018), www.pewresearch.org/fact-tank/2018/08/30/union-membership-2/; Lydia Saad, "Labor Union Approval Steady at 15-Year High," Gallup, August 30, 2018, https//:news.gallup.com/poll/241679/labor-union-approval-steady-year-high.aspx; "Millennials and Public Education in the United States," GenForward Survey (2018), genforwardsurvey.com/assets/uploads/2018/10/GenForward_2018_Education_Slides_FINAL_1539746737-1.pdf.
7. Vladimir Medencia, Matthew Fowler, and Cathy Cohen, "What Young Adults Think About the Economy—And Why It Matters for 2020," *Washington Post, Monkey Cage* (blog), June 4, 2019, www.washingtonpost.com/politics/2019/06/04/what-young-adults-think-about-economy-why-it-matters/; Harold Meyerson, "The Return of American Socialism" *American Prospect* (Fall 2018), prospect.org/article/return-american-socialism; and Hannah Hartig, "Stark Partisan Divisions in Americans' Views of 'Socialism,' 'Capitalism'," *Factank* (Pew Research Center), June 25, 2019, https://pewrsr.ch/2FxuzJ7.
8. Maddie Sach, "Why the Democrats Have Shifted Left over the Last 30 Years," *FiveThirtyEight* (blog), December 16, 2019, fivethirtyeight.com/features/why-the-democrats-have-shifted-left-over-the-last-30-years/.
9. Ted Gurr, *Why Men Rebel* (Princeton: Princeton University Press, 1970); J. C. Davies, "The J-Curve of Rising and Declining Satisfactions as a Cause of Some Great Revolutions and a Contained Rebellion" in *Violence in America: The History of Violence in America: Historical and Comparative Perspectives*, ed. Hugh Graham and Ted Gurr (New York: Praeger, 1969): 690–730.
10. Ray Quinn, "WV School Employee Strike Explained," *Charleston Gazette-Mail*, February 24, 2018, www.wvgazettemail.com/2018_wv_teachers_strike/wv-school-employee-strike-explained/article_5fcf9fbd-4594-5262-adbf-00dcad6adf2e.html. In the other noteworthy case of a statewide strike action, Florida teachers engaged in a mass resignation in 1968. Theresa Vargas, "The Day Florida Teachers Resigned en Masse in the Country's First Statewide Strike, " *Washington Post*, February 22, 2018, www.washingtonpost.com/news/retropolis/wp/2018/02/18/from-meek-to-militant-the-florida-teachers-strike-that-unsettled-a-nation-and-fueled-a-movement/. There have been a few instances of citywide general strikes in American history——the most noteworthy being Seattle in 1919, Minneapolis and San Francisco in 1934, and Oakland in 1946——but they all developed out of private-sector conflicts. Strikes against state governments have a different character and, until Teacher Spring, were rarer.
11. C. Wright Mills, "Letter to the New Left," *New Left Review* 1, no. 5 (September–October 1960): 18–23, https://newleftreview.org/issues/I5.
12. Dana Goldstein and Ben Casselman, "Teachers Find Public Support as Campaign for Higher Pay Goes to Voters," *New York Times*, May 31, 2018, www.nytimes.com/2018/05/31/us/politics/teachers-campaign.html; the 2018 Phi Delta Kappa/Gallup poll found that 73 percent of the general public and 78 percent of public school parents supported the 2018 Teacher Spring strikes, kappanonline.org/wp

-content/uploads/2018/08/PDK-Poll-2018.pdf. The 2019 Phi Delta Kappa/Gallup poll, taken after the 2019 strikes, showed no decline in public support for teacher strikes over issues of school funding, teacher pay, and teacher voice in educational decisions (pdkpoll.org/assets/downloads/2019pdkpoll51.pdf).

Similar results were found in statewide polls in 2018, as with the high-profile Los Angeles strike of 2019. Mason Stockstill, "Strong Majority of Los Angeles County Residents Supports Teachers' Strike, LMU Survey Finds," *LMU Newsroom*, January 15, 2019, newsroom.lmu.edu/2019/01/15/strong-majority-los-angeles-county-residents-supports-teachers-strike-lmu-survey-finds/.

13. Jon Shelton, *Teacher Strike! Public Education and the Making of a New American Political Order* (Champaign: University of Illinois Press, 2017).
14. William J. Bennett and Karen Nussle, "No, Teacher Strikes Do Not Help Students," *Education Week*, May 15, 2018, www.edweek.org/ew/articles/2018/05/16/no-teacher-strikes-do-not-help-students.html; Moriah Balingit, "Betsy DeVos to Oklahoma Teachers: 'Serve the Students,'" *Washington Post*, April 9, 2008, www.washingtonpost.com/news/education/wp/2018/04/09/betsy-devos-to-oklahoma-teachers-serve-the-students/; Arne Duncan, "Democrats in California Need to Lead on Education," *The Hill*, December 26, 2018, thehill.com/blogs/congress-blog/education/422847-democrats-in-california-need-to-lead-on-education.
15. *Time Magazine* covers, December 8, 2008, and September 13, 2018; Joel Klein, "The Failure of American Schools," *The Atlantic*, June 2011, www.theatlantic.com/magazine/archive/2011/06/the-failure-of-american-schools/308497/; Nick Hanauer, "Better Schools Won't Fix America," *The Atlantic*, July 2019, www.theatlantic.com/magazine/archive/2019/07/education-isnt-enough/590611/.
16. Families for Excellent Schools was found to have violated the Massachusetts campaign finance law in this campaign; heavy fines and the revelations of its major "dark money" donors forced it to close (Michael Levenson, "Pro-Charter School Group Pays State's Largest Campaign Finance Penalty," *Boston Globe*, September 11, 2017, www.bostonglobe.com/metro/2017/09/11/pro-charter-school-group-pays-state-largest-campaign-finance-penalty/uQlWnaSnOC6CeHma74cPqN/story.html; Kate Taylor, "Charter School Group, Known for Battling the Mayor, Will Close" *New York Times*, February 5, 2018, www.nytimes.com/2018/02/05/nyregion/families-excellent-schools-deblasio-closing.html).
17. The Walton Education Coalition was sponsored by the Walton family (founders and owners of Walmart). The Coalition memo in question was retrieved from www.documentcloud.org/documents/4442316-WaltonQuestion2Full.html.
18. Sarah Schwartz, "In Historic Win, Nationally Recognized Teacher Jahana Hayes Elected to U.S. House," *Education Week*, November 7, 2018, www.edweek.org/ew/articles/2018/11/06/in-historic-win-nationally-recognized-teacher-jahana.html; Sophia Bollag, "Charter School Backers Spent Millions on Statewide Races in 2018. They Still Lost Twice," *Sacramento Bee*, November 19, 2018, www.edweek.org/ew/articles/2018/11/19/charter-school-backers-spent-millions-on-california.html; David Callahan, "Not Just Philanthropy: For Top Charter School Backers, Political Giving Is Seen as Key" *Inside Philanthropy*, November 18, 2108, www.insidephilanthropy.com/home/2018/11/8/not-just-philanthropy-for-top-charter-school-backers-political-giving-is-seen-as-key.

19. Phil Kabler, "Despite Some Changes, Legislature Remains in GOP Hands," *Charleston Gazette-Mail*, November 7, 2018, www.wvgazettemail.com/election_2018/legislature_2018/despite-some-changes-legislature-remains-in-gop-hands/article_198669d2-95bc-5ffb-8366-19da469e6089.html; Eric Levitz, "Oklahoma Teachers Just Purged the Statehouse of Their Enemies," *Intelligencer*, August 29, 2018, nymag.com/intelligencer/2018/08/teachers-strikes-oklahoma-gop-primaries-house-2018-elections.html; Madeline Will, "With Successful Strikes Behind Them, Teachers Are Now Running for Office," *Education Week*, July 17, 2018, www.edweek.org/ew/articles/2018/07/18/with-successful-strikes-behind-them-teachers-are.html; Katie Reilly, "Most Teachers Running for Office Lost on Tuesday. Here's Why Educators Are Celebrating the 2018 Midterms Anyway," *Time Magazine*, November 9, 2018, time.com/5447995/teacher-education-2018-midterm-elections/; Madeline Will and Sarah Schwartz, "Dozens of Teachers Were Elected to State Office. Many More Fell Short," *Education Week*, November 9, 2018, www.edweek.org/ew/articles/2018/11/08/dozens-of-teachers-were-elected-to-state.html.
20. Alexia Fernández Campbell, "How the Teachers Strikes Gave Democrats a Win in Deep Red Kentucky," *Vox*, November 6, 2019, www.vox.com/identities/2019/11/6/20951459/kentucky-democrat-beshear-bevin-teachers.
21. Michael Leachman and Eric Figueroa, *K–12 School Funding Up in Most 2018 Teacher-Protest States, but Still Well Below Decade Ago* (Washington, DC: Center of Budget and Policy Priorities, March 6, 2019), www.cbpp.org/research/state-budget-and-tax/k-12-school-funding-up-in-most-2018-teacher-protest-states-but-still.
22. Eliza Shapiro, "How New York Stopped Being the Nation's Education Reform Capital," *Politico*, August 7, 2018, www.politico.com/states/new-york/albany/story/2017/08/07/how-new-york-stopped-being-the-nations-education-reform-capital-113548; and Eliza Shapiro, "With Democratic Wins, Charter Schools Face a Backlash in N.Y. and Other States" *New York Times*, November 9, 2018, www.nytimes.com/2018/11/09/nyregion/nyc-charter-schools.html.
23. Rachel Cohen, "The Charter Primary," *American Prospect*, July 15, 2019, prospect.org/article/charter-school-primary.
24. National Association of Charter School Authorizers, "Charter School Openings Have Slowed Dramatically," n.d., www.qualitycharters.org/policy-research/inside-charter-school-growth/openings/; Robin Lake, "Is Charter School Growth Flat-Lining?" *The Lens* (blog), www.crpe.org/thelens/charter-school-growth-flat-lining.
25. I draw here on Gramsci's theory of hegemony (*Selections from the Prison Notebooks of Antonio Gramsci*, ed. Quintin Hoare and Geoffrey Nowell Smith [London: Lawrence & Wishart) 1971]) and Habermas's theory of legitimation crisis (Jürgen Habermas, *Legitimation Crisis* [Boston: Beacon Press, 1975]).
26. For an examination of how charter schools departed from the original vision put forward by American Federation of Teachers President Al Shanker and what would have to be done to return to that vision, see Richard D. Kahlenberg and Halley Potter, "Restoring Shanker's Vision for Charter Schools," *American Educator* 38, no. 4 (Winter 2014–15), www.aft.org/ae/winter2014-2015/kahlenberg_potter.
27. For charter schools that remain true to that original vision, see the web site of the Coalition of Public Independent Charter Schools (CPICS), www.indiecharters.org/.

28. On how "small schools" were captured for market-based education reform, see different analyses by founders and leaders of the small schools movement, including Deborah Meier and Ann Cook, *Rethinking Schools*, 19, no. 4 (Summer 2005), www.rethinkingschools.org/issues/volume-19-no-4-summer-2005.
29. On this new philanthropy in education, see Joanne Barkan, "Got Dough? How Billionaires Rule Our Schools," *Dissent Magazine* 57, no. 1 (Winter 2011), www.dissentmagazine.org/article/got-dough-how-billionaires-rule-our-schools; and "Plutocrats at Work: How Big Philanthropy Undermines Democracy," *Dissent Magazine*, Fall 2013, www.dissentmagazine.org/article/plutocrats-at-work-how-big-philanthropy-undermines-democracy.
30. Barbara Hollingsworth, "Michelle Rhee's Five Year Plan," *Washington Examiner*, June 16, 2010, www.washingtonexaminer.com/michelle-rhees-five-year-plan; Ruth Wattenberg, "Don't Downplay Lessons from D.C. Schools Scandal," *Education Next* blog, March 7, 2001, www.educationnext.org/dont-downplay-lessons-washington-dc-public-schools-scandal/; Rachel Cohen, "How D.C. Became the Darling of Education Reform" *American Prospect*, April 19, 2017, prospect.org/article/how-dc-became-darling-education-reform.
31. Burnie Bond et al., *The State of Teacher Diversity in American Education* (Washington DC: Albert Shanker Institute, 2015), www.shankerinstitute.org/resource/teacherdiversity.
32. For an overview of charter schools, see Leo Casey, "The Charter School Challenge," *New Labor Forum* 24, no. 1 (Winter 2015), newlaborforum.cuny.edu/2015/01/17/the-charter-school-challenge/. On the failure of charter schools to educate their fair share of high-need students, see Gary Miron, "Charters Should Be Expected to Serve All Kinds of Students," *Education Next* 14, no. 4 (Fall 2014), www.educationnext.org/charters-expected-serve-kinds-students/; and Jack Buckley and Carolyn Sattin-Bajaj, "Are ELL Students Underrepresented in Charter Schools?," *Journal of School Choice*. 5, no. 1, (2011): 40–65, doi:10.1080/15582159.2011.548242.
33. See Philip Gleason et al., *The Evaluation of Charter School Impacts: Final Report*, NCEE 2010-4029 (Washington, DC: National Center for Education Evaluation and Regional Assistance, Institute of Education Sciences, US Department of Education, 2015), ies.ed.gov/ncee/pubs/20104029/pdf/20104029.pdf; Melissa Clark et al., "Do Charter Schools Improve Student Achievement?," *Educational Evaluation and Policy Analysis* 37, no. 4 (2015): 419–436, doi: 10.3102/0162373714558292.
34. For example, the unsuccessful 2018 referendum campaign to lift the cap on charter schools in Massachusetts was entirely focused on a subgroup of charter schools in Boston that produced higher test scores. The research supporting the campaign was designed in a way that excluded poorly performing charter schools from its purview.
35. Mark Dynarski and Austin Nichols, *More Findings About School Vouchers and Test Scores, and They Are Still Negative* (Washington, DC: Brookings Institution, July 13, 2017), www.brookings.edu/research/more-findings-about-school-vouchers-and-test-scores-and-they-are-still-negative/.
36. Matt Barnum, "In a Shift, More Education Reformers Say They're Worried About Schools' Focus on Testing," *Chalkbeat*, November 14, 2018, www.chalkbeat.org/posts/us/2018/11/13/education-reformers-shift-their-rhetoric-turning-on-testing/.

37. C. Kirabo Jackson, "The Full Measure of a Teacher: Using Value-Added to Assess Effects on Student Behavior," *Education Next* 19, no. 1 (Winter 2019): 63–68. For a general critique of the testing regime of No Child Left Behind and Race to the Top, see Dan Koretz, *The Testing Charade: Pretending to Make Schools Better* (Chicago: University of Chicago Press, 2017).
38. Valerie Strauss, "The Testing Opt-Out Movement Is Growing, Despite Government Efforts to Kill It," *Washington Post*, January 31, 2016, www.washingtonpost.com/news/answer-sheet/wp/2016/01/31/the-testing-opt-out-movement-is-growing-despite-government-efforts-to-kill-it/; Scott Levy, "Opt-Out Reflects the Genuine Concerns of Parents," *Education Next* 16, no. 4 (Fall 2016): 55–62, www.educationnext.org/opt-out-reflects-genuine-concerns-of-parents-forum-testing/.
39. John Chubb and Terry Moe, *Politics, Markets, and America's Schools* (Washington, DC: Brookings Institution, 1990), 47.
40. Albert O. Hirschman, *Exit, Voice, and Loyalty: Responses to Decline in Firms, Organizations, and States* (Cambridge, MA: Harvard University Press, 1970).
41. Domingo Morel, *Takeover: Race, Education, and American Democracy* (New York: Oxford University Press, 2018); Eve Ewing, *Ghosts in the Schoolyard: Racism and School Closings on Chicago's South Side* (Chicago: University of Chicago Press, 2018); Jelani Cobb, "What's Really at Stake When a School Closes?" *New Yorker*, August 31, 2015, www.newyorker.com/magazine/2015/08/31/class-notes-annals-of-education-jelani-cobb.
42. Bond et al., *The State of Teacher Diversity in American Education*.
43. Elissa Gootman and Robert Gebeloff, "Fewer Children Entering Gifted Programs," *New York Times*, October 29, 2008, www.nytimes.com/2008/10/30/nyregion/30gifted.html; Javier C. Hernández, "Racial Imbalance Persists at Elite Public Schools," *New York Times*, November 7, 2008, www.nytimes.com/2008/11/08/nyregion/08specialized.html; Sharon Otterman and Robert Gebeloff, "When 81% Passing Suddenly Becomes 18%," *New York Times*, August 1, 2010, archive.nytimes.com/www.nytimes.com/imagepages/2010/08/01/education/01schoools-graphic2.html; Sharon Otterman, "Top Public High Schools Admit Fewer Blacks and Hispanics," *New York Times*, February 11, 2011, cityroom.blogs.nytimes.com/2011/02/11/top-public-high-schools-admit-fewer-blacks-and-hispanics/.
44. Tina Moore, "'Life Isn't Always Fair', Mayor Bloomberg Says of NAACP Suit That Claims Blacks and Latinos Are Shut Out of Top City High Schools," *New York Daily News*, September 28, 2012, www.nydailynews.com/new-york/education/life-isn-fair-mayor-bloomberg-naacp-suit-claims-blacks-latinos-shut-top-city-high-schools-article-1.1170106.
45. Daniel J. Losen et al., *Charter Schools, Civil Rights and School Discipline: A Comprehensive Review* (Los Angeles: UCLA Civil Rights Project, 2016), www.civilrightsproject.ucla.edu/resources/projects/center-for-civil-rights-remedies/school-to-prison-folder/federal-reports/charter-schools-civil-rights-and-school-discipline-a-comprehensive-review/losen-et-al-charter-school-discipline-review-2016.pdf; Carly Berwick, "Zeroing Out Zero Tolerance," *The Atlantic*, March 17, 2015, www.theatlantic.com/education/archive/2015/03/zeroing-out-zero-tolerance/388003/.
46. Bruce Baker, *Exploring the Consequences of Charter School Expansion in US Cities* (Washington, DC: Economic Policy Institute, November 2016), www.epi.org/109218.

47. Kristina Rizga, "Why Did Black Lives Matter and the NAACP Call for an End to More Charter Schools?" *Mother Jones*, August 15, 2016, www.motherjones.com/politics/2016/08/black-lives-matter-naacp-moratorium-charter-schools/; Andre Perry, "Why the Black Lives Matter Movement Has to Take on Charter Schools," *Hechinger Report*, August 10, 2016, hechingerreport.org/why-the-black-lives-matter-movement-has-to-take-on-charter-schools/.
48. Klein, "The Failure of American Schools."
49. David Graham, "The Longer Trump Stays in Office, the More Americans Oppose His Views," *Atlantic*, August 19, 2019, www.theatlantic.com/ideas/archive/2019/08/how-trump-reshaping-american-opinion/596335/; Dylan Matthews, "Trump Has Changed How Americans Think About Politics," *Vox*, January 30, 2018, www.vox.com/policy-and-politics/2018/1/30/16943786/trump-changed-public-opinion-russia-immigration-trade.
50. Rachel Cohen, "Education Reform Democrats on Donald Trump," *American Prospect* blog, November 28, 2016, prospect.org/blog/tapped/education-reform-democrats-donald-trump; Eliza Shapiro, "At Odds over Trump, Democrats for Education Reform Chief Resigned from Success Board," *Politico*, August 14, 2017, www.politico.com/states/new-york/city-hall/story/2017/08/14/democrats-for-education-reform-chief-resigns-from-success-academy-board-113916.
51. Dana Goldstein, "What New York City's Biggest School Reformer Sees in Donald Trump," *New Yorker*, November 23, 2016, www.newyorker.com/news/news-desk/what-new-york-citys-biggest-school-reformer-sees-in-donald-trump; Sarah Darville, "Michelle Rhee 'Not Pursuing' Trump Post, but Urges Others to Help Him Succeed," *Chalkbeat*, November 22, 2016, www.chalkbeat.org/posts/us/2016/11/22/michelle-rhee-takes-herself-out-of-the-running-for-trump-post-but-urges-others-to-help-him-succeed/; Eva Moskowitz, Twitter post: twitter.com/moskowitzeva/status/821403806370058240; Cassi Feldman, "Why Charter School Leader Eva Moskowitz, a Democrat, Is Going to Bat for Betsy DeVos," *Chalkbeat*, March 23, 2017, www.chalkbeat.org/posts/ny/2017/03/23/eva-moskowitz-talks-about-betsy-devos-vouchers-discipline-and-how-the-tide-is-turning-for-charter-schools/.
52. Prominent on the Success Academy Board was its then chair, hedge fund tycoon Dan Loeb, who had gained notoriety for asserting that teacher unions and incoming New York State Senate Majority Leader Andrea Stewart-Cousins, an African American, had done more damage to communities of color than the Ku Klux Klan. Among Success Academy's leading financial backers and board members are Trump supporters Robert and Rebekah Mercer, John Paulson, and Julian Robertson. The Mercers were owners of Cambridge Analytica, which played a key role in the Trump campaign and facilitated connections with Russian intelligence during the 2016 presidential campaign. Until Steve Bannon's falling out with Trump, they had been key financial backers of his work, including his editorial direction of Breitbart News.
53. Eliza Shapiro, "Following Months of Criticism, Eva Moskowitz Distances Herself from Trump," *Politico*, August 17, 2017, www.politico.com/states/new-york/albany/story/2017/08/17/following-months-of-criticism-eva-moskowitz-distances-herself-from-trump-113998.

CHAPTER 4

1. A solid account of the UFT's multifaceted support of the civil rights movement can be found in Stephen Lazar, "In Solidarity with Those Which Share Our Purposes: The United Federation of Teachers and the Civil Rights Movement, 1963–1965" (unpublished manuscript, May 2018). In 1964, the UFT awarded King its highest honor, the John Dewey award. In 1967, during a difficult strike where the union was under attack from Black Power advocates H. Rap Brown and Floyd McKissick, King publicly supported the union's stance (Dr. Martin Luther King Jr. to Albert Shanker, September 13, 1967, box 69, folder 23 of UFT Records, Series I. [WAG022] Tamiment Library & Wagner Labor Archives, New York.)
2. On Layle Lane, see Jack Schierenbeck, "Lost and Found: The Incredible Life and Times of (Miss) Layle Lane," in the *American Educator* 24, no. 4 (Winter 2000–2001), www.aft.org/sites/default/files/periodicals/LostandFound_JackSchierenbeck.pdf.
3. On Bayard Rustin, see John D'Emilio, *Lost Prophet: The Life and Times of Bayard Rustin* (Chicago: University of Chicago Press, 2003). Daniel Perlstein's *Justice, Justice: School Politics and the Eclipse of Liberalism* (New York: Peter Lang, 2004) is the best of the literature that uses the frame of the 1968 strike to interpret Rustin's relationship with the UFT.
4. See Sandy Feldman, "In Her Own Words" (Washington, DC: American Federation of Teachers, 2005), www.uft.org/files/attachments/uft-sandy-feldman-memorial.pdf.; and "Sandy Feldman" in *Voices of Freedom: An Oral History of the Civil Rights Movement from the 1950s Through the 1980s*, ed. Henry Hampton and Steve Fayer (New York: Bantam Books, 1990), chapter 26: "Ocean Hill-Brownsville, 1967–68," 489. On the Route 40 Freedom Rides, see Global Nonviolent Action Database, "CORE's Route 40 Project: Maryland Campaign for Desegregation and US Civil Rights," nvdatabase.swarthmore.edu/content/cores-route-40-project-maryland-campaign-desegregation-and-us-civil-rights-1961.
5. On Parrish, see Lazar, "In Solidarity with Those Which Share Our Purposes."
6. On Hill, see Suzanne Popadin, "A Paragon of Activism: Fight for Civil and Workers' Rights Defines Life of Chapter's Founder," *New York Teacher*, March 6, 2019, https://www.uft.org/news/member-spotlight/paragon-activism.
7. Oral history of Nat LaCour, in possession of the author.
8. For the first half century of its existence, the AFT had a no-strike policy, as did the National Education Association (NEA). During this time, strikes were rare, and those that did occur—the most notable being a 1946 strike by the St. Paul Federation of Teachers—did not demand collective bargaining (Cheryl Carlson, "Strike for Better Schools: The St. Paul Public Schools Teachers' Strike of 1946," *Ramsey County History*, 43, no. 2. [Summer 2008]), www.rchs.com/wp-content/uploads/2015/11/RCHS_Summer2008_Carlson.pdf. Similarly, prior efforts at demonstrations in the nation's capital had been suppressed (Coxey's Army in 1894 and the Bonus Army of World War One veterans in 1932) or called off (Randolph's first March on Washington in 1941.) A national demonstration with large numbers of African Americans participating was without precedent; it stoked considerable fear before it occurred.
9. For accounts of the organizing of the 1960 UFT strike, see oral histories of George Altomare and Abe Levine, in possession of the author.

10. For accounts of the organizing of the 1963 March on Washington, see William P. Jones, *The March on Washington: Jobs, Freedom and the Forgotten History of Civil Rights* (New York: W. W. Norton, 2013); Charles Euchner, *Nobody Turn Me Around: A People's History of the 1963 March on Washington* (Boston: Beacon Press, 2010); David Lucander, *Winning the War for Democracy: The March on Washington Movement, 1941–1946* (Champaign: University of Illinois Press; 2014); and "The March on Washington, 1963" in Hampton and Fayer, *Voices of Freedom*.
11. In addition to Randolph, prominent members of NALC included Willoughby Abner and Horace Sheffield of the United Auto Workers, Ernst Calloway of the Teamsters, Charles Hayes and Addie Wyatt of the United Packinghouse Workers, Dick Parrish of the UFT and AFT, Cleve Robinson of District 65, and Maida Springer of the International Ladies Garment Workers Union. The origins of NALC lay in efforts to address racial discrimination and segregation within the labor movement. See Jones, *The March on Washington*, chapter 4.
12. A full description of the Delaney Card system can be found in its Wikipedia entry, en.wikipedia.org/wiki/Delaney_card.
13. Charles Payne, *I've Got the Light of Freedom: The Organizing Tradition and the Mississippi Freedom Struggle* (Berkeley: University of California Press, 1995).
14. A solid account of the mobilization of the Women's March can be found Marie Berry and Erica Chenoweth, "Who Made the Women's March" in *The Resistance: The Dawn of the Anti-Trump Opposition Movement*, ed. David Meyer and Sidney Tarrow (New York: Oxford University Press, 2018).
15. For classical collective action theory, the costs of such action outweighed its benefits, making it "irrational" for individuals to engage it (Mancur Olson, *The Logic of Collective Action: Public Goods and the Theory of Groups* [Cambridge, MA: Harvard University Press, 1965]). Without granting Olson's premises, it is worth noting that social media mobilization changes the terms of the equation, since it significantly lessens the costs of mobilizing collective action.
16. Aniko Bodroghkozy, *Equal Time: Television and the Civil Rights Movement* (Champaign, IL: University of Illinois Press, 2012).
17. Todd Gitlin, *The Whole World Is Watching: Mass Media in the Making and Unmaking of the New Left* (Berkeley: University of California Press, 2003).
18. Jon Shelton, *Teacher Strike! Public Education and the Making of a New American Political Order* (Champaign: University of Illinois Press, 2017).
19. Katerina Eva Matsa and Elisa Shearer, "News Use Across Social Media Platforms," *Pew Research Reports*, September 10, 2018, www.journalism.org/2018/09/10/news-use-across-social-media-platforms-2018/.
20. Zeynep Tufekci, *Twitter and Tear Gas: The Power and Fragility of Networked Protest* (New Haven: Yale University Press, 2017).
21. Hauke Brunkhorst, *Solidarity: From Civic Friendship to Global Legal Community* (Cambridge, MA: MIT Press, 2005).
22. On how social media shapes personal interactions, see Nancy Baym, *Personal Connections in the Digital Age* (Cambridge, MA: Polity Press, 2010).
23. The experiences of Black Lives Matter activists in various online efforts to disrupt their actions is instructive. See Karen Ross and Marcia Mundt, "What Black Lives Matter Activists Can Teach Us About the Pitfalls and Potential of Digital Organizing,"

Waging Nonviolence, March 26, 2019, wagingnonviolence.org/2019/03/the-pitfalls-and-potential-of-digital-organizing-according-to-black-lives-matter-activists/.

24. See, for example, the Twitter community of teachers of color built around the hashtag #educolor.
25. One way of viewing the relative ease with which protest movement connections over geographical distance can be made is that the process through which local protests become generalized, growing into regional and national movements, is greatly facilitated by social media. For an account of the generalization of local protests, see the analysis of the civil rights movement in Doug McAdam, Sidney Tarrow, and Charles Tilly, *Dynamics of Contention* (Cambridge: Cambridge University Press, 2004), chapters 1 and 2.
26. Anna North, "The Women's March Changed the American Left. Now Anti-Semitism Allegations Threaten the Group's Future," *Vox*, December 21, 2018, www.vox.com/identities/2018/12/21/18145176/feminism-womens-march-2018-2019-farrakhan-intersectionality.
27. Manuel Castells, *Networks of Outrage and Hope: Social Movements in the Internet Age* (Cambridge, MA: Polity Press, 2012), 15.
28. Danielle Allen, Joseph Kahne, and Ellen Middaugh, "Youth, New Media, and Participatory Politics," in *From Voice to Influence: Understanding Citizenship in A Digital Age*, ed. Danielle Allen and Jennifer Light (Chicago: University of Chicago Press, 2015).
29. Monica Anderson and Madhumitha Kumar, "Digital Divide Persists Even as Lower-Income Americans Make Gains in Tech Adoption," *Pew Research Center Fact-Tank*, May 7, 2019, pewrsr.ch/2vK1HIo.
30. On race, see Lisa Nakamura and Peter Chow-White, eds., *Race After the Internet* (New York: Routledge, 2012). Danah Boyd ("White Flight in Networked Publics: How Race and Class Shaped American Teen Engagement with MySpace and Facebook, in Nakamura and Chow-White, *Race After the Internet*, 203–222) and Eszter Hargittai ("Open Doors, Closed Spaces? Differentiated Adoption of Social Network Sites by User Background" in Nakamura and Chow-White, *Race After the Internet*, 223–245) speak directly to the question of racialized social media space. On gender, see Baym, *Personal Connections in the Digital Age*, 66–68.
31. Jürgen Habermas, *The Structural Transformation of the Public Sphere: An Inquiry into a Category of Bourgeois Society* (Cambridge, MA: MIT Press,1989). For sympathetic critiques of Habermas that point to the need to recognize the capacity for exclusion and domination in the bourgeois public sphere, see Nancy Fraser, "Rethinking the Public Sphere: A Contribution to the Critique of Actually Existing Democracy" and Seyla Benhabib, "Models of Public Space" in *Habermas and the Public Sphere*, ed. Craig Calhoun (Cambridge, MA: MIT Press, 1992).
32. The virtue of Zeynep Tufekci's *Twitter and Tear Gas*: The Power and Fragility of Networked Protest (New Haven, CT: Yale University Press, 2107) and Jen Schradie's *The Revolution That Wasn't: How Digital Activism Favors Conservatives* (Cambridge, MA: Harvard University Press, 2019) is that they provide a more balanced account of the impact of social media on protest movements.
33. Robert Michels, *Political Parties: A Sociological Study of the Oligarchical Tendencies of Modern Democracy* (Kitchener, ON: Batoche Books, 2001), 241.
34. In *Political Parties*, Michels discusses syndicalism and anarchism at some length

(208–217), arguing that they have an insufficiently complete and thorough going critique of organization, such that they think it is possible to escape its oligarchic tendencies.

35. Frances Fox Piven and Richard Cloward, *Poor People's Movements: How They Succeed, How They Fail* (New York: Vintage Books, 1979).
36. Piven and Cloward, *Poor People's Movements*, xv–xvi.
37. W. Lance Bennett and Alexandra Segerberg, *The Logic of Connective Action: Digital Media and the Personalization of Contentious Politics* (New York: Cambridge University Press, 2013).
38. The politics of Occupy are elaborated in a collection of writings from various activists from its ranks (Kate Khatib, Margaret Killjoy, and Mike McGuire, eds., *We Are Many: Reflection on Movement Strategy from Occupation to Liberation* [Baltimore: AK Press, 2012]). See also the account in Castells (*Networks of Outrage and Hope*, 159–219) which uncritically embraces Occupy's account of itself.
39. Jo Freeman, "The Tyranny of Structureless," 1972, www.jofreeman.com/joreen/tyranny.htm.
40. For an insightful analysis of the problematic nature of efforts to abolish "representative democracy" and establish pure "direct democracy," with the authoritarian consequences, see Nicos Poulantzas, "Towards A Democratic Socialism," in *State, Power, Socialism* (London: Verso Books, 2014), 251–265.
41. On this point, see Allen et al., "Youth, New Media, and Participatory Politics."
42. Hèla Yousfi, *Trade Unions and Arab Revolutions: The Tunisian Case of UGTT* (New York: Routledge, 2017).
43. Schradie, *The Revolution That Wasn't*, chapter 2.

CHAPTER 5

1. This is the view, for example, of Eric Blanc, *Red State Revolt: The Teachers' Strike Wave and Working-Class Politics* (New York: Verso, 2019). This perspective is often advocated for other protest movements. See, for example, Keeanga-Yamahtta Taylor, "Five Years Later, Do Black Lives Matter?," *Jacobin*, September 30, 2019, www.jacobinmag.com/2019/09/black-lives-matter-laquan-mcdonald-mike-brown-eric-garner.
2. Bayard Rustin, "From Protest to Politics: The Future of the Civil Rights Movement," in *Time on Two Crosses: The Collected Writings of Bayard Rustin* (1965; rept. San Francisco: Cleis Press, 2003).
3. Paul LeBlanc and Michael Yates, *A Freedom Budget for All Americans: Recapturing the Promise of the Civil Rights Movement in the Struggle for Economic Justice Today* (New York: Monthly Review Press, 2013). On Rustin's role in developing and promoting the Freedom Budget, see John D'Emilio, *Lost Prophet: The Life and Times of Bayard Rustin* (Chicago: University of Chicago Press, 2004), 430–436.
4. Rustin, "From Protest to Politics."
5. I distinguish here between governmental power and state power, which extends beyond the government and its subordinate agencies. A movement cannot contest state power, however, without first contesting the power to govern through electoral politics. See Richard Healey, "Organizing for Governing Power," paper of Grassroots Policy Project, 2015, grassrootspolicy.org/wp-content/uploads/2017/04/Organizing-for-Governing-Power-RH-copy-Web.pdf.

6. For a detailed overview of the evolving position of the AFL toward electoral politics, see Julie Greene, *Pure and Simple Politics: The American Federation of Labor and Political Activism* (New York: Cambridge University Press, 1998).
7. As quoted in Philip Foner, *The Policies and Practices of the American Federation of Labor, 1900–1909*. Volume III of *History of the Labor Movement in the United States* (New York: International Publishers, 1964), 282. Gompers's views evolved over time, and he would move away from his abstentionism: after World War I, he adopted a "reward your friends, punish your enemies" approach to electoral politics.
8. J. David Greenstone, *Labor in American Politics* (Chicago: University of Chicago Press, 1969), 29.
9. The AFL did not oppose protective workplace legislation that was limited to women and children workers, on the paternalistic grounds that women and children were incapable of defending themselves in the workplace.
10. For an overview of the Wobblies, see Melvin Dubofsky, *We Shall Be All: A History of the Industrial Workers of the World*, abridged edition (Urbana: University of Illinois Press, 2000).
11. Vincent St. John, "Political Parties and the I.W.W.," in *Rebel Voices: An I.W.W. Anthology*, ed. Joyce Kornbluh (Ann Arbor: University of Michigan Press, 1972).
12. Philip Taft and Philip Ross, "American Labor Violence: Its Causes, Character, and Outcome," in *The History of Violence in America: A Report to the National Commission on the Causes and Prevention of Violence*, ed. Hugh Graham and Ted Gurr (Washington, DC: National Commission on the Causes and Prevention of Violence, 1969), 221.
13. Sorel's conception of the "general strike" is developed fully in Georges Sorel, *Reflections on Violence* (Cambridge: Cambridge University Press, 2004).
14. Sorel, *Reflections on Violence*, 115.
15. Sorel, *Reflections on Violence*, 155.
16. Sorel, *Reflections on Violence*, 118.
17. Sorel, *Reflections on Violence*, 85.
18. Philip Foner, *The Industrial Workers of the World, 1905–1917*, vol. IV of *History of the Labor Movement in the United States* (New York: International Publishers, 1965), 159.
19. J. Anthony Lukacs, *Big Trouble: A Murder in a Small Western Town Sets Off a Struggle for the Soul of America* (New York: Simon and Schuster, 1977.)
20. Elizabeth Gurley Flynn, Walker Smith, and William Trautman, *Direct Action and Sabotage: Three Classic IWW Pamphlets from the 1910s* (Chicago: Charles Kerr, 1997); Ben Williams, "Sabotage" in Kornbluh, *Rebel Voices*, chapter 51; and Frank Bohn, "Some Definitions: Direct Action—Sabotage" in Kornbluh, *Rebel Voices*, chapter 52. For an overview of the idea of sabotage, including the connections between the French and American usages of the concept, see Dominique Pinsolle, "Sabotage, the IWW, and Repression: How The American Reinterpretation of a French Concept Gave Rise to a New International Conception of Sabotage," in *Wobblies of the World: A Global History of the IWW*, ed. Peter Cole, David Struthers, and Kenyon Zimmer (London: Pluto Press, 2017).
21. Flynn, Smith, and Trautman, *Direct Action and Sabotage*, 61.
22. Dubofsky, *We Shall Be All*, 96.
23. "The I.W.W. Decision," *The American Teacher* 7, no. 7 (September 1918): 138.
24. "The I.W.W. Decision."

25. An exception is Theodore Draper, *The Roots of American Communism* (Chicago: Ivan R. Dee, 1989), which discusses the connection in some detail.
26. Revolutionary syndicalists migrated into the Communist parties of Europe as well. See Ralph Darlington, *Radical Unionism: The Rise and Fall of Revolutionary Syndicalism* (Chicago: Haymarket Books, 2013).
27. The exceptions to this syndicalist approach were few and episodic, limited in time and place. During the Popular Front period, for example, the Communist Party would exercise real electoral influence in New York, particularly in New York City, where a hugely disproportionate share and concentration of its national membership resided. However, sectarian changes in party line and declines in party membership meant that this presence was not sustained for long.
28. See Kim Moody, *In Solidarity: Essays on Working-Class Organization and Strategy in the United States* (Chicago: Haymarket Books, 2014.) This model is most succinctly presented chapter 4 "The Rank-and-File Strategy," 75–161.
29. Kim Moody, *On New Terrain: How Capital Is Reshaping the Battleground of Class War* (Chicago: Haymarket Books, 2017), chapters 9 and 10; Kim Moody, "In Defense of the Rank-and-File Strategy," *Jacobin*, June 26, 2019, www.jacobinmag.com/2019/06/rank-and-file-strategy-kim-moody-labor-unions; and Kim Moody, "The Two Souls of Democratic Socialism," *New Politics* 16, no. 4 (Winter 2018), newpol.org/issue_post/two-souls-democratic-socialism/.
30. Eric Blanc, "Red State Strikes and Electoral Politics," in *Socialist Strategy and Electoral Politics*, electronic edition (New York: Verso Books, Haymarket Books, and *Jacobin*, 2019), https://www.haymarketbooks.org/books/1344-socialist-strategy-and-electoral-politics).
31. The best introduction to the life and work of A. J. Muste is Leilah Danielson, *American Gandhi: A. J. Muste and the History of Radicalism in the Twentieth Century* (Philadelphia: University of Pennsylvania Press, 2014). Despite the fact that it does not cover much after 1936, one should also consult Muste's own "Sketches for an Autobiography" in *The Essays of A. J. Muste*, ed. Nat Hentoff (New York: Bobbs-Merrill, 1967).
32. For a full account of the 1919 Lawrence strike and Muste's role in it, as well as the brief history of the Amalgamated Textile Workers union, see David Goldberg, *A Tale of Three Cities: Labor Organization of Protest in Paterson, Passaic, and Lawrence, 1916–1921* (New Brunswick, NJ: Rutgers University Press, 1989).
33. On Brookwood and the larger workers' education movement, see Richard Altenbaugh, *Education for Struggle: The American Labor Colleges of the 1920s and 1930s* (Philadelphia: Temple University Press, 1990); and Danielson, *American Gandhi*, chapters 3, 4, and 5.
34. Muste was for a number of years the chairman of the board of Manumit School. The New York City Teachers Union provided much of the educational expertise on that board, and Teachers Union president Henry Linville even assumed the directorship of the school in a particularly troubled moment. Both Brookwood and Manumit shared common sponsors and founders: the Christian pacifists and socialist William and Helen Fincke. The one published account of the Manumit School is Scott Walter, "Labor's Demonstration School: The Manumit School for Workers' Children, 1924–1932," ERIC Document ED473025, files.eric.ed.gov/fulltext/ED473025.pdf.

35. John Dewey, "Labor Politics and Labor Education," *New Republic*, January 9, 1929, newrepublic.com/article/93594/labor-politics-and-labor-education.
36. On "Third Period Stalinism," see Irving Howe and Lewis Coser, *The American Communist Party: A Critical History* (Boston: Beacon Press, 1957), chapters 5 and 6.
37. For a good account of the Toledo Auto-Lite strike, see Irving Bernstein, *The Turbulent Years: A History of the American Worker, 1933–1941* (Chicago: Haymarket Books, 2010), 218–228.
38. Christopher Phelps, *Young Sidney Hook: Marxist and Pragmatist* (Ithaca, NY: Cornell University Press, 1997), 104–132.
39. A. J. Muste, "The World Task of Pacifism," in *The Essays of A. J. Muste*, 220.
40. Muste, "The World Task of Pacifism," 225.
41. For the history of CORE, see August Meier and Elliott Rudwick, *CORE: A Study in the Civil Rights Movement, 1942–1968* (Champaign: University of Illinois Press, 1975). For Muste's role in the founding of CORE, see Danielson, *American Gandhi*, chapter 8; for Rustin's role, see D'Emilio, *Lost Prophet*, chapters 3 and 7.
42. *CORE*, 308.
43. Muste, "The World Task of Pacifism," 222.
44. Danielson, *American Gandhi*, 218 ff.
45. See A. J. Muste, *Nonviolence in an Aggressive World*, especially chapter 6, "Pacificism as Revolution Strategy–II" (New York: Harper and Brothers, 1940).
46. Michael Walzer, *The Revolution of the Saints: A Study in the Origins of Radical Politics* (Cambridge, MA: Harvard University Press, 1965).
47. Muste, *Nonviolence in An Aggressive World*, 102 ff.; A. J. Muste, "Of Holy Disobedience" and "Statement Made on 12/21/65 to the Federal Grand Jury," in *The Essays of A. J. Muste*.

CHAPTER 6

1. The AFT would drop its no-strike policy in 1963, and the NEA followed suit three years later.
2. Joseph Slater, *Public Workers: Government Employee Unions, the Law and the State, 1900–1962* (Ithaca, NY: Cornell University Press, 2004), chapter 1.
3. Marjorie Murphy, *Blackboard Unions: The AFT and the NEA, 1900–1980* (Ithaca, NY: Cornell University Press, 1990), 182–184. For a description of the St. Paul strike, see Cheryl Carlson, "Strike for Better Schools: The St. Paul Public Schools Teachers' Strike of 1946," *Ramsey County History* 43, no. 2 (Summer 2008), www.rchs.com/wp-content/uploads/2015/11/RCHS_Summer2008_Carlson.pdf. For a contemporaneous account of the teacher strikes of the late 1940s, see Albert Schiff, "Teachers' Strikes in the United States" *Phi Delta Kappan* 34, no. 4 (January 1953): 133–155.
4. Roger Seifert, *Teacher Militancy: A History of Teachers Strikes, 1896–1987* (London: Falmer Press, 1987), 59.
5. Exact numbers for teacher strikes are not available, as the US Department of Labor's Bureau of Labor Statistics did not break out public-sector strikes for most of those years. Based on a number of different sources, I have offered an estimate that is most likely understated. In *The Teacher Rebellion* (Washington, DC: Howard

University Press, 1985), Dave Selden, one of the organizers of the 1960 UFT strike who would later become president of the AFT, estimated that at least a thousand of the nation's seventeen thousand school districts would experience strikes and near strikes during the 1960s (p. 109). Marjorie Murphy reported more than three hundred teacher strikes during the 1960s, with the number increasing as the decade went on ("Militancy in Many Forms: Teachers Strikes and Urban Insurrections, 1967–74," in *Rebel Rank and File: Labor Militancy and Revolt from Below in the Long 1970s*, ed. Aaron Brenner, Robert Brenner, and Cal Winslow [New York: Verso, 2010], 231). According to John Lyons, "between July 1960 and June 1974, the country experienced over 1,000 teacher strikes involving more than 823,000 teachers ("American Federation of Teachers" in *Encyclopedia of U.S. Labor and Working Class History*, ed. Eric Arnesen [New York: Routledge, 2007], 90). Writing in 2009, Lyons estimated that "since the beginning of the collective bargaining era in 1960," there could well have been over three thousand teacher strikes of at least one day's duration ("Teacher Strikes" in *The Encyclopedia of Strikes in American History*, ed. Aaron Brenner, Benjamin Day, and Immanuel Ness [Armonk, NY: M. E. Sharpe, 2009], 252).

6. Richard Murphy, "Public Employee Strikes," in *The Crisis in Public Employee Relations in the Decade of the Seventies*, ed. Richard Murphy and Morris Sackman (Washington, DC: Bureau of National Affairs, 1970), 75.
7. Lyons, "American Federation of Teachers," 90; Ed Hurley, "Teacher Pay 1940–2000," www.nea.org/home/14052.htm.
8. Murphy, "Public Employee Strikes," 74.
9. Cal Winslow, "The Rebellion from Below," in *Rebel Rank and File*.
10. Jack Barbash, "Causes of Rank-and-File Unrest," in *Trade Union Government and Collective Bargaining: Some Critical Issues*, ed. Joel Seidman (New York: Praeger, 1970), 42.
11. Much has been written on the 1968 Ocean Hill Brownsville strike and 1970–1971 Newark strike. On Ocean Hill Brownsville, see the different perspectives of Richard Kahlenberg, *Tough Liberal: Albert Shanker and the Battle over Schools, Union, Race, and Democracy* (New York: Columbia University Press, 2007), chapters 4, 5, and 6; Daniel Perlstein, *Justice, Justice: School Politics and the Eclipse of Liberalism* (New York: Peter Lang, 2004); and Jerald Podair, *The Strike That Changed New York: Blacks, Whites, and the Ocean-Hill Brownsville Crisis* (New Haven, CT: Yale University, 2002); on Newark, see Steve Golin, *The Newark Teacher Strikes: Hopes on the Line* (New Brunswick, NJ: Rutgers University Press, 2002).
12. On the 1975 fiscal crisis and UFT strike, see Kim Phillips-Fein, *Fear City: New York's Fiscal Crisis and the Rise of Austerity Politics* (New York: Henry Holt, 2018); and Kahlenberg, *Tough Liberal*, chapter 10.
13. Jon Shelton, *Teacher Strike! Public Education and the Making of a New Political Order* (Chicago: University of Illinois Press, 2017).
14. Joseph McCartin, *Collision Course: Ronald Reagan, the Air Traffic Controllers, and the Strike That Changed America* (New York: Oxford University Press, 2011).
15. Jeremy Brecher, "The Decline of Strikes," in *The Encyclopedia of Strikes in American History*.
16. Largely on the basis of teacher and other public-sector strikes, the number of strikes in 2018 were the most since 2007 and the number of workers on strike was the most since 1986. That is movement in a positive direction, but it is still

movement concentrated among teachers and public-sector workers. It remains to be seen if that movement can be sustained and if it can spread to the private sector ("Major Work Stoppages in 2018" [Washington, DC: Bureau of Labor Statistics of U.S. Department of Labor, February 8, 2019], www.bls.gov/news.release/pdf/wkstp.pdf).

17. Reflecting the power of the city's labor movement, Mayor Robert Wagner settled the 1960 strike by appointing a three person committee of labor senior statesmen—Harry Van Arsdale, head of the New York City Central Labor Council; Jacob Potofsky, president of the Amalgamated Clothing Workers; and David Dubinsky, president of the International Ladies Garment Workers Union—to decide if teachers should have collective bargaining. There was little question that they would recommend collective bargaining, even though it was almost entirely unprecedented in public education. In the election campaign to be chosen as the collective bargaining agent, the UFT received key financial aid from the AFL-CIO's Industrial Union Department, then under the leadership of UAW President Walter Reuther, and a loan from the Amalgamated Bank, a labor bank owned by the Amalgamated Clothing Workers.

18. In *Divided Unions: The Wagner Act, Federalism, and Organized Labor* (Philadelphia: University of Pennsylvania Press, 2020), Alexis Walker makes a well-crafted argument that the failure to include public-sector workers in the National Labor Relations Act is responsible for the failure of their unions to establish a significant beachhead in the deep "red" states of the old Confederacy. Yet the fact that public-sector unionization efforts were hindered in the very same states where private-sector labor had been largely unsuccessful suggests that even inclusion in the NLRA would be no guarantee of better results.

19. Gerald Mayer, *Union Membership Trends in the United States* (Washington, DC: Congressional Research Service, 2004), digitalcommons.ilr.cornell.edu/cgi/viewcontent.cgi?article=1176&context=key_workplace; Megan Dunn and James Walker, *BLS Spotlight on Statistics: Union Membership in the United States* (Washington, DC: US Department of Labor, Bureau of Labor Statistics, 2016), digitalcommons.ilr.cornell.edu/cgi/viewcontent.cgi?article=2795&context=key_workplace; John Schmitt and Alexandra Mitukiewicz, *Politics Matter: Changes in Unionization Rates in Rich Countries, 1960–2010* (Washington, DC: Center for Economic and Policy Research, 2011), cepr.net/documents/publications/unions-oecd-2011-11.pdf.

20. David Plotke, *Building a Democratic Political Order: Reshaping American Liberalism in the 1930s and 1940s* (New York: Cambridge University Press, 1996); Kevin Boyle, *The UAW and the Heyday of American Liberalism* (Ithaca, NY: Cornell University Press, 1995); and Gary Gerstle and Steve Fraser, eds., *The Rise and Fall of the New Deal Order, 1930–1980* (Princeton, NJ: Princeton University Press, 1990).

21. Paul Krugman, *The Conscience of a Liberal* (New York: W. W. Norton, 2009), chapter 3; Thomas Piketty and Emmanuel Saez, "Income Inequality in the United States, 1913–1998," *Quarterly Journal of Economics* 118, no. 1 (February 2003), doi:10.1162/00335530360535135; and Timothy Noah, *The Great Divergence: America's Growing Inequality Crisis and What We Can Do About It* (New York: Bloomsbury, 2012).

22. Thomas Piketty and Emmanuel Saez, "The Evolution of Top Incomes: A Historical and International Perspective," *American Economic Review: Papers and Proceedings* 96, no. 2 (May 2006), doi:10.1257/000282806777212116.
23. Joshua Freeman, *Working-Class New York: Life and Labor Since World War II* (New York: New Press, 2001).
24. Georges Sorel, *Reflections on Violence* (Cambridge: Cambridge University Press, 2004), 123.
25. See, for examples of this view, Lois Weiner, *The Future of Our Schools: Teachers Unions and Social Justice* (Chicago: Haymarket Books, 2012); and James Gray Pope, Ed Bruno, and Peter Kellman, "The Right to Strike" in *Boston Review of Books*, May 22, 2017, bostonreview.net/forum/james-gray-pope-ed-bruno-peter-kellman-right-strike.
26. On the strike and republicanism, see Josiah Bartlett-Lambert, *"If the Workers Took a Notion": The Right to Strike and American Political Development* (Ithaca, NY: Cornell University Press, 2005). For a more general consideration of labor and republicanism, see Alex Gourevitch, *From Slavery to the Cooperative Commonwealth: Labor and Republican Liberty in the Nineteenth Century* (New York: Cambridge University Press, 2015); and David Montgomery, *Citizen Worker: The Experience of Workers in the United States with Democracy and the Free Market During the Nineteenth Century* (New York: Cambridge University Press, 1994). For an appreciation of the influence of civic republicanism on trade union and then Socialist Party leader Eugene Debs, see Nick Salvatore, *Eugene V. Debs: Citizen and Socialist* (Champaign: University of Illinois Press, 1984).
27. For an exposition of civic republicanism based on the idea of freedom as non-domination, see Philip Pettit, *Republicanism: A Theory of Freedom and Government* (New York: Oxford University Press, 1997).
28. Michael Honey, *Going Down Jericho Road: The Memphis Strike, Martin Luther King's Last Campaign* (New York: W. W. Norton, 2007).
29. Human Rights Watch, *Unfair Advantage: Workers' Freedom of Association in the United States under International Human Rights Standards* (New York: Human Rights Watch, 2000), www.hrw.org/reports/pdfs/u/us/uslbr008.pdf.
30. Elizabeth Anderson, *Private Government: How Employers Rule Our Lives (and Why We Don't Talk About It)* (Princeton, NJ: Princeton University Press, 2017).
31. Alexander Hertel-Fernandez, *Politics at Work: How Companies Turn Their Workers into Lobbyists* (New York: Oxford University Press, 2018).
32. Terence Powderly, *Thirty Years of Labor, 1859–1889* (Columbus, OH: Excelsior Printing House, 1889), 248, 250. On the Knights of Labor and solidarity, see Philip Dray, *There Is Power in a Union: The Epic Story of Labor in America* (New York: Anchor Books, 2011), 122ff.
33. Gourevitch, *From Slavery to the Cooperative Commonwealth*, chapter 5.
34. Danielle Allen, *Talking to Strangers: Anxieties of Citizenship Since* Brown v. Board of Education (Chicago: University of Chicago Press, 2004).
35. Michael Kernan, "Harry Bridges at 76," *Washington Post*, January 17, 1978, www.washingtonpost.com/archive/lifestyle/1978/01/17/harry-bridges-at-76/571e451f-96ca-48df-b413-e413ba70754d/.
36. Joe Burns, *Reviving the Strike: How Working People Can Regain Power and Transform America* (New York: IG Publishing, 2011); and *Strike Back: Using the Militant Tactics of Labor's Past to Reignite Public Sector Unionism Today* (New York: IG Publishing, 2014).

Burns's arguments against what he describes as "alternatives" to the strike are in chapters 4–6 of *Reviving the Strike*.

37. Micah Uetricht, "You Don't Get This Perfect Storm of Class Struggle Very Often: An Interview with Eric Blanc," *Jacobin*, July 5, 2019, www.jacobinmag.com/2019/07/teachers-strikes-bernie-sanders; Eric Blanc, *Red State Revolt: The Teachers' Strikes and Working-Class Politics* (New York: Verso, 2019).
38. Doug McAdam, *Political Process and the Development of Black Insurgency, 1930–1970* (Chicago: University of Chicago Press, 1999), 164 ff.
39. Marshall Ganz, *Why David Sometimes Wins: Leadership, Organization, and Strategy in the California Farm Worker Movement* (New York: Oxford University Press, 2009).
40. Jane McAlevey, *No Shortcuts: Organizing for Power in the New Gilded Age* (New York: Oxford University Press, 2016). The quotation is drawn from Sarah Freeman-Wolpert, "Labor organizer Jane McAlevey on why strikes are the only way out of our current crisis," *Waging Non-Violence* (blog), April 10, 2019, wagingnonviolence.org/2019/04/labor-organizer-jane-mcalevey-strikes-trump-era/.
41. Celine McNicholas, Margaret Poydock, and Lynn Rhinehart, *Unprecedented: The Trump NLRB's Attack on Workers' Rights* (Washington, DC: Economic Policy Institute, 2019), www.epi.org/files/pdf/177387.pdf.
42. Sidney Fine, *Sit-Down: The General Motors Strike of 1936–1937* (Ann Arbor: University of Michigan Press, 1969); and Nelson Lichtenstein, *The Most Dangerous Man in Detroit: Walter Reuther and the Fate of American Labor* (New York: Basic Books, 1995).
43. McCartin, *Collision Course.*
44. Erik Loomis, *A History of America in Ten Strikes* (New York: New Press, 2018).
45. McAlevey, *No Shortcuts*, chapter 4. McAlevey is by no means alone in her blind spots. Steven Ashby's and Robert Bruno's *A Fight for the Soul of Education: The Story of the Chicago Teachers Strike* (Ithaca: Cornell University Press, 2016) mentions the timing of the strike and the presidential race only in a few sentences in passing and only to suggest that some other teacher unionists around the country were opposed to the strike as a consequence. Similarly, one searches in vain for a mention of the strike's timing and the presidential race in Micah Uetricht's narrative of the strike. *Strike for America: Chicago Teachers Against Austerity* (New York: Verso Books, 2014).

CHAPTER 7

1. See chapter 3, note 11.
2. Christopher Dawson, "Before They Went on Strike, West Virginia Teachers Packed Bags to Make Sure Kids Didn't Go Hungry," *CNN Reports*, February 27, 2018, www.cnn.com/2018/02/26/us/iyw-striking-teachers-feed-students-trnd/index.html; and Max Zahn, "How Free Lunch and Daycare Are Bolstering the Oklahoma Teachers' Walkout," *Waging Non-Violence* (blog), April 10, 2018, wagingnonviolence.org/2018/04/oklahoma-teachers-walkout-free-lunch-daycare/.
3. Mary Cathryn Ricker, "Teacher-Community Unionism: A Lesson from St. Paul," *Dissent Magazine* 62, no. 3 (Summer 2015), www.dissentmagazine.org/article/teacher-community-unionism-lesson-st-paul; and Maurice BP-Weeks et al., "Before the Chalk Dust Settles: Building on the 2018 Teachers' Mobilization," *American Prospect*, April 24, 2018, prospect.org/article/chalk-dust-settles-building-on

-2018-teachers%e2%80%99-mobilization. There is a "bargaining for the common good" network, with teacher unions disproportionately represented; its website is: www.bargainingforthecommongood.org/.

4. Leo Casey, "The Educational Value of Democratic Voice," in *Collective Bargaining in Education: Negotiating Change in Today's Schools*, ed. Jane Hannaway and Andrew Rotherham (Cambridge, MA: Harvard Education Press, 2006).
5. One historical window into those developments is the important text of Charles Kerchner, Julia Koppich, and Joseph Weeres, *United Mind Workers: Unions and Teaching in the Knowledge Society* (San Francisco: Jossey-Bass, 1997).
6. Ricker, "Teacher-Community Unionism: A Lesson from St. Paul"; and St. Paul Federation of Teachers, *The Schools St. Paul Children Deserve* (St. Paul: SPFT, 2013), spfe28.org/wp-content/uploads/2017/08/The-Schools-Saint-Paul-Children-Deserve-.pdf.
7. For a solid introduction to the idea of the "community school," see Lee Benson et al., "The Enduring Appeal of Community Schools," *American Educator*, Summer 2009, www.aft.org/sites/default/files/periodicals/enduringappeal.pdf.
8. On Jane Addams, the Hull House, and John Dewey, see Louise Knight, *Citizen: Jane Addams and the Struggle for Democracy* (Chicago: University of Chicago Press, 2005), chapter 10; and Alan Ryan, *John Dewey and the High Tide of American Liberalism* (New York: W. W. Norton, 1995), chapter 4. On the broader settlement house movement, see Michael Friedman and Brett Friedman, *Settlement Houses: Improving the Social Welfare of America's Immigrants* (New York: Rosen, 2006).
9. John Dewey, "The School as Social Centre," in *John Dewey: The Middle Works*, vol. 2, ed. Jo-Ann Boydston (Carbondale: Southern Illinois Press, 1976), 80, 82.
10. Dewey, "The School as Social Centre," 91.
11. Michael Johanek and John Puckett, *Leonard Covello and the Making of Benjamin Franklin High School: Education as If Citizenship Mattered* (Philadelphia: Temple University Press, 2007).
12. See Leonard Covello, Simon Beagle, and Leon Bock, "The Community School in a Great Metropolis," in *The Crisis in Urban Schools* (New York: MSS Information Corporation, 1973). and Frances Butterfield, "A Neighborhood School," *American Teacher*, February 1948.
13. On the approach of Franklin to citizenship education, see Leonard Covello, "A High School and Its Immigrant Community–A Challenge and an Opportunity," *Journal of Educational Sociology* 9, no. 6 (February 1936): 331–346; and Lisa Rabin, "Community Service and Activism in Heritage Languages, New York City, 1915–1956," *Foreign Language Annals*, 44, no. 2 (Summer 2011): 338–352, doi:10.1111/j.1944-9720.2011.01138.x. On the Youthbuilders program, see Sabra Holbrook, "Citizens Already—The Youthbuilders Program," *High Points in the New York Public Schools* 25, no. 9 (November 1943); and Sabra Holbrook, *Children Object!* (New York: Viking Press, 1943).
14. Johanek and Puckett, *Leonard Covello and the Making of Benjamin Franklin High School*, chapters 5, 6, and 7.
15. The quoted phrase is from the subtitle of *Leonard Covello and the Making of Benjamin Franklin High School*. For the discussion of the concept of democratic citizenship that undergirded Benjamin Franklin High School, see chapters 1 and 9 of that book. See also Michael Johanek, "Preparing Pluribus for Unum: Historical

Perspectives on Civic Education," in *Making Civics Count: Citizenship Education for a New Generation*, ed. David Campbell, Meira Levinson, and Frederick Hess (Cambridge, MA: Harvard Education Press, 2012).

16. Covello, "A High School and Its Immigrant Community," provides an account of the earlier decades of this transformation.
17. For a view of the ethnic and racial conflicts in Harlem during the 1930s, see Nadia Venturini, "Over the Years People Don't Know: Italian-Americans and African-Americans in Harlem in the 1930s," in *Italian Workers of the World: Labor Migration and the Formation of Multiethnic States*, ed. Donna Gabaccia and Fraser Ottanelli (Urbana: University of Illinois Press, 2001).
18. Johanek and Puckett, *Leonard Covello and the Making of Benjamin Franklin High School*, 175.
19. The best overall account of DuBois's work is Diana Selig's *Americans All: The Cultural Gifts Movement* (Cambridge, MA: Harvard University Press, 2008). DuBois's autobiography, *All This and Something More: Pioneering in Intercultural Education* (Bryn Mawr, PA: Dorrance and Company, 1984) should also be consulted. On DuBois's units at Benjamin Franklin, see Shafali Lal, "1930s Multiculturalism: Rachel Davis DuBois and the Bureau for Intercultural Education," *Radical Teacher* 69 (May 2004), 21, newschoolhistories.org/wp-content/uploads/2019/02/ContentServer.pdf. Zoë Burkholder provides an anachronistic reading of Davis's work, faulting it for not adopting the insights of anti-racist education that were developed decades later (*Color in the Classroom: How American Schools Taught Race, 1900–1954* [New York: Oxford University Press, 2011], chapter 3).
20. Rachel Davis DuBois, "Intercultural Education at Benjamin Franklin High School," *High Points in New York City Public Schools* 19, no. 10 (December 1937): 23–29; and Nicholas Montalto, "Multicultural Education in the New York City Public Schools, 1919–1941," in *Educating an Urban People: The New York City Experience*, ed. Diane Ravitch and Ronald Goodenow (New York: Teachers College Press, 1981), 71–73.
21. For the story of the Franklin film series and Keliher's role in it, see Lisa M. Rabin, "The Social Uses of Classroom Cinema: A History of the Human Relations Film Series at Benjamin Franklin High School in East Harlem, New York City, 1936–1955," *The Velvet Light Trap* 72 (Fall 2013): 58–71, doi:10.7560/VLT7206; Craig Kridel, "Educational Film Projects of the 1930s: Secrets of Success and the Human Relations Film Series," in *Learning with the Lights Off: Educational Film in the United States*, ed. Devin Orgeron, Marsha Orgeron, and Dan Streible (New York: Oxford University Press, 2012); and Craig Kridel, "Examining the Educational Film Work of Alice Keliher and the Human Relations Series of Films and Mark May and the Secrets of Success Program" (research report, Rockefeller Foundation Archive Center, 2010), www.rockarch.org/publications/resrep/kridel.php.
22. Davison Douglas, *Jim Crow Moves North: The Battle over Northern School Segregation, 1865–1954* (Cambridge: Cambridge University Press, 2005); and Adina Back, "Exposing the 'Whole Segregation Myth': The Harlem Nine and New York City's School Desegregation Battles," in *Freedom North: Black Freedom Struggles Outside the South, 1940–1980*, ed. Jeanne Theoharis and Komozi Woodward (New York: Palgrave Macmillan, 2003). In New York City, the Harlem Nine were in the forefront of these efforts in the late 1950s. See Melissa Weiner, *Power, Protest, and the Public*

Schools: Jewish and African American Struggles in New York City (New Brunswick, NJ: Rutgers University Press, 2012), 53–65.

23. The UFT (and its predecessor organization, the Teachers Guild) were participants in the main citywide organization seeking school integration during the 1950s, the Intergroup Committee on New York's Public Schools. The UFT would provide key organizational support to Bayard Rustin when he organized the February 3, 1964, school boycott of over 450,000 students demanding the integration of New York City schools, which remains the largest demonstration for school integration in American history (oral history of George Altomare, in possession of author).
24. Diane Ravitch, *The Great School Wars: A History of the New York City Public Schools* (New York: Basic Books, 1974), 257.
25. For a number of northern examples of white flight, see Thomas Sugrue, *Sweet Land of Liberty: The Forgotten Struggle for Civil Rights in the North* (New York: Random House, 2008), 163–189. On white flight in the South, see Kevin Kruse, *White Flight: Atlanta and the Making of Modern Conservatism* (Princeton, NJ: Princeton University Press, 2005).
26. In chapters 24 and 25 of *The Great School Wars*, Diane Ravitch lays out the problems faced by desegregation plans for the New York City public schools, absent an accompanying plan to address the inequities in teaching and learning conditions between schools.
27. The UFT had originally called the program "Effective Schools," but added "more" to mollify the NYC Board of Education, which did not want to concede that its schools were not already "effective." These descriptions of the MES program come from the May 15, 1964, *Report of the Joint Planning Committee for More Effective Schools of the New York City Public Schools* (the committee was joint in that it had representatives of the schools superintendent, the Council of Supervisors and Administrators [the supervisors union] and the UFT) and a 1965 document, "The More Effective Schools Program in New York City: A Summary Statement," written by Si Beagle, chair of the UFT's More Effective Schools Committee.
28. A study of MES schools showed that where students continued their education without disruption, there were significant positive effects, but where students moved in and out of MES schools, there was a significant loss of those effects (Richard Kahlenberg, *Tough Liberal: Albert Shanker and the Battle over Schools, Union, Race, and Democracy* [New York: Columbia University Press, 2007], 78). If the MES program had been brought to scale in all of New York City's inner-city schools rather than restricted to a small number of pilots, the problem of transience would be at least partially abated, since students would be moving from one MES school to another.
29. UFT President Al Shanker would bus his own son so he could attend a MES pre-K program.
30. Shanker told the UFT's Delegate Assembly that it was not enough to get "pretty good salary and welfare provisions" if the union did not get "anything to help the children to learn and read," and the assembly overwhelmingly voted down the Board's offer, until they came back with an increase in funding that could be used for MES schools (Kahlenberg, *Tough Liberal*, 78). The *New York Times* quote is from Deborah Meier, "New York City Teachers' Strike," *Midstream* (December 1967), deborahmeier.files.wordpress.com/2018/04/1968_newyorkteachersstrike.pdf.

31. Kahlenberg, *Tough Liberal*, 71–88.
32. Martin Luther King Jr. to Albert Shanker, September 13, 1967, box 69, folder 23 of UFT Records, Series I (WAG022) Tamiment Library & Wagner Labor Archives, New York.
33. As quoted in Karen Ferguson, *Top Down: The Ford Foundation, Black Power, and the Reinvention of Racial Liberalism* (Philadelphia: Pennsylvania University Press, 2013), 128.
34. John Kucsera and Gary Orfield, *New York State's Extreme School Segregation: Inequality, Inaction and a Damaged Future* (Los Angeles: UCLA Civil Rights Project, 2014), www.civilrightsproject.ucla.edu/research/k-12-education/integration-and-diversity/ny-norflet-report-placeholder/Kucsera-New-York-Extreme-Segregation-2014.pdf.
35. Samuel Abrams, *Education and the Commercial Mindset* (Cambridge, MA: Harvard University Press, 2016).
36. The engagement process between the parents and community organizers of CC9 and the teachers and leaders of the UFT is described in considerable detail in Michael Fabricant's *Organizing for Educational Justice: The Campaign for Public School Reform in the South Bronx* (Minneapolis: University of Minnesota Press, 2010). The book captures the hard work that had to be done by both sides to build a partnership. Unfortunately, the original design of the "lead teacher" position, in which selection committees of parents and teachers would choose the teachers, was undone by Chancellor Joel Klein, who gave the school principal complete authority in selection, removing parents and teachers from any meaningful role. With this change, it quickly became a patronage position and lost its educational value. When school budgets were cut in the wake of the Great Recession, the position disappeared in all but a handful of schools.
37. Meredith Kolodner, "Unity Breeds Power For UFT, Parents," *The Chief*, July 13, 2007, maketheroadny.org/unity-breeds-power-for-uft-parents/.
38. Kalena Thomhave, "West Virginia Teachers Won Their Strike. Now, They're Rebuilding the Local Economy," *American Prospect*, Spring 2018, prospect.org/infrastructure/west-virginia-teachers-won-strike.-now-rebuilding-local-economy./ The different programs of Reconnecting McDowell can be view on its web site: mcdowell.connections.aft.org/.
39. The fullest account of the community partnership work and organizing that undergirded the Los Angeles strike can be found in Leigh Dingerson, *Building the Power to Reclaim Our Schools* (Los Angeles: Reclaim Our Schools–Los Angeles, 2019), reclaimourschoolsla.org/wp-content/uploads/2019/07/0719-Reclaim-our-Schools-Case-Study.Report-pg_p-002.pdf.
40. Reclaim Our Schools–Los Angeles, "A Vision to Support Every Student," reclaimourschoolsla.org/wp-content/uploads/2013/08/Reclaim-Our-Schools-LA-A-Vision-to-Support-Every-Student-December-2016.pdf.
41. King and Rustin were particularly helpful in helping the UFT extract itself from a serious difficulty involving its demand over the "disruptive child." City and board officials saw the issue as one that could be used as a wedge issue against the union; they misrepresented the demand, claiming it would allow teachers to expel students from their classes solely on their own authority, when the actual proposal included a due process procedure that involved the student's parent. On the basis of this misrepresentation, many in the community came to believe the proposal

would be used to exclude African American and Latino students from class. King and Rustin intervened to allow the UFT to clarify its demand. It must be noted, however, that if the UFT had partnered with local community in the formulation of its demands in 1967, this major misstep could have been avoided.

CHAPTER 8

1. Saul Alinsky, *Rules for Radicals* (New York: Random House, 1971).
2. Kim Bobo, Jackie Kendall, and Steve Max, *Organizing for Social Change: Midwest Academy Manual for Activists* (Santa Ana, CA: Forum Press, 2001).
3. *A Troublemaker's Handbook 2: How to Fight Back Where You Work and Win*, ed. Jane Slaughter (Detroit: Labor Notes, 2005). See also Alexandra Bradbury, Mark Brenner, and Jane Slaughter, *Secrets of a Successful Organizer* (Detroit: Labor Notes, 2016).
4. John Dewey, "My Pedagogic Creed," in *John Dewey: The Early Works, 1882–1898*, vol. V, ed. Jo-Ann Boydston (Carbondale: Southern Illinois Press, 1972), 93.
5. In this crucial respect, Dewey's understanding of education differs from libertarian and anarchist conceptions such that outlined in A. S. Neill's *Summerhill School: A New View of Childhood* (New York: St. Martin's Press, 1992), in which education is entirely self-directed.
6. Danielle Allen, *Talking to Strangers: Anxieties of Citizenship Since* Brown v. Board of Education (Chicago: University of Chicago Press, 2004).
7. Allen, *Talking to Strangers*, 93.
8. Clayton Sinai, *Schools of Democracy: A Political History of the American Labor Movement* (Ithaca, NY: ILR Press, 2006).
9. Leo Casey, "The Civic Power of Unions and the Anti-Union Political Agenda," *Shanker Institute Blog*, April 20, 2016, www.shankerinstitute.org/blog/civic-power-unions-and-anti-union-political-agenda.
10. Like all democratic institutions, unions can be corrupted from their purpose. But the existence of corrupted unions tells us no more about their democratic purpose than the existence of corrupted democratic governments tells about their democratic purpose.
11. James Paul Gees, *Introducing Discourse Analysis: From Grammar to Society* (New York: Routledge, 2018), chapter 5.
12. David Snow, "Identity Dilemmas, Discursive Fields, Identity Work, and Mobilization: Clarifying the Identity-Movement Nexus" in *The Future of Social Movement Research: Dynamics, Mechanisms, and Processes*, ed. Jacquelien van Steklenburg, Conny Roggeband, and Bert Klandermas (Minneapolis: University of Minnesota Press, 2013); and Frederick Mayer, *Narrative Politics: Stories and Collective Action* (New York: Oxford University Press, 2014).
13. These are the same set of assumptions that undergird Marx's notion of an economic class "in itself" that develops consciousness of itself, becoming a political class "for itself":

    > [E]conomic conditions had first transformed the mass of the people of the country into workers. The domination of capital has created for this mass a common situation, common interests. This mass is thus already a class as

against capital, but not yet for itself. In the struggle, of which we have pointed out only a few phases, this mass becomes united, and constitutes itself as a class for itself. The interests it defends become class interests. But the struggle of class against class is a political struggle (Karl Marx, *The Poverty of Philosophy* in the *Collected Works of Marx and Engels*, vol. VI [London: Lawrence and Wishart, 1976], 211.)

14. Readers with an interest in this subject may consult Ernesto Laclau and Chantal Mouffe, *Hegemony and Socialist Strategy: Toward a Radical Democratic Politics* (London: Verso Books, 1985). I made a similar argument, with a close textual reading of Marx, in Leo Casey, *Confronting the State of the "Iron Cages": The Problem of State Authoritarianism in Modern Democratic and Socialist Political Theory* (PhD dissertation,University of Toronto, 1989).
15. Laclau and Mouffe, *Hegemony and Socialist Strategy*. I draw heavily on Laclau and Mouffe for my general approach here.
16. For overviews of that literature, see James Jasper, "Emotions and Social Movements: Twenty Years of Theory," *Annual Review of Sociology* 37 (2011), doi:10.1146/annurev-soc-081309-150015. One informative collection on the subject is Jeff Goodwin, James Jasper, and Francesca Polletta, eds., *Passionate Politics: Emotions and Social Movements* (Chicago: University of Chicago Press, 2001). Deborah Gould's *Moving Politics: Emotion and ACT UP's Fight Against AIDS* (Chicago: University of Chicago Press, 2009) provides an exemplary analysis of emotion in the organization ACT UP.
17. Martha Nussbaum, *Political Emotions: Why Love Matters for Justice* (Cambridge, MA: Harvard University Press, 2013).
18. It is worth pointing out here that research in cognitive science has shown that emotions play a role in cognition itself, so that our understanding of our interests can never be purely "objective," but has an important emotional dimension.
19. See Kathleen Casey, *I Answer with My Life: Life Histories of Women Teachers Working for Social Change* (New York: Routledge, 1993), 107–153; Michele Foster, *Black Teachers on Teaching* (New York: New Press, 1998); and Gloria Ladson-Billings, *The Dreamkeepers: Successful Teachers of African American Children* (San Francisco: Jossey-Bass, 1994), 54–77.
20. See William E. Connolly, *The Terms of Political Discourse* (Princeton, NJ: Princeton University Press, 1983), 9–44.
21. See, for example, Gabriel Winant, "Why Are So Many White-Collar Professionals in Revolt?," *The Guardian*, May 27, 2018, www.theguardian.com/commentisfree/2018/may/27/why-are-so-many-white-collar-professionals-in-revolt. On this count, it is instructive to follow the evolution of Bob Peterson, founding editor of *Rethinking Schools* and past president of the Milwaukee Teacher Association, who over the course of a number of years moved from a hostility to teacher professionalism, to a position that views it as an improvement over "industrial unionism" but still lacking, to a position that fully integrates professionalism into a progressive conception of teacher unionism: "Which Side Are You On?," *Rethinking Schools* 8, no. 1 (Autumn 1993), www.rethinkingschools.org/magazine/special-collections/the-role-of-teacher-unions/which-side-are-you-on); "A New Vision of Teacher Unionism" *Rethinking Schools* 11, no. 4 (Summer 1997), www.rethinkingschools.org/articles/a-new-vision-of-teacher-unionism; "Survival

and Justice: Rethinking Teacher Union Strategy" in *Transforming Teacher Unions: Fighting for Better Schools and Social Justice*, ed. Michael Charney and Bob Peterson (Milwaukee: Rethinking Schools, 1999); and "A Revitalized Teacher Union Movement," *Rethinking Schools* 29, no. 2 (Winter 2014/15), www.rethinkingschools.org/articles/a-revitalized-teacher-union-movement-reflections-from-the-field.

CHAPTER 9

1. Geraldine Clifford, *Those Good Gertrudes: A Social History of Women Teachers in America* (Baltimore: Johns Hopkins press, 2014); Dana Goldstein, *The Teacher Wars: A History of America's Most Embattled Profession* (New York: Random House, 2014); and Madeline Grumet, *Bitter Milk: Women and Teaching* (Amherst: University of Massachusetts Press, 1988).
2. See Nel Noddings, *Caring: A Feminine Approach to Ethics and Moral Education* (Berkeley: University of California Press, 1986); and *The Challenge to Care in Schools: An Alternative Approach to Education* (New York: Teachers College Press, 1992); Renee Prillman, Deborah Eaker-Rich, and Doris M. Kendrick, eds., *The Tapestry of Caring: Education as Nurturance*, (Norwood, NJ: Ablex Publishing, 1994); and Deborah Eaker-Rich and Jane Van Galen, eds., *Caring in an Unjust World: Negotiating Borders and Barriers in School* (Albany: State University of New York Press, 1996).
3. Carol Gilligan, *In a Different Voice: Psychological Theory and Women's Development* (Cambridge, MA: Harvard University Press, 1982); and *Making Connections: The Relational World of Adolescents at Emma Willard School* (Cambridge, MA: Harvard University Press, 1982).
4. The main target of Gilligan's critique was Lawrence Kohlberg's pathbreaking work in moral psychology, summarized in his *Essays on Moral Development* (New York: Harper and Row, 1984). Kohlberg had extended Piaget's theory of cognitive development into the sphere of moral reasoning, positing that there were universal, sequential stages of moral cognitive development. The Kohlberg model was strongly Kantian in inspiration; it was based on the Kantian work of John Rawls's *A Theory of Justice* (Cambridge, MA: Harvard University Press, 1971). Like Kant and Rawls, Kohlberg thought that the highest stage of moral development was based on abstract moral reasoning—one starts from a categorical imperative and, using moral reasoning, arrives at a universal principle of justice that must be followed. Gilligan noted that all of the subjects of Kohlberg's initial research had been male, leading to a gendered view of moral reasoning.
5. The broad strokes of the critique I offer here have been made by a number of different feminist critics operating from different theoretical perspectives. See, for example, Seyla Benhabib, "The Generalized and Concrete Other: The Kohlberg-Gilligan Controversy and Feminist Theory" in *Feminism as Critique: On the Politics of Gender*, ed. Seyla Benhabib and Drucilla Cornell (Minneapolis: University of Minnesota Press, 1987), chapter 5; Iris Young, "Impartiality and the Civic Public: Some Implications of Feminist Critiques of Moral and Political Theory," in *Feminism As Critique*, chapter 4; and Chantal Mouffe, "Feminism, Citizenship and Radical Democratic Politics" in *Feminists Theorize the Political*, ed. Judith Butler and Joan Scott (New York: Routledge, 1992).

6. John Dewey, *School and Society* in *John Dewey: The Middle Works, 1899–1901*, vol. I, ed. Jo-Ann Boydston (Carbondale: Southern Illinois Press, 1976), 5.
7. Megan Boler, *Feeling Power: Emotions and Education* (New York: Routledge, 1999).
8. Pedro Noguera, *The Trouble with Black Boys: Reflections on Race, Equity, and the Future of Public Education* (San Francisco: Jossey-Bass, 2008); A. Wade Boykin and Pedro Noguera, *Creating the Opportunity to Learn: Moving from Research to Practice to Close the Achievement Gap* (Alexandria, VA: ASCD, 2011); Na'ilah Suad Nasir, Jarvis Givens, and Christopher Chatmon, eds., *"We Dare Say Love": Supporting Achievement in the Educational Life of Black Boys* (New York: Teachers College Press, 2019).
9. Michelle Fine, *Framing Dropouts: Notes on the Politics of an Urban High School* (Albany: State University of New York Press, 1991).
10. David Cecelski, *Along Freedom Road: Hyde Country, North Carolina, and the Fate of Black Schools in the South* (Chapel Hill: University of North Carolina Press, 1994); Vanessa Walker, *Their Highest Potential: An African American School Community in the Segregated South* (Chapel Hill: University of North Carolina Press, 1996); and Van Dempsey and George Noblit, "Caring and Continuity: The Demise of Caring in an African-American Community, One Consequence of School Desegregation" in *Caring in Unjust World.*
11. Sandra Harding ("The Curious Coincidence of Feminine and African Moralities: Challenges for Feminist Theory" in *Women and Moral Theory*, ed. Eva Kittay and Diana Meyers [New York: Rowman and Littlefield, 1987]) points out a number of parallels in moral theories and world views rooted in gender and race and suggests that have common roots in responses to oppression based on gender and race.
12. Sweet Honey in the Rock, "On Children," on *Selections, 1978–1988*, Flying Fish Records, 2009.
13. See Sari Biklen, "Teachers' Perspectives on the Mother's Gaze," *School Work: Gender and the Cultural Construction of Teaching* (New York: Teachers College Press, 1995).
14. Leo Casey, "How to Make Teacher Caring Effective," *New York Teacher*, November 17, 2005.
15. For overviews of this movement, see Michelle Fine and Janis Somerville, eds., *Small Schools, Big Imaginations: A Creative Look at Urban Public Schools* (Chicago: Cross City Campaign for Urban School Reform, 1998); and Michael Klonsky, *Small Schools: The Numbers Tell a Story: A Review of the Research and Current Experience* (Chicago: Small Schools Workshop, University of Illinois at Chicago, 1995). For a look at a particular model school, see Deborah Meier, *The Power of Their Ideas: Lessons for America from a Small School in Harlem* (Boston: Beacon Press, 1995). The arguments for small schools are made well by two of Meier's essays, "Small Schools, Big Results," *American School Board Journal* 192, no. 7 (July 1995), deborahmeier.files.wordpress.com/2012/02/1995_smallschools.pdf; and "The Big Benefits of Small Schools," *Educational Leadership* 54, no. 1 (September 1996), www.ascd.org/publications/educational-leadership/sept96/vol54/num01/The-Big-Benefits-of-Smallness.aspx.
16. On how "small schools" were captured by philanthropy, see *Rethinking Schools* 19, no. 4 (Special Issue, Summer 2005).
17. Andy Hargreaves, *Changing Teachers, Changing Times: Teachers' Work and Culture in the Post-Modern Age* (New York: Teachers College Press, 1994), chapter 7.

18. David Stuit and Thomas Smith, "Teacher Turnover in Charter Schools" (research brief, National Center on School Choice, 2010), files.eric.ed.gov/fulltext/ED543582.pdf.
19. This insight is reinforced by the analysis of Huriya Jabbar et al., "Teacher Power and the Politics of Union Organizing in the Charter Sector," *Educational Policy* 34, no. 1 (2020): 211–238, doi:10.1177/0895904819881776.

CHAPTER 10

1. For a sophisticated analysis of the rise of professionalism in the American context that summarizes this literature, see Magalai Sarfatti Larson, *The Rise of Professionalism: Monopolies of Competence and Sheltered Markets* (New Brunswick, NJ: Transaction Publishers, 2013). Larson reflects back on her earlier work (*The Rise of Professionalism* was originally written in early 1970s) and applies it to teaching in the valuable "Looking Back and a Little Forward: Reflections on Professionalism and Teaching as a Profession," *Radical Teacher*, no. 99 (Spring 2014), radicalteacher.library.pitt.edu/ojs/radicalteacher/article/view/112/71.
2. For an overview of the literature on teacher organizations, professionalism and Progressive Era reforms, see Wayne Urban, "Organized Teachers and Educational Reform During the Progressive Era: 1890–1920," *History of Education Quarterly* 16, no. 1 (Spring 1976): 35–52, doi:10.2307/367781. For an examination of these developments in Chicago, see Robert L. Reid, *The Professionalization of Teachers: The Chicago Experience, 1895–1920* (PhD dissertation, Northwestern University, 1968). For similar developments in New York City, consult Diane Ravitch, *Great School Wars: A History of the New York City Public Schools, 1805–1973* (New York: Basic Books, 1988).
3. Raymond Callahan, *Education and the Cult of Efficiency: A Study of the Social Forces That Have Shaped the Administration of the Public Schools* (Chicago: University of Chicago Press, 1962); and Jal Mehta, *The Allure of Order: High Hopes, Dashed Expectations, and the Troubled Quest to Remake American Schooling* (New York: Oxford University Press, 2013).
4. Frederick Winslow Taylor, *The Principles of Scientific Management* (New York: Harper and Brothers, 1919), 40.
5. Christina Collins, *"Ethnically Qualified": Race, Merit, and the Selection of Urban Teachers, 1920–1980* (New York: Teachers College Press, 2011), chapter 4. In his memoirs, Irving Howe wrote that he chose not to become a New York City high school teacher, as his father had wished, because he did not believe he could pass the Examiner's oral exams that were designed to "eliminate Jewish candidates." (*A Margin of Hope: An Intellectual Biography* [New York: Harcourt, Brace and Jovanovich, 1982], 10.)
6. An examination of early teacher union history shows that a conception of teacher professionalism was at its center. This was not a peculiarly American phenomenon: based on their observations of the British National Union of Teachers, prominent Fabian Society members Sidney and Beatrice Webb concluded that all unions "will more and more assume the character of professional associations . . . Each Trade Union will find itself, like the National Union of Teachers, more and more concerned with raising the standard of competency in its occupation, improving the

professional equipment of its members, 'educating their masters' as to the best way of carrying on the craft, and endeavoring by every means to increase its status in public estimation" (Sidney and Beatrice Webb, *Industrial Democracy* [London: Longmans, Green & Co., 1902], 826).

7. It is telling that the main focus of the literature is on breaking the power of teachers and their unions, with alternative ideas of teacher professionalism presented almost as an afterthought. See Michael Podgursky, "Collective Bargaining and Education Policy," *Flypaper* (blog of the Fordham Institute), May 22, 2002, fordhaminstitute.org/national/commentary/collective-bargaining-and-education-policy; Sol Stern, "How Teachers' Unions Handcuff Schools," *City Journal of Manhattan Institute* (Spring 1997), www.city-journal.org/html/how-teachers%E2%80%99-unions-handcuff-schools-12102.html; Caroline Hoxby, "Changing the Profession," *Education Next*, Spring 2001, www.educationnext.org/changing-the-profession/; and Chester E. Finn Jr., "The End of Teacher Tenure?" *Defining Ideas* (blog of the Hoover Institution), May 23, 2017, www.hoover.org/research/end-teacher-tenure.
8. See chapter 9, note 16.
9. Myron Lieberman's *Education as a Profession* (Englewood Cliffs, NJ: Prentice-Hall, 1956), 297–333 and 241–255, invokes a number of these regressive interpretations.
10. An examination of contending discourses of teacher professionalism in other national contexts can be found in Pamela Osmond-Johnson, "Discourses of Teacher Professionalism: 'From Within' and 'From Without' or Two Sides of the Same Coin?," *Canadian Journal of Educational Administration and Policy*, no. 185 (2018):61–72, https://journalhosting.ucalgary.ca/index.php/cjeap/article/view/42966/40385; and Sølvi Mausethagen and Lise Granlund, "Contested Discourses of Teacher Professionalism: Current Tensions Between Education Policy and Teachers' Union," *Journal of Education Policy* 27, no. 6 (2012): 815–833, doi:10.1080/02680939.2012.672656.
11. Jake Jacobs, "What's Behind New York's Charter School End Run Around Teacher Certification?," *The Progressive*, March 1, 2018, progressive.org/public-school-shakedown/new-yorks-charter-school-end-run-of-teacher-certification-180301/.
12. See the web site of the National Board for Professional Teaching Standards, www.nbpts.org.
13. Donald A. Schön, *The Reflective Practitioner: How Professionals Think in Action* (New York: Basic Books, 1983) and *Educating the Reflective Practitioner: Toward a New Design for Teaching and Learning in the Professions* (San Francisco: Jossey-Bass, 1987).
14. Doug Lemov, *Teach Like a Champion: 49 Techniques That Put Students on a Path to College* (San Francisco: Jossey-Bass, 2010).
15. Lemov, *Teach Like a Champion*, 7.
16. In a very brief discussion, *Teach Like a Champion* offers as an exemplar of good questioning technique a rapid-fire exchange between a teacher and a single student that is focused on whether a particular sentence is run-on. The pedagogical reason for being able to identify run-on sentences—clarity of communication—is never addressed, and there is no discussion of how to rewrite the sentence in a way that would better communicate its main ideas; there is no time for the student to think about his answers, as one question follows on the next in an almost cross-examination style; no other students in the class are involved in the exchange, when

good questioning technique would have looked to have several students involved in answering questions; and the dialogue actually includes a "whiplash" question ("And so the predicate must have what?") that is generally known as a poor questioning technique because it starts in the form of a declarative sentence and then, at the very end, suddenly becomes a question, throwing off the student's train of thinking (Lemov, *Teach Like A Champion*, 243).

17. On teacher evaluation, see Linda Darling-Hammond, *Getting Teacher Evaluation Right: What Really Matters for Effectiveness and Improvement* (New York: Teachers College Press, 2013). On school accountability, see Linda Darling-Hammond, Linda Pittenger, and Gene Wilhoit, "Accountability for College and Career Readiness: Developing a New Paradigm," *Education Policy Analysis Archives* 22, no. 86 (2014), epaa.asu.edu/ojs/article/view/1724.
18. W. D. Hawley, "The Education of Japanese Teachers: Lessons for the United States?," ERIC Clearinghouse ED280830 (1986), files.eric.ed.gov/fulltext/ED280830.pdf; and N. Sato and Milbrey McLaughlin, "Context Matters: Teaching in Japan and the United States," *Phi Delta Kappan* 73, no. 5 (December 1991),: 359–366.
19. Andy Hargreaves and Michael Fullan, *Professional Capital: Transforming Teaching in Every School* (New York: Teachers College Press, 2012); Linda Darling-Hammond et al., *Professional Learning in the Learning Profession: A Status Report on Teacher Development in the United States and Abroad* (Dallas: National Staff Development Council, 2009), learningforward.org/docs/default-source/pdf/nsdcstudytechnicalreport2009.pdf; American Federation of Teachers, *A Guide to Engaging Members Through Professional Development and Learning* (Washington DC: AFT, 2018), www.aft.org/sites/default/files/engagingmembersthroughplguide.pdf.
20. See, for example, the Quest Center of the Chicago Teachers Union (www.ctuf.org/questcenter/), the Teacher Center of New York City's United Federation of Teachers (www.ufttc.org), the Teacher Center of the Washington Teachers Union (www.wtulocal6.org/wtu-professional-development/) and the national professional development of the American Federation of Teachers (www.aft.org/education/well-prepared-and-supported-school-staff/aft-professional-development-program).
21. Despite Lipsky's and Foucault's claims that their paradigms are applicable to schools, both the terms of their analysis and examples they choose are drawn overwhelmingly from other institutions; moreover, there is an absence of any concept of collective action on the part of the professionals in their work; see Michael Lipsky, *Street-Level Bureaucracy: Dilemmas of the Individual in Public Service* (New York: Russell Sage, 2010); and Michael Foucault, *Power/Knowledge: Selected Interviews and Other Writings, 1972–1977* (New York: Pantheon Book, 1972) and *Discipline & Punish: The Birth of the Prison* (New York: Pantheon Books, 1978).
22. Ivan Illich, *Deschooling Society* (New York: Harper and Row, 1971).
23. Walter Lippman, *Public Opinion* (New York: Harcourt Brace, 1922); and *The Phantom Public* (New York: Harcourt Brace, 1925).
24. John Dewey, *The Public and Its Problems*, in *John Dewey: The Later Works, 1925–1953*, vol. II, ed. Jo-Ann Boydston (Carbondale: Southern Illinois Press, 1984), 364.
25. On Dewey and democratic professionalism, see Albert Dzur, *Democratic Professionalism: Citizen Participation and the Reconstruction of Professional Ethics, Identity, and Practice* (University Park: Pennsylvania State University Press, 2008); and *Rebuilding Public*

Institutions Together: Professionals and Citizens in a Participatory Democracy (Ithaca, NY: Cornell University Press, 2018).

26. As Michael Walzer puts it: "So science and social science generate a kind of power, useful and even necessary in particular institutional settings; but this power is always limited by sovereignty, itself generated and informed by the larger knowledge of social meanings. Doctors and teachers (and wardens and even generals) are submitted to the 'discipline' of citizens" (*Spheres of Justice: A Defense of Pluralism and Equality* [New York: Basic Books, 1983], 290).
27. For schools that seek to fulfill this Deweyan vision of places of democracy, see Deborah Meier, *The Power of Their Ideas: Lessons for America from a Small School in Harlem* (Boston: Beacon Press, 1995).
28. For a model of democratic professionalism that highlights these "hard" issues, see Gary Anderson and Michael Ian Cohen, *The New Democratic Professional in Education: Confronting Markets, Metrics and Managerialism* (New York: Teachers College Press, 2018). Lisa Delpit's *Other People's Children: Cultural Conflict in the Classroom* (New York: New Press, 1995) remains essential reading on questions of pedagogy and students of color.

CHAPTER 11

1. Before the collective bargaining era, AFT locals were often geographically based, with public school and private school teachers, K–12, and higher education faculty all being members of a single local.
2. See, for example, Kathleen Casey, *I Answer with My Life: Life Histories of Women Teachers Working for Social Change* (New York: Routledge, 1993), 99–100.
3. For the history of American trade unionism and craft unionism before the split between the AFL and CIO, see David Montgomery, *The Fall of the House of Labor: The Workplace, The State and American Labor Activism, 1865–1925* (New York: Cambridge University Press, 1987); and Bruce Laurie, *Artisans into Workers: Labor in Nineteenth-Century America* (New York: Noonday Press, 1989).
4. On race/immigration and craft unionism, see David Roediger, *The Wages of Whiteness: Race and the Making of the American Working Class* (London: Verso, 1991); Julius Jacobson, ed., *The Negro and the American Labor Movement* (Garden City, NY: Doubleday, 1968); and Alexander Saxton, *The Indispensable Enemy: Labor and the Anti-Chinese Movement in California* (Berkeley: University of California Press, 1971).

   On gender and craft unionism, see Ileen DeVault, *United Apart: Gender and the Rise of Craft Unionism* (Ithaca, NY: Cornell University Press, 2004); Alice Kessler-Harris, "Where Are the Organized Women Workers?" in *A Heritage of Her Own: Towards a New Social History of American Women*, ed. Nancy Cott and Elizabeth Peck (New York: Simon and Schuster, 1979); and Alice Kessler-Harris, *Out to Work: A History of Wage-Earning Women in the United States* (New York: Oxford University Press, 1982).
5. H. M. Gitelman, "Adolph Strasser and the Origins of 'Pure and Simple' Trade Unionism" in *The Labor History Reader*, ed. Daniel Loeb (Urbana: University of Illinois Press, 1985). Gitelman's argument, which has also been made by others with reference to Samuel Gompers, is that Strasser broke with his socialist roots and comrades and adopted a narrow "pure and simple" trade unionism because the

relative weakness of the American labor movement made it impossible for him to realistically conceive of a successful, broader socialist movement.

6. For an analysis of why industrial unionism was pivotal in the organization of mass production industries, see David Brody, "The Emergence of Mass-Production Unionism," in *Workers in Industrial America: Essays on the Twentieth Century Struggle* (New York: Oxford University Press, 1980).
7. While growing up in the automobile manufacturing town of Dearborn, Michigan, a suburb of Detroit, Selden had worked summers in auto factories; a Socialist, he had done volunteer work for the UAW while teaching in Dearborn schools. Trachtenberg had worked and been a union activist in a Buffalo, New York, factory organized by the UAW, where he had gone after graduating from the City College of New York as part of a "colonization" effort of the Shachtmanite Workers Party. The two were coauthors of an influential internal strategy document, "Little Guild, Big Guild," which made the argument that the Teachers Guild, the predecessor organization of the UFT, needed to move beyond its debating society culture and adopt the organizational ethos of unions like the UAW ("Little Guild, Big Guild," box 5, folder 23, UFT Records (WAG 022), Series I: Teachers Guild/Teachers Union Records, Subseries I-B Teacher Guild Records, Tamiment Library & Wagner Labor Archives, New York University).
8. Prior to the collective bargaining era, many teacher union locals included principals and other supervisory staff. Some of the leading figures in New York City's United Federation of Teachers and its predecessor Teachers Guild—Abe Lefkowitz, Charlie Cogen, Leonard Covello, and Si Beagle, among others—had been principals and assistant principals. But this proved untenable in an era where teachers would be filing grievances against school supervisors; the UFT decided that supervisors could not be members and they organized their own union.
9. This was the view of Karl Marx, and it has been influential on the left. "The various interests and conditions of life within the ranks of the proletariat are more and more equalized," Marx wrote in the *Communist Manifesto*, "in proportion as machinery obliterates all distinctions of labor," and that homogenization is a precondition for the emergence of working-class power. From within this perspective, industrial unionism is a logical and indispensable supersession of craft unionism. Karl Marx and Friedreich Engels, "The Manifesto of the Communist Party" in *Karl Marx, The Revolution of 1848: Political Writings*, vol. I, ed. David Fernbach (London: Penguin Books, 1973), 75.
10. Harry Braverman, *Labor and Monopoly Capital: The Degradation of Work in the Twentieth Century* (New York: Monthly Review Press, 1974).
11. See the analysis of Michael Apple, especially his *Education and Power* (New York: Routledge, 1982) and *Teachers and Texts* (New York: Routledge, 1989); Kathleen Densmore's "Professionalism, Proletarianization and Teacher Work" in *Critical Studies in Teacher Education: Its Folklore, Theory, and Practice*, ed. Thomas Popkewitz (London: Falmer Press, 1987); and Jenny Ozga and Martin Lawn, *Teachers, Professionalism and Class* (London: Falmer Press, 1981).
12. See Steve Marglin, "What Do Bosses Do?" *Review of Radical Political Economics* 6, no. 2 (1974): 60–112; Katherine Stone, "The Origins of Job Structure in the Steel Industry," *Review of Radical Political Economics* 6, no. 2 (1974): 113–173; Richard Edwards, *Contested Terrain: The Transformation of the Workplace in the Twentieth Century* (New

York: Basic Books, 1979); and Michael Burawoy, *Manufacturing Consent: Changes in the Labor Process under Monopoly Capitalism* (Chicago: University of Chicago Press, 1979).

13. Richard Ingersoll, *Who Controls Teachers' Work? Power and Accountability in America's Schools* (Cambridge, MA: Harvard University Press, 2003).
14. See the pathbreaking work of William H. Sewell, *Work and Revolution in France: The Language of Labor from the Old Regime to 1848* (New York: Cambridge University Press, 1980); and Gareth Stedman Jones, *Languages of Class: Studies in English Working Class History, 1832–1982* (New York: Cambridge University Press, 1983). For an overview of the "new labor history," see the essays in Lenard Berlanstein, ed., *Rethinking Labor History: Essays on Discourse and Class Analysis* (Urbana: University of Illinois Press, 1993).
15. In this respect, see the analysis of Elliot Krause, *Death of the Guilds: Professions, States and the Advance of Capitalism, 1930 to the Present* (New Haven, CT: Yale University Press, 1997). That Krause sees modern professions and their organizations as descendants of the guilds is very suggestive of the link between craft unionism and professionalism. More problematic is Krause's contention that professionalism—and the tradition of the guilds—is now dying (see Thomas Haskell, "The New Aristocracy," *New York Review of Books*, December 4, 1997, www.nybooks.com/articles/1997/12/04/the-new-aristocracy/).
16. On the centrality of classical republican discourse in the early American labor movement, see David Montgomery's *Citizen Worker: The Experience of Workers in the United States with Democracy and the Free Market During the Nineteenth Century* (New York: Cambridge University Press, 1993). Nick Salvatore's *Eugene V. Debs: Citizen and Socialist* (Urbana: University of Illinois Press, 1982) reveals the central role of republican thought in the development of the leading American trade unionist and socialist Eugene Debs. On the "labor republican" struggles to defend workers control over the labor process, see Alex Gourevitch, "Labor Republicanism and the Transformation of Work," *Political Theory* 41, no. 4 (2013): 591–617, doi:10.1177/0090591713485370.
17. Steve Babson, *Building the Union: Skilled Workers and Anglo-Gaelic Immigrants in the Rise of the UAW* (New Brunswick, NJ: Rutgers University Press, 1991).
18. For discussions of teaching as a craft, see Alan Tom, *Teaching as a Moral Craft* (New York: Longman, 1984); Maxine Greene, "How Do We Think About Our Craft?" in *Rethinking School Improvement: Research, Craft, and Concept*, ed. Ann Lieberman (New York: Teachers College Press, 1986); Thomas Popkewitz, "The Craft of Study, Structure, and Schooling," *Teachers College Record* 74, no. 2 (December 1972): 155–165, www.tcrecord.org/content.asp?contentid=1513; Thomas Popkewitz, "Craft and Community as Metaphors of Social Inquiry Curriculum," *Educational Theory* 27, no. 4 (Fall 1977): 310–321, doi:10.1111/j.1741-5446.1977.tb00785.x; and Joseph McDonald, *Teaching: Making Sense of an Uncertain Craft* (New York: Teachers' College Press, 1992). Michael Huberman's "The Model of the Independent Artisan in Teachers' Professional Relations" (in *Teachers' Work: Individuals, Colleagues and Contexts*, ed. Judith Warren Little and Milbrey McLaughlin [New York: Teachers College Press, 1993]) uses the images of craft and artisans in its discussion of teacher work, but in ways that diverge from the analysis I am making here. Huberman sees the artisan as an atomistic individual, rather than one who is grounded in and part

of communities. While the current conditions of teacher work certainly have an individuating dynamic, and while that dynamic influences how teacher "artisans" view themselves, these categories of teacher identity reflect the aspirations as much as the reality of teacher work. And the concept of "artisan" is not separable from the potential and real communities of artisans who provide it with meaning.

19. Esther Quintero, ed., *Teaching in Context: The Social Side of Education* (Cambridge, MA: Harvard Education Press, 2017).
20. *What Matters Most: Teaching for America's Future—Summary Report of the National Commission on Teaching and America's Future* (New York: 1996), 5, files.eric.ed.gov /fulltext/ED395931.pdf. For a more recent assessment, see American Federation of Teachers, *Raising the Bar: Aligning and Elevating Teacher Preparation and the Teaching Profession* (Washington, DC: AFT, 2013), www.aft.org/sites/default/files/news/ raisingthebar2013.pdf. For a look at what works in teacher education in the academy, see Linda Darling-Hammond, *Powerful Teacher Education: Lessons from Exemplary Programs* (San Francisco: John Wiley, 2006).
21. Jack Schneider, "Rhetoric and Practice in Pre-Service Teacher Education: The Case of Teach for America," *Journal of Education Policy* 29, no. 4 (2014): 425–442, doi:10. 1080/02680939.2013.825329.
22. Richard Ingersoll, et al., *Seven Trends: The Transformation of the Teaching Force* (University of Pennsylvania: Consortium for Policy Research in Education, 2018), repository .upenn.edu/cpre_researchreports/108/.
23. For a full description of teacher residency programs, see the website of the National Center for Teacher Residencies, nctresidencies.org/. For the research, see Roneeta Guha, Maria Hyler, and Linda Darling-Hammond, "The Teacher Residency: A Practical Path to Recruitment and Retention," *American Educator* 41, no. 1 (Spring 2017), www.aft.org/ae/spring2017/guha_hyler_and_darling-hammond; and Kathleen Tindle et al., "The Urban Teacher Residency Program: A Recursive Process to Develop Professional Dispositions, Knowledge, and Skills of Candidates to Teach Diverse Students," *Educational Considerations* 38, no. 2 (2011): 28–35, doi:10.4148/0146-9282.1132.
24. On the need for teachers of color, see Burnie Bond et al., *The State of Teacher Diversity in American Education* (Washington DC: Albert Shanker Institute, 2015), www. shankerinstitute.org/resource/teacherdiversity.
25. See Susan Moore Johnson with The Project on the Next Generation of Teachers, *Finders and Keepers: Helping New Teachers Survive and Thrive in Our Schools* (San Francisco: Jossey-Bass, 2004), chapters 9 and 10; Ellen Moir et al., *New Teacher Mentoring: Hopes and Promise for Improving Teacher Effectiveness* (Cambridge, MA: Harvard Education Press, 2009); and Jennifer Dubin, "Coaching Them Through It: How San Antonio Supports First-Year Teachers," *American Educator* 42, no. 3 (Fall 2018), www.aft.org/ae/fall2018/dubin.
26. On PAR, see Susan Moore Johnson et al., *A User's Guide to Peer Assistance and Review* (Cambridge, MA: Project on the Next Generation of Teachers, Harvard Graduate School of Education, 2008), www.gse.harvard.edu/~ngt/par/resources/users _guide_to_par.pdf.; Susan Moore Johnson et al., *Teacher to Teacher: Realizing the Potential of Peer Assistance and Review* (Washington, DC: Center for American Progress, 2010), cdn.americanprogress.org/wp-content/uploads/issues/2010/05/pdf/ par.pdf; Jennifer Goldstein, *Peer Review and Teacher Leadership: Linking Professionalism*

and Accountability (New York: Teachers College Press, 2010); American Federation of Teachers, *Peer Assistance and Review: Pathways to Growth: Lessons from Five Districts* (Washington, DC: AFT, 2016), www.aft.org/sites/default/files/parreport0316.pdf.

27. A highly ideological critique of PAR, focused as much on teacher union's defense of public education as PAR itself, can be found in Myron Lieberman's *Teachers Evaluating Teachers: Peer Review and the New Unionism* (New Brunswick, NJ: Transaction Publishers, 1998). A "left" attack on PAR, rooted in a dogmatic industrial unionism that views differentiation of skill and responsibility among teachers as a threat to solidarity, can be found in Joel Jordan, "Behind Teacher 'Peer Review,'" Solidarity website, August 31, 1999, solidarity-us.org/p912/.

CHAPTER 12

1. Margaret Haley, "Why Teachers Should Organize," *Journal of Education* 60, no. 13 (September 1904): 215–216, doi:10.1177/002205740406001303.
2. See Kate Rousmaniere's aptly named biography, *Citizen Teacher: The Life and Leadership of Margaret Haley* (Albany: State University of New York Press, 2005).
3. Margaret Haley, *Battleground: The Autobiography of Margaret Haley* (Urbana: University of Illinois Press, 1982), 270.
4. John Dewey, *Democracy and Education* in *John Dewey: The Middle Works, 1899–1901*, vol. IX, ed. Jo-Ann Boydston (Carbondale: Southern Illinois Press, 1980).
5. See Alvin Gouldner, *The Future of Intellectuals and the Rise of the New Class* (New York: Continuum Books, 1979); Russell Jacoby, *The Last Intellectuals: American Culture in the Age of Academe* (New York: Basic Books, 1987); Thomas Bender, *New York Intellect: A History of Intellectual Life in New York City, from 1750 to the Beginnings of Our Time* (New York: Random House, 1987); and Alan Wald, *The New York Intellectuals: The Rise and Decline of the Anti-Stalinist Left from the 1930s to the 1980s* (Chapel Hill: University of North Carolina Press, 1987).
6. As quoted in Antonio Gramsci, *Selections from the Prison Notebooks*, ed. Quintin Hoare and Geoffrey Nowell Smith (New York: International Publishers, 1971), 9:

> All men are intellectuals, one could therefore say: but not all men have in society the function of intellectuals.*
>
> When one distinguishes between intellectuals and non-intellectuals, one is referring in reality only to the immediate social function of the professional category of the intellectuals, that is, one has in mind the direction in which their specific professional activity is weighted, whether towards intellectual elaboration or towards muscular-nervous effort. This means that, although one can speak of intellectuals, one cannot speak of non-intellectuals, because non-intellectuals do not exist . . .
>
> The problem of creating a new stratum of intellectuals consists therefore in the critical elaboration of the intellectual activity that exists in everyone at a certain degree of development, modifying its relationship with the muscular-nervous effort toward a new equilibrium, and ensuring that the muscular-nervous effort itself, in so far as it is an element of a general practical activity, which is perpetually innovating the physical and social world, becomes the foundation of a new and integral conception of the world.

* Thus, because it can happen that everyone at some time fries a couple of eggs or sews up a tear in a jacket, we do not necessarily say that everyone is a cook or a tailor.

On this question, see Seymour Martin Lipset, *Political Man: The Social Bases of Politics* (New York: Doubleday Press, 1960), 333. I do not, however, endorse Lipset's hierarchical differentiation between the creators, the distributors, and the appliers of culture.

7. Gramsci, *Selections from the Prison Notebooks*, 9.
8. In education theory, the "hidden curriculum" is generally seen as "norms and values that are implicitly, but effectively, taught," often without a teacher being fully aware of what she is doing (Michael Apple, *Ideology and Curriculum* [Boston: Routledge, 1979], 78; see also Michael Apple and Nancy King, "What Do Schools Teach?" in *The Hidden Curriculum and Moral Educationi*, ed. Henry Giroux and David Purpel [Berkeley, CA: McCutchan Publishing Corporation, 1983]). The assumption in this view is that the norms and values in question reinforce and reproduce the power of elites. But norms and values–and more importantly, skills and knowledge that are not subject specific, but crucial to democratic citizenship–can be taught by teachers in a conscious, self-aware fashion, which is what I am suggesting a democratic pedagogy does.
9. Chantal Mouffe, *Agonistics: Thinking the World Politically* (London: Verso, 2013); and William Connolly, *Identity\Difference: Democratic Negotiations of Political Paradox* (Minneapolis: University of Minnesota Press, 2002).
10. George Counts, *Dare the School Build a New Social Order?* ed. Wayne Urban (Carbondale: Southern Illinois University Press, 1978).
11. Benjamin Franklin High School is discussed in chapter 7, and the Manumit School was mentioned in chapter 5. While Benjamin Franklin itself is extraordinarily well documented, there were a number of leading teacher unionists who were principals of other schools, where they worked to organize them along democratic practices.
12. Michael Johanek and John Puckett, *Leonard Covello and the Making of Benjamin Franklin High School: Education as If Citizenship Mattered* (Philadelphia: Temple University Press, 2007).
13. Although the Coalition of Essential Schools ceased organization operations in 2017, it continues as an informal network, and its web site documents its historical work; see essentialschools.org/. For the Performance Standards Consortium, see performanceassessment.org/; for the Internationals Network, see: internationalsnps.org/; for the Bard Early College High School network, see: bhsec.bard.edu/.
14. Deborah Meier, *The Power of Their Ideas: Lessons for America from a Small School in Harlem* (Boston: Beacon Press, 1995).
15. The New York State Court of Appeals defined the state constitution's guarantee of a "sound, basic education" in terms of the skills necessary to enable students to function productively "as civic participants capable of voting and serving on a jury." While this may seem at first to be a minimal understanding, when one considers the knowledge and skill required to perform those two civic duties, it is quite robust. For a discussion of the case and its implications, see Michael Rebell, *Flunking Democracy: Schools, Courts, and Civic Participation* (Chicago: University of Chicago Press, 2017).

16. Amy Gutmann, *Democratic Education* (Princeton: Princeton University Press, 1987), 44–45.
17. The opposition between state and civil society is central to modern Western political theory, from Hobbes onward. This opposition takes different forms in different theorists, depending upon the way in which the power of the state with respect to civil society was conceptualized. See Michael Walzer, "The Civil Society Argument" in *Dimensions of Radical Democracy: Pluralism, Citizenship, Community*, ed. Chantal. Mouffe (London: Verso, 1992); Charles Taylor, "Invoking Civil Society," in *Philosophical Arguments* (Cambridge, MA: Harvard University Press, 1995); and John Keane, *Democracy and Civil Society* (London: Verso, 1988).
18. Max Weber's well-known definition of the modern state—"a compulsory association which organizes domination" and holds "a monopoly on the legitimate use of physical force within a given territory"—highlights this coercive aspect ("Politics as a Vocation," in *From Max Weber: Essays in Sociology*, ed. H. Gerth and C. Wright Mills [New York: Oxford University Press, 1972], 82–83, 78). It must be noted that the distinction I am drawing here between a "coercive state" and a "consensual civil society" is by no means absolute and should not be overstated. Many institutions of civil society such as public schools rely, for example, on the state for their funding and legal authority; similarly, the democratic state clearly requires a popular consensus to exercise its coercive power. But in a general way, the state monopolizes the means of coercion, and civil society is consensual.
19. Gutmann, *Democratic Education*, 51.
20. Leo Casey, "When Privatization Means Segregation: Setting the Record Straight on School Vouchers," *Dissent Magazine*, August 9, 2017, www.dissentmagazine.org/online_articles/private-school-vouchers-racist-history-milton-friedman-betsy-devos.

CONCLUSION

1. Samuel Bowles and Herbert Gintis, *Schooling in Capitalist America: Educational Reform and the Contradictions of Economic Life* (New York: Basic Books, 1976).
2. Bowles and Gintis, *Schooling in Capitalist America.*
3. See Michael Katz, *The Irony of Early School Reform: Educational Innovation in Mid-Nineteenth Century Massachusetts* (Cambridge, MA: Harvard University Press, 1968); Michael Katz, *Class, Bureaucracy, and Schools: The Illusion of Educational Change in America* (New York: Praeger Publishers, 1971); and Joel Spring, *Education and the Rise of the Corporate State* (Boston: Beacon Press, 1972).
4. See, for example, Ivor Goodson and Ian Dowbiggin, "Docile Bodies: Commonalities in the History of Psychiatry and Schooling," in *Foucault and Education: Disciplines and Knowledge*, ed. Stephen Ball (London: Routledge, 1990); and AnnMarie Wolpe, "Schools, Discipline and Control" in *Education and Social Change*, ed. Len Barton and Stephen Walker (New York: Croom Helm, 1985), 152–175.
5. It is the merit of Dennis Carlson's work that it insists on the political subjectivity of teachers; see *Teachers and Crisis: Urban School Reform and Teachers' Work Culture* (New York: Routledge, 1992) and "Teachers as Political Actors: From Reproductive Theory to the Crisis of Schooling," *Harvard Educational Review* 57, no. 3 (August 1987): 283–308, doi:10.17763/haer.57.3.k74471m582v30526.

Acknowledgments

THIS BOOK EXAMINES the Teacher Insurgency that emerged from the teacher strikes of 2018 and 2019, with a particular focus on the strategic and organizing issues it raised. The reader will quickly discover, however, that the questions I address in this book are not limited to these particular strikes or moment in history. Rather, they are grounded in a long historical arc of teacher collective action and teacher unionism in the United States that dates back to the first decades of the twentieth century and in the intersections between teacher organizing and the history of the labor, civil rights, and other democratic movements. For three and a half decades, I have been a participant in that history as a teacher, a unionist, and a political activist. During this time, I was privileged to be entrusted with positions of leadership by the teachers with whom I worked.

Much of what I have written reflects the insights I have acquired over those years, so I will begin by acknowledging my debts to my students, who always kept me grounded, and to those who walked the long trail with me: my fellow educators at Clara Barton High School in the Crown Heights section of Brooklyn and Bard High School Early College on the Lower East Side of Manhattan, who provided much love and support over many years; my comrades in New York City's United Federation of Teachers (UFT), the UFT's Alliance of Charter School Teachers (UFT-ACTS), and the American Federation of Teachers (AFT), who have been at my side in the many battles we fought together; and my colleagues at the Albert Shanker Institute, a think tank affiliated with the AFT that I have had the honor of leading for the last eight years.

Over this time, I have discussed the ideas contained in this book with a number of friends and comrades and learned from them (and, in a number of cases, from their published work). They include: Danielle Allen, Joanne Barkan, Jules Bernstein, Jack Clark, Ann Cook, Larry Cohen, Randy Garton, Jonathan Gyurko, Richard Healey, Janella Hinds, Bob Hughes, Jeff Isaac, Kombiz Lavasany, Steve Lazar, Mark Levinson, Harold Meyerson, Deborah Meier, Chantal Mouffe, Michael Mulgrew, Barbara Pallazzo, Shaun Richman, Christine Rowland, Joe Schwartz, John Soldini, Claire Sylvan, Miles Trager, and Rich Yeselson. Two friends deserve special mention: Gerry Hudson and I became friends and comrades close to forty years ago, in the early days of Democratic Socialists of America, and have traded ideas ever since as we each followed our own paths in our respective unions. Since I came to work at the Shanker Institute and the AFT, Jessica Smith has been a friend and a comrade at every turn, ever supportive of the work we do.

A group of friends and comrades provided not only instructive dialogue on the issues, but also vital feedback on and assistance with this book. They are Burnie Bond, Matt Di Carlo, my brother Stephen Casey, Eric Chenoweth, Asher Huey, Phil Kugler, Charles Lenchner, Ann Mitchell, Bob Morgenstern, Emilee O'Brien, Esther Quintero, Vicki Thomas, Marla Ucelli-Kashyap, and Rob Weil.

Many years ago, I started working on the ideas put forth in the third section of this book as a founding fellow of the Teacher Policy Institute, organized by my friend Ellen Meyers, and benefited from the feedback of the many accomplished teachers in that project.

I missed the counsel of my sister Kathleen Casey, and friends Genie Kemble and Glenn Scott while writing this book, as they passed away before it came into being, but I benefited from many conversations with them on these subjects over the years.

Jeff Henig had the idea that I should write a book, and at Harvard Education Press, Caroline Chauncey had patience and the faith that I would deliver it—even as it took much longer to write than either of us had anticipated.

One close friend whom I have known for this entire journey has deeply shaped my thinking on the questions addressed in this book. A few short years after I began teaching and Randi Weingarten became UFT counsel, she and I met on the steps of a courthouse when I filed legal action against the New York City Board of Education for doing construction work on asbestos-containing materials in my school without following the legally mandated health and safety protocols. In the process of working together to clean up the school and finish its renovations without further disruption, we became friends. We have worked together in the decades that followed, on everything from co-teaching classes to organizing coalitions and demonstrations to advocating for education into democratic citizenship. When you work with someone as long as I have worked with Randi, and on as many different projects as we did, the influence of that person on your ideas is so pervasive that it becomes difficult to know exactly where it begins and ends.

For over a quarter of a century, my daughters, Shannon, Sherraine, and Sandia Ashley, have brought much love to my life, fortifying me for the often-difficult struggles in the world. And Winsome Johnson, whom I first met at the UFT, has been a loving life partner for those same years, sharing me with the students I taught and cared for and the teachers I have been proud to serve without complaint. This book is dedicated to her.

About the Author

LEO CASEY is the Executive Director of the Albert Shanker Institute, a strategic think tank affiliated with the American Federation of Teachers. He taught and worked in New York City public high schools for twenty-eight years. During this time, he was a union activist and leader, serving for six years as a Vice President of New York City's United Federation of Teachers. In that role, he led the union's organizing in charter schools. Casey has won a number of awards for his teaching and was named the 1992 Social Studies Teacher of the Year for the American Teacher Awards. For ten years, his students—all of color, and predominantly immigrants and girls—won city and state championships in the "We the People" civics competition, twice placing fourth in the nation. Casey has worked with teachers in Tanzania and Russia on the development of civics education, and with teachers in China on promoting critical pedagogical methods. He has written extensively on civics, education, unionism and politics, in both print and on-line publications. Casey holds a PhD in political science from the University of Toronto.

Index